AN ENTREPRENEU

OF THE

Traditional theories of the firm have concentrated on such topics as technology, evolution, transaction costs and property rights whilst failing to account for one of the most fundamental aspects of the market process: entrepreneurial activity. Using an approach consistent with the modern Austrian School, Frédéric Sautet brings a fresh perspective to the economics of the firm by developing the open-ended theories initiated by Mises and Hayek.

An Entrepreneurial Theory of the Firm makes a thorough and comprehensive enquiry into the nature of the relationship that exists between firms and markets, with separate, in-depth explorations of both the existence and inner organization of the firm. Sautet develops a model that explains the emergence of the firm in the market process as the result of entrepreneurial activity in the context of genuine uncertainty and rivalrous competition. The Austrian angle enables him to provide a theory that is both alternative and complementary to established viewpoints.

This original, provocative work offers a thorough and convincing theory that encompasses a wealth of existing literature and leads it in an entirely new direction. It will inspire and be of great interest to economic scholars, particular within the fields of Austrian economics and theory of the firm.

An Entrepreneurial Theory of the Firm includes a foreword by Israel M. Kirzner.

Frédéric Sautet works for the New Zealand Treasury.

FOUNDATIONS OF THE MARKET ECONOMY
Edited by Mario J. Rizzo
New York University
and
Lawrence H. White
University of Georgia

A central theme of this series is the importance of understanding and assessing the market economy from a perspective broader than the static economics of perfect competition and Pareto optimality. Such a perspective sees markets as causal processes generated by the preferences, expectations and beliefs of economic agents. The creative acts of entrepreneurship that uncover new information about preferences, prices, and technology are central to these processes with respect to their ability to promote the discovery and use of knowledge in society.

The market economy consists of a set of institutions that facilitate voluntary cooperation and exchange among individuals. These institutions include the legal and ethical framework as well as more narrowly "economic" patterns of social interaction. Thus the law, legal institutions, and cultural or ethical norms, as well as ordinary business practices and monetary phenomena, fall within the analytical domain of the economist.

AN ENTREPRENEURIAL
THEORY OF THE FIRM

Frédéric E. Sautet
with a foreword by Israel M. Kirzner

London and New York

First published 2000
by Routledge
2 Park Square, Milton Park, Abingdon, Oxon, OX14 4RN

Simultaneously published in the USA and Canada
by Routledge
270 Madison Ave, New York NY 10016

Reprinted 2001, 2002

Transferred to Digital Printing 2006

Routledge is an imprint of the Taylor & Francis Group

Typeset by BC Typesetting, Bristol

British Library Cataloguing in Publication Data
A catalogue record for this book is available from the British Library

Library of Congress Cataloging in Publication Data
Sautet, Frédéric.
An entrepreneurial theory of the firm/Frédéric Sautet;
with a foreword by Israel M. Kirzner.
p.   cm. – (Foundations of the market economy series)
Includes bibliographical references and index.
1. Industrial organization (Economic theory).
2. Transaction costs.   I. Title.   II. Series.
HD2326 .S265 2000
338.5–dc21
99-058068

ISBN10: 0–415–22977–4 (hbk)
ISBN10: 0–415–77108–0 (pbk)

ISBN13: 978–0–415–22977–7 (hbk)
ISBN13: 978–0–415–77108–5 (pbk)

À la mémoire de mon père Jean-Paul et de mes grands-pères Camille et Eugène, et pour l'amour de ma grand-mère Eugénie, de ma mère Maryse et de ma sœur Caroline.

CONTENTS

CONTENTS

FIGURES

FOREWORD

Dr Frédéric Sautet's book offers the economics profession an outstanding contribution in two distinct respects. It presents, first of all, a satisfyingly rich theory of the firm, going beyond the existing literature in a fresh and original direction. Secondly, Dr Sautet's study provides us with an example *par excellence* of the way in which the insights developed in modern Austrian economics can be illuminatingly applied to new areas of inquiry. We have every reason to hope and expect that this impressive work will stimulate further progress along each of these two dimensions.

Building on foundations laid down in the mid-twentieth century by Mises and by Hayek, modern Austrian economics has, in recent decades, succeeded in introducing the profession to an understanding of economic processes in the framework of *open-endedness*. The dominant approach to microeconomics sees markets as the arena within which individual decisions interact against the background of iron-clad given limits to the possible, represented by *already*-recognized opportunities (the circumstance that these opportunities have, at the outset of analysis, already been recognized, is not itself modified by the concession that what is known is qualified by the element of risk). The "open-ended" environment, on the other hand, to which the Austrians have drawn attention, is one in which relevant opportunities may exist without their having, at the outset of analysis, already been recognized; there are *no* known limits to the possible. An economics that seeks to grapple with the real-world circumstance of open-endedness must transcend an analytical framework that cannot accommodate genuine surprise. Austrian economics has sought to accomplish this goal by focusing attention on the nature and function of pure entrepreneurial discovery. It has, paradoxically enough, turned out to be the case that significant features of real-world markets, in particular the *orderliness* of markets, have become understandable precisely by the introduction of this creative, unpredictable, entrepreneurial element – the very element which, from a mainstream perspective, appears to pose *a threat* to theoretical orderliness, let alone determinacy.

Dr Sautet has skilfully deployed his deep understanding of and appreciation for the open-endedness of the entrepreneur-inspired market process, to create a fresh perspective on the emergence and the operation of the firm. Carefully and critically sifting through the large modern literature on the theory of the firm, he has judiciously identified what in that literature can, and what cannot, be incorporated into an open-ended perspective on the world. By pursuing this perspective with tenacity and insight, Dr Sautet has been able convincingly to explain features of the modern economy of firms, which can only with difficulty, if at all, be accounted for by existing approaches to the theory of the firm. He is thoroughly appreciative of the contributions of those approaches (since they offer valuable insights, the relevance of which is not lost in the open-ended environment). But, his own new perspective on the firm is able not only to retain those insights, it is able significantly to extend our economic understanding in illuminatingly new ways. In this research he has joined a group of gifted scholars who have already published valuable work on the theory of the firm, work that draws on related Austrian insights. The comprehensiveness and thoroughness of Sautet's contribution being published here, establishes him as one of the foremost researchers in this field.

Both scholars in the area of the theory of the firm and scholars in Austrian economics will be able to derive important benefit from the rich intellectual fare with which Dr Sautet presents us here. The proof validating this assertion will, I am confident, be provided by the new research which, in the years ahead, will be inspired by Dr Sautet's splendid book.

Israel M. Kirzner
June 1999

ACKNOWLEDGMENTS

Ever since I came across Ronald Coase's famous article *The Nature of the Firm* during my years as an undergraduate student at the Université de Paris Dauphine, I have been deeply interested in what economists call the theory of the firm (or how economics accounts for the existence of business organizations and their internal structures), especially in the way Ronald Coase and his followers understand the subject. This interest survived my years of undergraduate school and I eventually decided to write my doctoral dissertation on this subject. This book was born out of my doctoral dissertation.

I owe an immense intellectual debt to Professor Pascal Salin who introduced me to what I would call "sound economic science" while I was studying monetary economics under his auspices. Professor Salin is one of the great figures of economics I have had the honor of knowing during my life as a student – he exercised a decisive influence on my choice to become an economist. I am forever grateful to Professor Salin, who became my mentor during my formative years, for his profound influence on my thinking. Professor Salin's intellectual legacy underlies the present work.

Exploring the theory of the firm from an Austrian approach was a rare opportunity that was given to me by Professor Mario Rizzo. In 1995, he agreed to supervise my work during my stay at New York University as a visiting doctoral student (and subsequently as a post-doctoral researcher) in the Austrian Economics Program. I owe Professor Rizzo an immense debt of gratitude for his influence on my understanding of economics and classical liberalism and for his effort (as a co-editor of the *Foundations of the Market Economy* series) to help me turn my doctoral dissertation into a book. I can say that without Professor Rizzo's help, this book would not have existed.

During three and a half years at New York University, I have had the privilege and the invaluable opportunity to work under the auspices of Professor Israel Kirzner. Toward Professor Kirzner, who was extremely attentive in commenting upon each draft of the dissertation manuscript and whose work influenced the present book enormously, I feel eternally indebted. Professor Kirzner's work on the entrepreneurial understanding of competition is one of the most important developments in economics in the last few decades. By developing Mises's and Hayek's theories of the market process, Professor Kirzner gave economists an invaluable set of tools for understanding the nature of competition. I would also like to thank Professor Kirzner from the bottom of my heart for accepting to write a generous foreword to the present book, I feel deeply honored.

While at New York University, I also had the unique chance to work under the guidance of Professor Peter Boettke (now Professor at George Mason University). To Professor Boettke, who read and commented on every draft of the dissertation manuscript and from whom I learnt the "Boettkean" way of understanding economics, I owe an immense intellectual debt.

I presented drafts of the three chapters of the dissertation manuscript to the Austrian Economics Colloquium at New York University. I would like to express my gratitude to the participants of the Colloquium for their very constructive comments. In particular I would like to thank the Austrian faculty and senior research scientists of New York University, Professor Israel Kirzner, Professor Mario Rizzo, Professor Peter Boettke and Dr David Harper. I would also like to thank the Faculty Research Fellows of the New York University Austrian Economics Program, William Butos (Trinity College), Young Back Choi (St John University), Sandford Ikeda (The State University of New York), Roger Koppl (Farleigh Dickinson University) and Joseph Salerno (Pace University), as well as the graduate students I studied with at New York University: Yisok Kim, Gilberto Salgado and Glen Whitman. I am particularly indebted to Gilberto Salgado who was my flatmate during my years at New York University and with whom I had endless discussions about economics in general and the concept of entrepreneurship in particular. I would also like to thank Father James Sadowsky (SJ) with whom I had numerous fruitful discussions on the nature of knowledge and on the content of economic science.

This book would not have become a reality without the help of the other members of my doctoral dissertation committee (in addition to

Professors Salin, Rizzo and Boettke). First and foremost, Jacques Raiman, who helped me understand many aspects of the structure of organizations while I was working at Générale de Service Informatique (GSI, which had Jacques Raiman as CEO). GSI (now ADP) helped me finance my trip to the USA and I am forever grateful to Jacques Raiman and many other people in this company (especially Yves Stucki and Anvarali Jiva) for this opportunity. I also wish to thank Professor Nicolai Foss, from the Copenhagen Business School, for his important influence on this work, his comments on my dissertation draft and for agreeing to be a member of my doctoral dissertation committee. Last, but not least, I would like to thank Professor Daniel Pilisi, from the Université de Paris Dauphine, for agreeing to stand in my committee and for his comments on my draft dissertation.

My intellectual development, which led to the existence of this book, was also influenced by three remarkable individuals: Professor Bertrand Lemennicier (Université de Paris Assas), Henri Lepage (Institut Euro 92) and Professor Philippe Nataf (Université de Paris Dauphine). It is thanks to Henri Lepage's work and teaching at the Université de Paris Dauphine that I discovered the work of Ronald Coase. I am grateful to the three of them for their influence on my career.

My dear friends Véronique de Rugy, Philippe Chamy and Philippe Lacoude have been (and still are) irreplaceable intellectual companions and their influence on this work is beyond words. I wish to thank them for their friendship and their beneficial influence on my work.

I would also like to thank Professor Lawrence White (as a co-editor of the *Foundations of the Market Economy* series) for his support for the publication of the present book, Alan Jarvis of Routledge for his patience and support, as well as Professor Peter Lewin (University of Texas at Dallas, USA), Professor Stavros Ioannides (Panteion University in Athens, Greece), Professor Richard Langlois (University of Connecticut, USA) and Professor Peter Klein (University of Georgia, USA) for the fruitful discussions I had with them on the theory of the firm.

I would like to give a special thanks to Patrick Nolan and Mary-Ellen Fogarty from the New Zealand Treasury, both of whom provided assistance by working after hours. Patrick Nolan made numerous corrections and editorial suggestions that immensely improved the style and readability of the manuscript. Mary-Ellen Fogarty provided needed research assistance.

I wish to thank wholeheartedly the organizations and the people who made my studies at New York University possible. While a visiting doctoral student, I received study and research grants from the Sarah Scaife Foundation, the Earhart Foundation and the Institute for Human Studies (Claude R. Lambe Foundation). During my year as a post-doctoral researcher, I received financial support from the Bradley Foundation. I wish to thank the individuals whose financial generosity made this work possible, for without them the exploration of new intellectual ventures would not be a reality.

In addition to the economists named above, my intellectual development owes primarily to Ludwig von Mises and Friedrich A. Hayek. Mises's achievements in economics are unparalleled and Hayek gave the economic profession a unique and broad understanding of the economic problem. We may stand on the shoulders of giants to try to see further than they themselves did. Thus, one of the main challenges for Austrian economists for the years to come is to develop explanations of the ways entrepreneurship is embedded into the institutional structure of the market system and how this structure influences the discovery process. I hope the present work represents a contribution to this research program and that it helps to improve the understanding of the workings of the market system. Responsibility for the errors of this book is my own.

I gratefully acknowledge permission from Kluwer Academic publishers to reproduce material first written by Richard Langlois in *Constitutional Political Economy* (1995). I would also like to thank MIT Press for the permission to reproduce material originally written by Alfred Chandler in *Strategy and Structure* (1990). Finally, I want to express my gratitude to Prentice Hall International Inc. for permission to publish material originally written by Paul Milgrom and John Roberts in *Economics, Organization and Management* (1992).

I dedicate this book to my family. To the memory of my father, Jean-Paul, who left us far too early, to my grandfathers, Camille and Eugène, who gave me strength and belief, to my grandmother, Eugénie, my mother, Maryse and my sister, Caroline, for their love unbounded.

Frédéric E. Sautet
Wellington, New Zealand
September 1999

Scientific knowledge is judgement about things that are universal and necessary, and the conclusions of demonstration, and all scientific knowledge, follow from first principles.

Aristotle (*Nicomachean Ethics*, Book iv: Chapter 6)

GENERAL INTRODUCTION

The problem of entrepreneurship for economists is that the best-developed and best-understood part of economic theory – neoclassical economics – is really mathematics. Business firms in that system are merely formulas, "production function". There are no people, no institutions; it is a timeless paradigm of resources shifting back and forth according to changes in relative prices and costs. This has meant that entrepreneurship, the most forceful, dramatic, and obvious phenomenon in all of economic life, has perforce been ignored by theoretical economists in their story of how economic events happen.

Jonathan R. Hughes (1986 [1965]: x)

As the title of my book – *An Entrepreneurial Theory of the Firm* – shows, the goal of this work is to introduce the "most forceful, dramatic, and obvious phenomenon in all economic life" (Hughes 1986 [1965]: x) – namely entrepreneurship – into the theory of the firm. Indeed, the economic theory of the firm, like most of the rest of economic theory, does not really make room for entrepreneurial activity and thus does not account for the most fundamental aspect of the market process.

Firms have always puzzled economists. They are an empirical phenomenon that must be explained along with other phenomena that constitute the market system. However, firms have never been really incorporated in conventional economic theory, thus my purpose in the following pages is to give an explanation for the emergence and the growth of firms in the marketplace that would be consistent with the approach of the modern Austrian school[1]. This is an inquiry into the nature of the relationship that exists between firms and markets.

There is more than one theory explaining the existence of organizations in economics. Some theories are technologically oriented, some deal with transaction costs, and others take an evolutionary view. Following Coase and Williamson, I think that technological factors and economies of scale can certainly explain the existence of industrial plants, but they do not explain the phenomenon of the firm itself. Moreover, the neoclassical theory of the market does not make room for the firm and may lead to various explanations that have no real organizing principle, to use Franklin Fisher's (1991) term.

In the first chapter, I will explore what I call the "market theory problem" and then assess the tradition started by Coase – namely transaction cost economics – in the light of the market theory problem. This will serve as a foil, or contrast, against which I will develop my entrepreneurial theory of the firm in Chapters 2 and 3. Since, as Demsetz (1995) explains, the existence and inner organization of the firm are different problems that should be studied separately, I shall deal with the issue of the existence (or more exactly, the emergence) of the firm in Chapter 2, and its inner organization (in relation to its growth) in Chapter 3.

In Chapter 2, I develop a model of the emergence of the firm. I argue that entrepreneurial activity and its effect on the market process, rather than the existence of information costs, explains the emergence of the firm. In fact, I develop a model of the firm in which transaction costs are assumed to be equal to zero. This assumption allows me to link a number of the different aspects of entrepreneurial activity: (a) the problem of the exploitation of a profit opportunity; (b) the activities of other entrepreneurs in the market; and (c) the existence of the firm. I consequently explain the emergence of the firm in the market process as the result of entrepreneurial activity in the context of genuine uncertainty.

In Chapter 3, I explore the growth of the firm. I assess the capabilities view (especially through the work of Edith Penrose) and I develop an entrepreneurial explanation of the growth of the firm. I then use this entrepreneurial explanation to reformulate Alfred Chandler's and Oliver Williamson's accounts of the emergence of the multidivisional corporation.

My analysis takes place in an unhampered market in which property rights are definable and enforced. I recognize that property rights are an essential element of the understanding of the business firm, but they do not constitute the core of my analysis. Instead, I focus on the role of the entrepreneurial function in the marketplace in relation to the existence of the firm. My emphasis is on developing "a theory of the market [that] provide[s] insight into the course of events set in motion by the state of market disequilibrium" (Kirzner 1973: 70). This emphasis allows me to develop an entrepreneurial theory of the firm that is both an alternative and a complement to the currently accepted theories of the firm. I wish the reader to realize that, to explain the phenomenon of the firm, organizational economics must be regenerated and enriched with an entrepreneurial understanding of market competition.

Note on the text

The date in square brackets in some references refers to the date of publication of the first edition of the work.

1

THE ECONOMICS OF THE FIRM, THE MARKET THEORY PROBLEM AND TRANSACTION COST ECONOMICS

> Economists usually ascribe the order which competition produces as an equilibrium – a somewhat unfortunate term, because such an equilibrium presupposes that the facts have already all been discovered and competition therefore has ceased.
>
> Friedrich A. Hayek (1978: 184)

> Presumably it is the existence of a considerable measure of order and stability in the real economic world around us that engenders faith that equilibrium can in fact be realized, but here it is most important to remember that the conditions of the real world are not those of perfect competition and that, if they were, it might no longer be possible for this order to be produced.
>
> George B. Richardson (1990 [1960]: 12)

INTRODUCTION

The realm of economic theory is to explain what can be observed as the result of human actions in the market system. More specifically, there is an aspect of reality that has to be explained by economists: the existence of long term hierarchical contracting relations, commonly called firms. Although there are many aspects of reality, other than firms, which require economic explanations, explaining why human activities take place within firms rather than directly in the marketplace is a question that economics cannot avoid.

There are four basic explanations of the existence of the firm in the marketplace. The purpose of this chapter is briefly to present these rationales and to assess those that are relevant to my entrepreneurial theory of the firm. This will allow me to use the relevant approaches as a foil, or a contrast, with my own view of the problem.

THE FOUR RATIONALES OF THE FIRM

Understanding the different approaches to the firm, and their similarities and differences is complex. However, four main categories of the different approaches to the firm can be found in the literature (Alchian and Woodward 1988; Holmström and Tirole 1989).

1 A first approach is a technological explanation. Firms exist because certain definite production processes cannot be separated, they have to be performed together. The rationale of the firm is that it makes sense to bind the individuals who perform these operations together.

2 A second approach is to deny (more or less) that firms have a distinct nature. Firms and markets can be viewed as having the same nature. There is no basic difference between the power of customers to stop patronizing a store and the power of an employer to fire his or her employees. The same types of actions are available to both and it is a delusion to think that there is a fundamental difference of nature between the two. Firms are just a certain kind of market contract (Cheung 1983).

3 A third view is to explain that there are costs associated with the use of the price mechanism and therefore it is sometimes efficient to avoid the direct use of the market system and to isolate certain relationships within a firm (Coase 1993a [1937]). The transaction costs view has been developed in two related directions (Alchian and Woodward 1988: 66; Langlois and Robertson 1995: 27): the measurement–cost approach on the one hand, and the asset-specificity approach on the other. The first direction emphasizes issues surrounding administering, directing, negotiating and monitoring the performances of teams (Alchian and Demsetz 1972). The second direction emphasizes (post-)contractual agreements issues: moral hazard, holdup, bounded rationality and opportunism (Williamson 1985).

4 A fourth approach revolves around the notion of rent and evolutionary theory. It says that the source of the firm is to be found in the existence of potential rents that can be created by a team of individuals working together. In order to capture these rents, one must establish a firm, that is to say a long-term bidding relationship among the members of the team which will be governed

by some kind of hierarchy. Rents can also be related to capabilities or capacities, which are, in a way, the most precious assets a firm may possess (Penrose 1995 [1959]). This body of theory is also intertwined with evolutionary (Foss 1997b) and knowledge-based views of the firm. These theories rest on a series of assumptions describing the behavior of individuals (or groups of individuals) in relation to their environment. It is assumed that there is an environmental mechanism that interacts with individuals' past behavior and internal properties. An evolutionary approach is meaningful as it emphasizes individuals' imperfect understanding of the environment and the adaptation of group members to local circumstances ("routines" and "capabilities", for instance, are biological analogies). Thus, even if an optimization approach is convenient in some cases, understanding agents as problem solvers that can adapt to circumstances is more fruitful. This fourth approach argues that firms emerge because they are the locus of accumulation of specialized and idiosyncratic resources. Thus, accumulation of resources occurs independently of contractual considerations, these theories therefore stand out in contrast to the "contractual approach" (the third view).

Following Williamson (1975, 1985) one can argue that the first view of the firm is not really part of economics, even if it has some influence on economic issues. At most, the first view can explain the existence of production plants, but not why these technical processes must take place within the same firm, instead of in the marketplace. It also cannot explain why unrelated or remotely related technical processes can be found within the same firm. As a consequence, I will not deal with the technological approach in the following pages.

The second approach, which denies a specific nature to the firm, provides little value in the development of an economics of the firm. In this work, I will follow a Coasean approach in the sense that the firm will be seen as an island of planning in which individuals are end-related, rather than means-related as in the marketplace (Hayek 1976). That is to say, the firm can be said to have a goal (or many goals) given by its chief officer (the one who chooses), whereas the marketplace, in and of itself, has no specific goal. I reject the view that claims there is no economic problem of the firm (firms are just special cases of more general instances, markets).

The third and the fourth views are relevant to my quest to develop an entrepreneurial theory of the firm. They are valid rationales of the firm and therefore will be the focus of study of this first chapter (although I will not study the transaction costs approach as two separate lines of thought, but as a single body). However, as I show below, these approaches are limited. Thus, the goal of my analysis is to enrich and complete these views, which do not describe the reality of the living economy as they cannot account for the emergence of the firm in an entirely satisfying manner. This is why I find a *market theory problem* (henceforth MTP) in the modern literature on the firm.

THE MARKET THEORY PROBLEM

In order to present my view of the MTP, I first need to introduce an analysis of the ways in which the concept of equilibrium is (or has been) used in economics. We will then see the different characteristics of the MTP and how these characteristics apply to transaction cost economics and resource-based theory.

The use of the equilibrium concept in modern economics

Following Kirzner (1973), Fink and Cowen (1985), Cowan and Rizzo (1996), Boettke (1997a, 1997b) and Machovec (1995), I would like to show that what I call the market theory problem can be seen, to a certain extent, as part of a bigger problem of contemporary modern economics: the misuse of equilibrium analysis in the understanding of the competitive process. Until the 1930s, the perfect competition model was used as a method of contrast to enlighten the positive role of institutions in the market economy (Boettke 1997b). That is the way Ludwig von Mises (1966: 236–50) thinks economists should proceed, for the only way to understand the complexity of a changing world is by isolating the change under study and keeping the rest of the world constant (in a mental experiment[1]). The formalist revolution that took place from the 1940s onward witnessed the emergence of new uses of the concept of equilibrium. As well as an ideal type, the concept of equilibrium came to be used as a description of reality (descriptive use) and as a critical standard (indictment) (Boettke 1997b: 22–3).

In the ideal-type[2] version, equilibrium is used as a foil, i.e. a method of contrast (Boettke 1997b), which has no other purpose than allowing the economist to think in a simple and clear way – by abstracting from change and by introducing a specific factor conducive of change. This is the *argumentum a contrario* (Mises 1966: 250)[3]. In this approach, "equilibrium is a postulate *that is not necessarily effected in the real world*" (Boettke 1997b: 44). This approach is entirely realistic in the sense that economists do not use assumptions as instruments in order to predict certain results, they try to isolate change in order to understand the complexity of the economy.

The use of equilibrium as a description of reality was demonstrated by the Chicago school in the 1950s and 1960s, which, under the influence of George Stigler and Milton Friedman, came to understand equilibrium in a different and more subtle way.

- Equilibrium can be used as a *description of reality*. Models of competition are not simply used in mental experiments, they are supposed to represent an accurate description of what the world is. As Melvin Reder explains in his discussion of the notion of tight prior equilibrium: "in applied work, adherents of [tight prior equilibrium] have a strong tendency to assume that, in the absence of sufficient evidence to the contrary, one may treat observed prices and quantities as good approximations to their long-run competitive equilibrium values. Call this the 'good approximation assumption'" (Reder, 1982: 12). In this view, real-world markets, as Boettke puts it, "act as if they were in competitive equilibrium" (Boettke 1997b: 23). The assumption is that markets are *always* in equilibrium, for if we include the relevant costs in the analysis, an efficient-always situation obtains. Economic problems are therein perceived in terms of costs and benefits, and the goal of economics is to understand the relevant costs without committing the fallacy of comparing an ideal state with incomplete observations about the world.

- This use of equilibrium as a description of the world was completed by the use of equilibrium as an *instrumental approach* aimed at predictions. As Reder puts it: "Hard use of the good approximation assumption is a hallmark of Chicago applied research; but the assumption is not tested directly. Instead of investigating the descriptive accuracy of this assumption, or the precise extent of the resources misallocation caused by its failure to hold exactly the Chicago style is to treat it as a maintained hypothesis [i.e. not tested] and apply it, using the resulting research findings as a test of [tight prior equilibrium]" (Reder 1982: 12–13). As Friedman (1953) explains in *Essays in Positive*

Economics, the use of equilibrium becomes purely instrumental, for it is aimed at explaining – predicting – the effects of certain changes in the economy. This approach does not need to have assumptions that conform to reality, for even if the assumptions are totally unrealistic, the goal is to be able to predict. Just like in the description of reality approach, the instrumental use of equilibrium sees markets in equilibrium always[4]. The economy is perceived as an ontologically-closed universe in which every economic aspect of human life can be seen as the result of rational choice under constraints, if the relevant costs are included[5].

The various types of Keynesian schools of thought have come to use the equilibrium concept as an indictment, i.e. a standard for criticizing reality (Boettke 1997b). This version of equilibrium does not make room for adjustment processes but still maintains that what the models describe can be attained through deliberate state intervention. In this view, the model is seen as a benchmark against which the real world must be assessed. Indeed, there are imperfections in reality and the role of models is to highlight them so that they can be corrected. "The desire [in the 1930s] to build a new science dedicated to evaluating comparative positions of static general equilibrium," writes Machovec, "led neoclassical economists to adopt the perfectly competitive endstate as a normative 'benchmark'" (Machovec 1995: 159). The modern versions of the indictment approach also see the economy as an ontologically-closed universe in which every economic aspect of human life can be seen as the result of rational choice under constraints. Grossman and Stiglitz's paradox is a good example. Assessing the work of Hayek, they contend that if prices are sufficient statistics (as they think Hayek says), nobody will have the incentive to produce information that could be obtained for free, just by looking at prices. As a result, a "noisy" equilibrium will arise where prices do not convey all the available information[6].

According to Boettke (1997b), modern economics has sacrificed the heuristic value of equilibrium analysis on the altar of formalism. As a result, most modern economic theory navigates between, on the one hand, an equilibrium-always world in which adjustment processes are assumed away, and, on the other hand, a market-failure approach which contends that departures from equilibrium are not only possible but also definitive[7].

What is the Market Theory Problem?

The MTP is the *inconsistency* involved in trying to answer questions that would not exist in an equilibrium-always world. This implies that the MTP exists in theories that use the equilibrium concept as a benchmark (i.e. as an indictment), as a description of reality or as an instrument (as in the positivist approach of the Chicago school). The MTP is therefore characterized by the absence of the fundamental attributes present in the modern Austrian theory of the market process (which uses the equilibrium concept as a foil). This is important, for the MTP occurs when the analysis tries to cope with the problems tackled by the Austrian approach, without using its necessary attributes. As a method of contrast, I identify below a series of concepts that represent the core of the Austrian market theory and show that their absence represents the distinguishing marks of the MTP.

Uncertainty

As we saw above, the Chicago use of the equilibrium concept entails the notion of an equilibrium-always world. This view replaced the old notion of competition around the period of the Second World War, thereby replacing Marshallian economics and the classical notion of competition as a rivalrous process (Machovec 1995). The economy is seen as being in a state of permanent equilibrium provided that the relevant costs are included in the analysis. An equilibrium-always theory entails a closed view of the universe. In such a system, there is no room for genuine uncertainty.

A usual reference for the definition of uncertainty is Kenneth Arrow's work.

> Uncertainty means that we do not have a complete description of the world which we fully believe to be true. Instead, we consider the world to be in one or another of a range of states. Each state of the world is a description that is complete for all relevant purposes. Our uncertainty consists in not knowing which state is the true one.
>
> Arrow (1974: 33)

However, a definition of uncertainty where there is only uncertainty over which state of the world is true does not help us understand the economic problem[8].

10

Austrian economists understand genuine uncertainty as Knight saw it. Knightian uncertainty means that genuine changes can take place within the system under study. These changes are not determined by the state of the system at any moment and cannot be assigned (objective or subjective) probabilities. Therefore, they cannot be modeled and are beyond the realm of prediction: the universe is open-ended[9]. An open-ended view of the universe entails that new knowledge can come into existence within the system, for sheer ignorance and genuine error are possible[10]. As Brian Loasby (1976), quoting Karl Popper, shows, the notions of objective and subjective probabilities are in themselves quite controversial[11]. He also argues that economists, when they deal with uncertainty, generally do not understand it the way the layman does. As Loasby puts it: "When someone says that he is uncertain, what he usually means is not just that he doesn't know the chances of various outcomes [subjective probability], but that he doesn't know what outcomes are possible [Knightian uncertainty]" (Loasby 1976: 9).

For Mises, the "uncertainty of the future is already implied in the very notion of action. That man acts and that the future is uncertain are by no means two independent matters, they are only two different modes of establishing one thing" (Mises 1966: 105). Moreover, "entrepreneur means acting man in regard to the changes occurring in the data of the market" (Mises 1966: 255). Following Kirzner, we recognize the tendency for individuals to come to notice that which is in their interest to notice, and this tendency resides in their entrepreneurial alertness (which can also be interpreted as individuals' capacity to imagine the future). "Alertness must, importantly, embrace the awareness of the ways the human agent can, by imaginative, bold leaps of faith, and determination, in fact *create* the future for which his present acts are designed" (Kirzner 1985a: 56).

In the market, the incentive for entrepreneurial activity is largely provided by the existence of pure profit opportunities. These opportunities, in fact, correspond to gains obtained from acting in accordance with the realized future. An individual's alertness is switched on by the prospect of pure profit and that enables him/her to find his/her way in an uncertain world. With alertness, individuals can pierce the fog of Knightian uncertainty and discover opportunities for pure profit. As we saw above, in this view, profit is not a residual as in the Knightian view, it is a gain obtained as a consequence of a correct anticipation of the future. In Knight's view, there is no such revenue, for the future, if truly uncertain, is unknowable, and if predictable, it excludes the existence of pure profit. What Knight did not perceive is that action in the face of uncertainty requires, as Kirzner explains, "a degree of alertness to what is 'around the corner' (i.e. hidden behind the fog of uncertainty) – in other words, it requires the exercise of the human entrepreneurial propensity" (Kirzner 1985a: 97).

Although he maintains the same distinction, Richard Langlois endorsed a different terminology, for he thinks that the concept of "Knightian uncertainty" is not clear enough in Knight's own writings[12]. According to Langlois and Robertson, uncertainty has two meanings:

> The first, which we can call *structural uncertainty*, arises when a firm needs to base its decisions on judgments about future outcomes that are as yet unknowable. The second type of uncertainty, which we term *parametric uncertainty*, arises from the possibility of a range of market imperfections including bounded rationality and opportunism. Whereas it is possible to adopt strategies to insure against parametric uncertainty, or at least to mitigate its effects, structural uncertainty cannot be eliminated strategically.
>
> Langlois and Robertson (1995: 18)[13]

Equilibrium and disequilibrium analysis

Some economists advocate the following view: all the changes can be modeled for they have already taken place. Changes are not genuine changes, but instantaneous adjustments. Chicagoans George Stigler and Gary Becker, for instance, argue that markets are always efficient and that there is an optimal level of ignorance. Prices are parametric and pure profit does not exist. External shocks are necessary for relative prices to change. In other words, the system is confined with the amount of information it possesses in the first place. In this approach, competition is a state and not a process. This view of equilibrium is the direct product of the transformation of the notion of competition in economics. "Acceptance of the Robbinsian definition of economics – with its exclusive emphasis on the allocation of given means – forced economists," writes Machovec, "to divorce entrepreneurship from their social vision, which, in turn, altered the way we have cast our analysis of economic development, industrial organization, international trade, and comparative systems" (Machovec 1995: 125). One may then say that the equilibrium-always view is an outcome of the pure competition approach.

Equilibrium as a critical standard can be another distinguishing mark of the MTP (especially in some empirical claims made by the transaction cost school). As we saw above, in this understanding of equilibrium, the model is seen as a benchmark against which the real world must be assessed. There are no real adjustment processes but, contrary to the equilibrium-always view, non-efficient situations can be found in the world and must therefore be corrected. Departures from the equilibrium state are inherent to the market system: they are due to human imperfection. What seemed to be an efficient equilibrium situation in the description view, is a non-efficient equilibrium situation in the indictment one (because frictions, i.e. human imperfections, in the real world lead the economy to sub-optimal states).

Disequilibrium analysis is the keystone of the modern Austrian economic explanation of the market. In this view, equilibrium is an ideal type that is used as a foil to isolate the implications of the existence of a certain phenomenon. Economic phenomena can only be understood by the *argumentum a contrario* provided by the notion of equilibrium. As Mises puts it: "in order to analyze the problems of change in the data and of unevenly and irregularly varying movement, we must confront them with a fictitious state in which both are hypothetically eliminated" (Mises 1966: 247)[14]. It is because Austrian economists use the equilibrium concept as a method of contrast that they can isolate sources of change in the market and show that a disequilibrium approach provides better explanations to the phenomena we seek to understand through economic enquiry. Equilibrium seen as a description of reality misses the point: it renders economists blind to the adjustment processes taking place in the market.

Information and the Hayekian Knowledge Problem (HKP)

Another way of describing the MTP is to show how the issue of knowledge is treated in the neoclassical theory of the market. The equilibrium-always use of the equilibrium concept requires information to be considered as a commodity: it is a "bookshelf approach." However, as Hayek showed, the problem is not that information is costly to obtain, but that it is dispersed and must be discovered. The real economic problem is not so much the allocation of known resources, but the discovery of dispersed knowledge[15]. As Hayek puts it in a famous passage:

> The peculiar character of the problem of a rational economic order is determined precisely by the fact that the knowledge of the circumstances of which we must make use never exists in concentrated or integrated form but solely as the dispersed bits of incomplete and frequently contradictory knowledge which all the separate individuals possess. The economic problem of society is thus not merely a problem of how to allocate "given" resources – if "given" is taken to mean given to a single mind which deliberately solves the problem set by these "data." It is rather a problem of how to secure the best use of resources known to any of the members of society, for ends whose relative importance only these individuals know. Or, to put it briefly, it is a problem of the utilization of knowledge which is not given to anyone in its totality.
>
> Hayek (1948 [1945]: 77–8)

As we will see below, Kirzner (1992a) elaborated the implications of the Hayekian understanding of information which came to be known as the Hayekian Knowledge Problem (henceforth HKP). As Kirzner (1985a; 1992a) shows, this HKP stems from the existence of Knightian uncertainty and genuine ignorance. A theory, which is oblivious to the HKP, rests on a narrow view of knowledge[16]. It cannot address the fundamental issue of adjustment except in two ways: adjustments are either instantaneous or impossible without state intervention (i.e. equilibrium is either used as a description or as an indictment). Moreover, the context in which decisions are being made is crucial to the nature of the information at stake. As Boettke puts it: "It is not just that information is costly to obtain, but that it is *different information* if it is stimulated by a context of rivalrous, private-property exchange. The knowledge actors rely on to make decisions is not universal and abstract, as it must be if it is to be replicated through either bureaucratic planning or political deliberation" (Boettke 1997b: 36).

Entrepreneurship

A direct implication of the lack of the HKP in mainstream economic theory is the absence of adequate consideration of the role of the entrepreneur in the market system. In the standard uses of the equilibrium concept (as a description of the world and as a benchmark), there are no real adjustment processes taking place because there is no entrepreneurship. In *The Emergent Firm*, Neil Kay explains that in the neoclassical theory of the market, "[t]he assumption of rationality and the existence of marginalist profit maximizing rules couched in the perfect knowledge assumption ensures that the entrepreneur has no real discretion over questions of resource allocation. These assumptions result in the treatment of the entrepreneur as an automaton" (Kay 1984: 57). Indeed, the role of the entrepreneur is a puzzle for neoclassical economics. As William Baumol puts it: "The entrepreneur is at once one of the most intriguing and . . . the most elusive . . . characters that constitutes the subject of economic analysis" (Baumol 1993: 2)[17].

In the process view, the entrepreneur's role is to bridge the gaps in knowledge that exist in the market and which are revealed by disequilibrium prices. These are gaps between a state of full (*ex ante* and *ex post*) coordination of plans (equilibrium) and the real state of ignorance and dissatisfaction of individuals in the market place (disequilibrium). Entrepreneurial action is action that tends to lead to a greater coordination of individuals' plans in the economy.

Cost-benefit analysis

A final consequence of the uses of equilibrium in modern industrial organizations is that pure cost-benefit analysis is predominant. By its very nature, cost-benefit analysis must find a common yardstick (usually money magnitudes) to compare costs and benefits across individuals. One problem with this approach is that it takes costs (and benefits) as objectively measurable. Another problem is that there is no discovery. In other words, opportunities have already been noticed and the information framework is given (even if information is only given in probabilistic terms). In a cost-benefit analysis, discovery issues are neglected and any approach in terms of market process is rejected. This type of analysis is pervasive in modern mainstream economics, since the main focus of the discipline is on optimization. Although it is undoubtable that cost-benefit analysis is useful, its intensive use blinds economists to the real economic problem. Indeed many problems in the theory on modern industrial organization are due to this way of thinking[18].

Concluding remarks

As we saw above, the MTP is the *inconsistency* involved in trying to answer questions that would not exist in an equilibrium-always world. In other words, standard competition theory can only provide certain answers and cannot solve problems that involve the use of the equilibrium concept as a foil. This is why theories taking place in an equilibrium-always world will be limited in their capacity to cope with the very problems implied by the use of the neoclassical theory of the market.

A theory that is subject to the MTP possesses some or all of the following characteristics: (a) equilibrium is used as an instrument (in the Chicago sense), as a description of reality or as a benchmark and, therefore, there is no disequilibrium analysis; (b) true adjustment processes are absent; (c) information is treated as a commodity; (d) there is no genuine uncertainty (and, as a consequence, no true ignorance); (e) knowledge does not have to be discovered; and (f) there is no entrepreneurship (for there is no HKP and there are no disequilibrium prices).

If, for a given theory, we find some or all of the features described above (while the theory tries to cope with their consequences), we can affirm that there is a MTP. As I explain in the introduction above, the Coasean theory of the firm and Williamson's transaction costs economics will serve as a method of contrast to my approach (see also Cowen and Parker 1997: 71–4).

THE MTP AND TRANSACTION COST ECONOMICS

Introduction

The MTP is present in many models of industrial organization. The modern theories of the firm basically stand on an inconsistency, in that they try to answer questions that would not exist in an equilibrium-always world.

In his review essay on the *Handbook of Industrial Organization*, Franklin Fisher couches his thoughts in terms of a series of stylized facts. First, "[i]ndustrial organization has no organizing principle," he writes; second, "[t]he principal result of theory is to show that nearly anything can happen'; and third, "[s]tripped-down models of the theory often fail to provide helpful guides for the analysis of real situations" (Fisher, 1991: 207–9). In other words, models of industrial organization proceed from different aspects of economic theory and are so unrealistic in their assumptions that: (a) they can almost explain contradictory phenomena, and (b) they cannot really shed light on actual situations[19]. Fisher's three propositions are certainly valid, but the central problem is that, behind the veil of confusion of modern neoclassical industrial organization, there is one principle: the neoclassical theory of the market[20]. All these theories rely on pure competition either as an instrument or as a benchmark (i.e. as a predictive model or as an indictment)[21].

Transaction cost economics is a special case within modern industrial organizations. It does not really share the technological aspect of most organizational theories and therefore relies heavily on economic principles (asset specificity and cost-benefit analysis for instance). Just like many other theories in industrial organization, the economics of a transaction cost does rely, to a certain extent, on the use of the neoclassical conception of competition (i.e. the allocative paradigm and the use of the equilibrium concept either as a pure description of reality or as a critical standard) as the *background* of its analysis. However, in the case of transaction cost economics – and that is where the MTP is – standard competition theory is used in an analysis which, in fact, was "designed" to cope with the very problems implied by the use of the neoclassical theory of the market. Because the contractual approach has been so heavily present in the theory of the firm, most of this chapter focuses on showing how the MTP can be found in this body of economics. This chapter will also touch upon the resource-based approaches because they represent one of the best alternatives to mainstream organizational theories.

Ronald Coase's analysis and the MTP

Introductory remarks: the existence of marketing costs

In his lecture delivered upon receiving the Nobel Prize in economics, Ronald Coase (1992) reminds us that Lionel Robbins explains, in *An Essay on the Nature and Significance of Economics*, that organizations lie outside the scope of economics. As we know, Robbins became one of the fathers of the neoclassical theory of competition and his views on organization had a certain impact on the development of the theory of the firm. However, although Coase was a student at the London School of Economics (LSE) in the 1930s, where Robbins was teaching, a larger influence on Coase was Arnold Plant, who "argued that competition would provide all the coordination needed" (Coase 1993b [1988]: 38) for the economic system to function. As Coase explains, it was because "Plant's point of view seemed to leave obscure the role of business management" (Coase 1993b [1988]: 38) that he started to inquire about organizations. Coase

(1993c [1988]: 52) himself said that he was in a search of a more realistic theory, taking into account the existence of firms as important actors of the market. It is interesting to examine certain aspects of Coase's theory in order to understand how his approach both broke free from Robbins' point of view and remained under its influence.

Coase's (1993a [1937]) paper *The Nature of the Firm* is based on the observation that most economic theory of his day was oriented towards the understanding of the market system, i.e. that all the necessary coordination between economic actors is done by the price mechanism[22]. This observation led Coase to ask: "But in view of the fact that it is usually argued that co-ordination will be done by the price mechanism, why is such organization necessary? Why are there these 'islands of conscious power'?" (Coase 1993a [1937]: 19).

Coase developed a new theory because he was able to identify a key idea and to understand its logical implications. He understood that "the distinguishing mark of the firm is the supersession of the price mechanism" (Coase 1993a [1937]: 20). Resources within the firm are not allocated through changes in relative prices but through the use of some authority (the "entrepreneur"). This implies that there must be, in some cases, advantages in replacing a market transaction by one taking place within a firm[23]. This led Coase to think that if a certain course of action does not take place when it could have, it must be because there are costs attached to it. Indeed, "[t]he main reason why it is profitable to establish a firm," explains Coase, "would seem to be that there is a cost of using the price mechanism" (Coase 1993a [1937]: 21). Within firms, individuals economize on the costs attached to market transactions. These costs are linked to the discovery of the relevant prices and to "negotiating and concluding a separate contract for each exchange transaction" (Coase 1993a [1937]: 21). Transaction costs are greatly reduced within the firm because the need for a series of short-term contracts is substituted with one contract[24].

One can argue that Coase's theory is based on the perfect competition framework. This point has been the center of argument of the Boudreaux–Holcombe/Foss "debate". The former explain that Coase's theory is based on the general equilibrium framework where "the goods to be produced and the methods of production are given" (Boudreaux and Holcombe 1989: 148). The latter explains (Foss 1993a: 270–3) that two different underlying ontological views can be identified in Coase's work. The first one is a closed ontological view – where no genuine uncertainty exists in the model – corresponding to that of Boudreaux and Holcombe. The second one corresponds to an open-ended economic universe where indeterminist processes are operative[25]. This debate indicates that there is a certain ambiguity in Coase's work, as his argument can cut two ways, depending on the interpretation of Coase's use of the concept of equilibrium.

Coase's struggle against the pure competition paradigm

In the 1930s, perfect competition became the established paradigm without providing an explanation for the existence of firms in the market. With the exception of Knight, economists of that period dropped firms from their economic inquiry in order to keep their theory coherent. Coase's concern with firms meant he had to question market competition theory in order to develop a satisfying explanation. Coase introduced the concept of marketing (i.e. transaction) costs[26] in his analysis because he wanted to understand the origins of actual market and legal institutions that could not be explained by the pure competition paradigm. In that sense, Coase used the equilibrium concept as a method of contrast, with which he could assess reality and show that institutions have a role to play in a world of transaction costs. As Boettke puts it: "Viewed as a practitioner of counterfactual thought experiments, what Coase was focusing on (in both his 1937 paper on the theory of the firm and his 1960 paper on the problem of social costs) was the origin of actual market and legal institutions as mechanisms for coping with real-world positive transaction costs" (Boettke 1997b: 21).

However, while introducing transaction costs into the picture, Coase chose, to a certain extent, to keep his theory of the market within the walls of the neoclassical approach. Nicolai Foss gives three reasons why Coase seems to accept the neoclassical analysis: (1) all inputs and outputs are given; (2) the behavior of agents is neoclassical; and (3) he basically uses comparative static analysis (Foss 1994b: 46–7). Indeed, by focusing on the role of various legal arrangements and institutions, he opened the door, on the one hand, to a comparative institutional program of research (equilibrium as a foil) and, on the other hand, to a pure cost-benefit approach (equilibrium as an instrument or a critical standard). However, as Boettke explains, "Coase's project, however, has been largely misunderstood by formalist neoclassical economics. Instead of highlighting the functional significance of real-world institutions in a world of positive transaction costs, Coase's work has been interpreted as describing the welfare implications of a zero-transaction-cost world"

(Boettke 1997b: 21). Coase had to face many difficulties in making his view understood among economists, and given the dominance of the pure competition paradigm after the war, it is not surprising that Coase's work came to be interpreted mostly in cost-benefit terms (i.e. in an instrumental or indictment use of equilibrium)[27].

Coase's use of the equilibrium concept

The difficulty facing Coase was that "[a]ccording to Kaldor [1934a], it is one of the assumptions of static theory that 'All the relevant prices are known to all individuals'. But this is clearly not true of the real world" (Coase 1993a [1937]: 31)[28]. Coase then explains that there must be a cost of using the price mechanism and the most obvious one is "that of discovering what the relevant prices are," yet Coase was aware that the costs of discovering the relevant prices could not be incorporated in the perfect competition framework. Thus, he clearly uses the equilibrium concept as a method of contrast with which he shows the necessity of transaction costs in the real world. That is why he may appear to sustain a contradiction: the existence of the costs of using the market in the perfect competition framework where all individuals know all the relevant prices[29].

Following Boettke (1997b), I contend that one cannot understand Coase's theory of the market unless one understands that he uses the equilibrium concept as a method of contrast. That is why Foss clearly finds an ongoing struggle against the closed view of the universe in the work of Coase. Coase knows that individuals must somehow handle unexpected change in the system and that pure competition does not provide room for such change. Genuine change and the role of costs can only be understood by the *argumentum a contrario* provided by the equilibrium concept.

In a recent paper, Coase (1993d [1988]) explains the existence of firms first by using an equilibrium model in which they are absent. "In such a system," writes Coase, "the allocation of resources would respond directly to the structure of prices, but a great part of the available resources would be absorbed in making the arrangements for the contract needed to bring about these transactions and in providing the information on the basis of which decisions would be made." Coase then allows firms to exist in the system. "In effect this means that it will be profitable to organize a firm when its costs of operating . . . are less than the transaction costs that would be incurred in a complete market system, since this difference is the source from which the higher return to factors and the lower prices for products will come" (Coase 1993d [1988]: 65–6). It seems, in this passage, that Coase uses the equilibrium construct as a method of contrast and that information costs are fundamental to the firm.

In a 1964 comment, Coase makes it clear that economics should not use equilibrium as a description of reality (or as an indictment), but as a method to judge alternative arrangements.

> Contemplation of an optimal system may provide tech-
> niques of analysis that would otherwise have been missed
> and, in certain special cases, it may go far to providing a
> solution. But in general its influence has been pernicious.
> It has directed economists' attention away from the main
> question, which is *how alternative arrangements will actually
> work in practice*. It has led economists to derive conclusions
> for economic policy from a study of an abstract of a
> market situation. It is no accident that in the literature . . .
> we find a category "market failure" but no category "govern-
> ment failure." Until we realize that we are choosing between
> social arrangements which are all more or less failures, we are
> not likely to make much headway.
>
> Coase (1964: 195, emphasis added)

Coase does not use the equilibrium concept as an instrument, a description of reality or as an indictment. He seems to be consistent in his use of the equilibrium concept and what he wants to show. Thus, the first criterion of the MTP does not apply to his work.

Contracts and adjustment processes

Associated with the idea of economizing on marketing costs is a theory of the form and role of contracts within the firm. Coase understands that the main advantage of a transaction taking place within a firm is that it allows for adaptation to unforeseen future contingencies. It is because general long-term contracts are preferable, in certain cases, to market transactions (i.e. short-term contracts in Coase's terms) that firms come into existence. As Coase puts it:

> [T]he service which is being provided is expressed in general
> terms, the exact details being left until a later date. All that
> is stated in the contract is the limits to what the person
> supplying the commodity or service is expected to do. The

details of what the supplier is expected to do is not stated in the contract but is decided later by the purchaser [sic]. When the direction of resources (within the limits of the contract) becomes dependent on the buyer in this way, that relationship which I term a "firm" may be obtained. A firm is likely therefore to emerge in those cases where a very short-term contract would be unsatisfactory.

Coase (1993a [1937]: 21)

Coase's focus on the notion of contract is fundamental because, by paying attention to contracting issues, he opens an entirely new field of economic research that was absent from the neoclassical agenda until his work: the links between contracts and the forms of exchange. The nature of the contract among parties becomes, with Coase, a fundamental issue: it is linked to the existence of transaction costs[30].

The question is then: does the theme of flexibility in the employment contract signal an adjustment process? Coase's work can very well be understood as taking place in a static world in which there are no genuine adjustment processes. As Foss puts it: "[Coase's theory] is largely a static affair that pays little or no attention to the creation of markets, and assumes that inputs, outputs and technology are given so that the economic problem has only to do with combining these in a transaction cost minimizing manner" (Foss 1994a: 57). It is also true that one can interpret the flexibility introduced by long term employment contracts as a feature of the open-ended universe. "[W]hat really separates [the firm] from the market [in Coase's paper] is the extent to which contracts are open-ended," writes Foss (1994b: 47). Indeed, one can argue that the theme of flexibility (such as that in employment contracts) is the direct result of the use of the equilibrium concept as a foil. Flexibility can definitely be interpreted as signaling a true adjustment process, for it allows for adaptations to unforeseen contingencies. Coase seems to be consistent in his use of the equilibrium concept and in what he wants to show, for he incorporates the possibility of true adjustment processes where they are needed. The second criterion of the MTP does not really apply to Coase's work.

Information

The very fact that Coase sees the firm as an institution that allows for unforeseen contingencies conveys the idea that information is not a commodity. The way he treats the problem of the limits of the firm can shed light on the nature of information in his work.

"[W]hy, if by organizing one can eliminate certain costs and in fact reduce the cost of production, are there any market transactions at all? Why is not all production carried on by one big firm?" (Coase 1993a [1937]: 23). To answer these questions, Coase developed a theory of the limits of the firm that is based on the identification of three anti-integration mechanisms. (a) First, there are costs associated with the management of the firm. "[A]s the firm gets larger, there may be decreasing returns to the entrepreneur function, that is, the costs of organizing additional transactions within the firm may rise" (Coase 1993a [1937]: 23). This first counter-force to the expansion of the firm draws on what we may call "bureaucratic costs", which will become a central theme of Williamson's theory. (b) The second counter-force is "that as transactions which are organized [within the firm] increase, the entrepreneur fails to place the factors of production in the uses where their value is greatest, that is, fails to make the best use of the factors of production" (Coase 1993a [1937]: 23). This second counter-mechanism calls on a theory of "entrepreneurial failure" (or management failure). It is surprisingly non-neoclassical in its spirit (if Coase really means "genuine failure" and "genuine entrepreneurship') and seems to be relevant to an Austrian understanding of the firm. However, it remains somewhat undeveloped in the transaction costs approach[31]. (c) The third counter-force is that "the supply price of one or more of the factors of production may rise" (Coase 1993a [1937]: 23). It is not clear what Coase really has in mind here, but it seems to show that the variation of input prices is a determining factor of firm-size limit (which is relevant, to a certain extent, to an Austrian approach).

Even if none of the above ideas are further developed in Coase's work, it is important to notice that the concept of "entrepreneurial failure" can convey the idea that information is not a commodity. Individuals can be truly mistaken with respect to the content of their knowledge (information has to be discovered). Unfortunately, it is very difficult to infer from Coase's work a theory of information, and many interpretations are possible. However, it is possible to defend a non-commodity approach of information in the work of Coase. He seems to be consistent in his use of the concept of information and what he wants to show.

Uncertainty

Coase addresses the issue of uncertainty very briefly in his article. As he puts it: "The question of uncertainty is one which is often considered to be very relevant to the study of the equilibrium of the firm. It seems improbable that a firm would emerge without the existence of uncertainty" (Coase 1993a [1937]: 22). However, Coase does not really address the topic, for he turns to Frank Knight's rationale for the firm (the guaranteeing view) and shows that it is irrelevant to the problem he is considering and claims that Knight does not give an answer to the make-or-buy question (Coase 1993a [1937]: 22 and 26–7). Whether this is true or not is not so much the question here. What is unfortunate is that Coase does not address the issue of uncertainty in more depth in his article, even if he acknowledges uncertainty as a necessary factor. It is therefore extremely difficult to decide whether true uncertainty is what he has in mind or not.

The entrepreneur

As Boudreaux and Holcombe put it, in Coase's theory "the goods to be produced and the methods of production are given" (Boudreaux and Holcombe 1989: 148). Entrepreneurial activity, at least as Austrian economists understand it, has to do with discovering the goods to be produced and the methods to produce them. Coase sees the entrepreneur as a manager, for the firm is a "system of relationships which comes into existence when the direction of resources is dependent on an entrepreneur" (Coase, 1993a [1937]: 22). The entrepreneur is a resource allocator who decides how to organize transactions within the firm and who makes the make-or-buy decision. In Coase's framework, there are costs and diminishing returns to management: the entrepreneur-manager is a Robbinsian maximizer (a Robbinsian manager) whose work is to carry on an optimal level of make-or-buy decisions.

Concluding remarks

Coase insists in his work that the view of the firm he puts forward is realistic (which is a concern that he expresses in the opening comments) and manageable: it provides a theory of the existence of the firm (a static and dynamic equilibrium analysis) and a research agenda to investigate the effects changes in the economic system have on transaction costs (Coase 1993a [1937]: 30). Coase's view is extremely powerful because it is based on fundamental economic principles and it opens the door to comparative institutional analysis. As he explains himself, his understanding of the firm "is tractable by two of the most powerful instruments of economic analysis developed by Marshall, the idea of the margin and that of substitution, together giving the idea of substitution at the margin" (Coase 1993a [1937]: 18).

Even if Coase uses equilibrium as a method of contrast, he does not abstract from change, uncertainty, cost and time in order to show that there is a HKP and that the economy is better understood in disequilibrium. Moreover, his view of information is somewhat unclear and the absence of disequilibrium analysis reinforces the absence of the entrepreneur. The behavior of individuals is quite neoclassical and we cannot see how agents could deal with disequilibrium prices and genuine uncertainty if they are expected to behave as Robbinsian maximizers.

Coase's case with respect to the MTP is difficult to assess. It is clear, as many authors have shown (see, for instance, Foss 1994b; Boudreaux and Holcombe 1989), that there is an ongoing struggle within Coase. It seems that Coase tried to extend the neoclassical approach of the market by introducing transaction costs in his analysis, while continuing to use the equilibrium concept as a method of contrast. Using this method, he was able to convey the idea that the firm could be the locus of certain genuine adjustments that could not take place otherwise. However – and this remark is not meaningless – he did not pursue his analysis to its logical end, for he kept his theory within the walls of the neoclassical theory of the market. Uncertainty is almost ignored, which implies that there is no HKP and that, eventually, we do not really know if his world is open-ended or not (i.e. if prices are in disequilibrium). The struggle in Coase lies in the fact that although he clearly realized the limits of the neoclassical model, he continued to use this model to underpin his own analysis. However, there is a more satisfying view of the world depicted by Arnold Plant at the London School of Economics: the entrepreneurial understanding of competition.

Oliver Williamson's transaction cost economics and the MTP

Introductory remarks

Oliver Williamson recognized, more than any other economist in the last 30 years, the importance of transaction costs in the study of the firm. He considers that transaction costs economics can: (a) explain the emergence of the firm and its limits; (b) show that many non-standard contracting forms of organization are efficient relative to other forms of contractual arrangements; and (c) explain the internal organization of the firm in terms of governance structure. Williamson contends, following Coase, that transaction costs economics can explain the emergence, the existence and the evolution of organizations by showing that they result from a constant search for economizing on transaction costs on the part of individuals. His research program over the past 20 years or so has been to show that organizational diversity finds its rationale in the economizing of transaction costs and that it gives rise to new falsifiable claims about the origins of non-standard contracting behaviors.

Williamson has, for a long time, been a strong believer in the power of economic science to explain the existence of organizations. As he himself explains in the preface of *Markets and Hierarchies*:

> The study of economic organization commonly proceeds as though market and administrative modes of organization were disjunct. Market organization is the province of economists. Internal organization is the concern of organization specialists. And never the twain shall meet. *Markets and Hierarchies* maintains that one can understand the powers and limits of market and internal modes of organization only by examining each in relation to the other.
>
> Williamson (1975: ix)

With this goal in mind from the beginning, Williamson contends that his approach stands in contrast both to the technological view and to its derivative, the production costs understanding of the firm[32] (which are well-accepted views in mainstream economic theory). For these reasons, Williamson does not really stand inside the neoclassical approach to economics, he is clearly one of the contenders of the new institutionalist school.

Foss (1993a, 1994b) explains that one can identify two traditions in the modern Coasean approach: (a) nexus-of-contract and (b) governance. Foss thinks that these two approaches result from the two ontological views he identifies in Coase's article, as shown above. "A convenient perspective on contemporary theories of the firm," writes Foss, "is that some of these have taken their lead from Coase the proponent of an 'open' ontology, whereas others have

26

open vs. closed ontology.

followed Coase the proponent of a 'closed' ontology" (Foss 1993a: 271). Peter Klein and Foss contend that Williamson's work belongs to the first category. As Klein puts it, the:

> transaction cost framework incorporates non-maximizing behavior (bounded rationality); true "structural" uncertainty or genuine surprise (complete contracts are held not to be feasible, meaning that all *ex post* contingencies cannot be contracted upon *ex ante*); and process or adaptation over time (trading relationships develop over time, typically undergoing a "fundamental transformation" that changes the terms of trade).
>
> Klein (1996: 22)

However, even if some aspects of Williamson's work could indeed correspond to an open-ended approach, one can still identify a MTP in his work.

Opportunism: do only incentives matter?

As Williamson explains, "many differences among alternative approaches to the study of economic organization owe their origins to underlying differences in the behavioral assumptions" (Williamson 1985: 44). Following Frank Knight, Williamson acknowledges the importance of "opportunism" in the study of human behavior, for he thinks that this assumption is consistent with human nature. As Williamson puts it: "By Opportunism I mean self-interest seeking with guile. This includes but is scarcely limited to more blatant forms, such as lying, stealing, and cheating. Opportunism more often involves subtle forms of deceit. . . . Opportunism refers to the incomplete or distorted disclosure of information, especially to calculated efforts to mislead, distort, disguise, obfuscate, or otherwise confuse" (Williamson 1985: 47). Human agents are in general given to opportunism[33]. Human beings will sometimes seek their own immediate self-interest at the expense of others, thereby undermining the possibility of credible commitments.

This assumption is fundamental because "were it not for opportunism, all behavior could be ruled governed" (Williamson 1985: 48). Opportunism forces parties to devise safeguards to protect themselves in transactions (in firms – i.e. superior governance structures within which transactions are organized – or with the realignment of contract incentives, for example). Moreover, without opportunism there are no surprises in the execution of promises and "[i]ssues of economic organization thus turn on technological features (e.g. scale economies), there being no problematic behavior to rule deviance among human actors" (Williamson 1985: 49). It is because of the introduction of opportunism, according to Williamson, that we can no longer regard the firm as a production function and vertical integration as a purely technological problem (Williamson 1985: 65).

Williamson puts opportunism (along with bounded rationality) at the center of his analysis. This calls for one remark: Williamson's theory of the firm and integration depends almost exclusively on a behavioral assumption. Therefore, if there is a change in the assumption, then the theory loses some of its explanatory power. It is true that what is interesting in Williamson's approach is precisely the fact that he develops an analysis on what seems to be realistic assumptions, but the question here is to know whether or not human nature is opportunistic the way he describes it. The firm is one of the safeguards devised to protect individuals from opportunistic behavior on the part of others. As we saw above, if people were totally honest, "all behavior could be ruled governed" (Williamson 1985: 48). This implies that, in a totally honest world, firms would not exist because any contract would be self-enforcing. Conversely, the existence of firms is then a pure contracting problem. As Williamson puts it: "Transaction cost economics poses the problem of economic organization as a problem of contracting" (Williamson 1985: 20). However, although it is true that behavioral assumptions of this kind (and the theory of integration constructed upon these assumptions) are important, (Robbinsian) incentive problems are not the most fundamental economic problem. As we will see in the subsequent chapter, even if people were honest (i.e. transaction costs were zero), firms would still be needed[34].

Herbert Simon's and Oliver Williamson's views of bounded rationality

The way in which Williamson uses the assumption of rationality is surely the major difference between his work and neoclassical economics[35]. He considers, following Herbert Simon, that human agents are rational but only in a limited way. "Bounded rationality is the cognitive assumption on which transaction cost economics relies" (Williamson 1985: 45). Bounded rationality differs from the usual maximizing approach in the sense that it integrates the relevant costs and certain limits to rationality (i.e. cognitive limits). Simon revolted against the use of rationality in neoclassical micro-economics. Complete rational appraisal by individuals of all available alternatives is an impossible task to perform, according to Simon. The reason is that such a task is beyond human cognitive faculties. What is novel in Simon's analysis (with respect to the mainstream's view) is that the calculational (or appraisal) problem does not arise because of a search problem, it arises because of a cognitive capacity limitation[36]. He infers from this analysis that agents do not maximize but try to attain a "satisficing" minimum. In this view, maximizing behavior cannot be used as a tool of economic analysis. As Williamson puts it: "An economizing orientation is elicited by the intended rationality part of the definition [individuals are intend-edly rational, but only limitedly so], while the study of institutions is encouraged by conceding that cognitive competence is limited" (Williamson 1985: 45).

The assumption of bounded rationality is crucial, for instance, to the study of contracts, for it shows that comprehensive contracting is unrealistic[37]. The implication of bounded rationality is that individuals will economize on their (bounded) rationality in their decision processes on the one hand, and by setting up governance structures on the other[38]. However, the fact that Williamson endorses Simon's concept of bounded rationality does not mean that he follows Simon's views on other grounds (he does not use Simon's "satisficing" hypothesis).

According to Foss, the use of bounded rationality by Williamson is a mark of an open-ended universe. "[B]oundedly rational agents can actively search for new solutions, new means-ends-structures, new satisficing levels etc. . . . ," writes Foss, "[t]his implies that models employing assumptions of bounded rationality cannot be models characterized by what Bhaskar calls 'intrinsic closure'" (Foss 1994b: 53). Clearly, Williamson uses a concept of bounded rationality intertwined with a Coasean framework: "Economizing on transaction costs essentially reduces to economizing on bounded rationality" (Williamson 1985: 32).

Two types of criticism can be made against the case of bounded rationality: first, a specific criticism against Williamson's use of bounded rationality (as developed in Geoffrey Hodgson), and second, a more general one against the concept itself (as developed by Esteban Thomsen).

Hodgson's critique

According to Hodgson, it seems that Williamson equates the search for minimum transaction costs and the concept of bounded rationality. Indeed, "Williamson adopts," explains Hodgson, "the orthodox, cost minimizing interpretation of Simon and not the one which clearly prevails in Simon's own work. In Williamson's work 'economizing on transaction costs' is part of global, cost-minimizing behavior, and this is inconsistent with Simon's idea of bounded rationality" (Hodgson 1989: 254). According to Hodgson, it seems fair to have doubts about the correct use of Simon's concept of bounded rationality by Williamson because "the fact that the cost calculus remains supreme in his theory means that he has not broken entirely from the orthodox assumption of maximization" (Hodgson 1989: 254). Nevertheless, a case can be made against Hodgson's criticism if we understand that Williamson uses the term "economizing" in the sense of "reducing." This means that Williamson uses bounded rationality in order to explain why, even though parties want to reduce transaction costs (as the parties are rational), they cannot eliminate them. However, the problem is that this view still assumes a closed-universe as Thomsen shows.

Thomsen's critique

Thomsen's (1992) criticism of the concept of bounded rationality in Simon's and in Williamson's works is far more profound because it is directly linked to the type of market theory they sustain. In fact, in Simon's work, bounded rationality can be linked to the issue of complexity (Simon 1957). Simon's argument goes like this: the world is so complex that agents (a) cannot assess all the alternatives in their environment, and (b) cannot optimize, even in terms of an imperfect level of decision à la Stigler. Agents use simplifying devices. If agents maximize, they maximize with respect to a very simplified model of reality in which only a small part of the environment is taken into account. In this small representation of reality, the agent chooses the most satisfying alternative by scanning his/her environment (satisficing). The ignorance of agents in Simon's work is due to the complexity of the world. It is exactly in this sense that Williamson interprets the concept: "Bounds on rationality are interesting . . . only to the extent that the limits of rationality are reached – which is to say, under conditions of . . . complexity" (Williamson 1975: 22).

In contrast to Williamson, Thomsen sees the issue of bounded rationality due to complexity in the following way:

> In the market-process approach, . . . facts, even if they are few and simple, have to be noticed, discovered, by alert, active agents. What complexity does is increase the likelihood that instances of "sheer" ignorance will happen, making a discovery process even more necessary. It is not that the number of facts will become so unmanageably large as to saturate the human mind, but that it becomes much more probable that many facts will not be noticed at all. In this view, the facts do not "hit" the individuals "in the face" while they act as passive receptacles of knowledge. Nor are these facts there simply to be seen by anyone who merely "scans" the environment.
>
> Thomsen (1992: 77)

Bounded rationality is not (necessarily) an instance of the open-ended character of the universe. The type of ignorance that has to be overcome by agents in the theories of Simon and Williamson does not have to do with the discovery of genuine information, but with the fact that the mind is limited in face of the complexity of the world[39]. "Simon's notion of satisficing [and of bounded rationality] may turn out to be of doubtful validity," writes Thomsen, because "[i]ndividuals would not need to scan: their attention could be drawn directly to the most worth while alternative" (Thomsen 1992: 130). The problem is that Simon has not understood the nature of profits and their role in the market process for the reason that, though he criticizes the notion of rationality, he still endorses the neoclassical theory of the market[40]. As Thomsen explains, Simon accepts the neoclassical view that prices convey all the necessary information because they are information summaries: they provide accurate knowledge to satisficing price-takers. Simon endorses the mainstream interpretation of Hayek's view of the role of prices. However, in order to sustain this approach, Simon must think of prices as equilibrium prices, because these are the prices that could possibly convey all the necessary information (Thomsen 1992: 81–2). There is a MTP in Williamson's analysis of bounded rationality, for he uses Simon's understanding, which is itself subject to criticisms from the approach of Austrian economists[41].

The equilibrium concept

Williamson's use of the equilibrium concept is complex. His notion of change is fundamental as it gives us a hint on his use of the equilibrium concept and the existence of adjustments. Williamson's theory allows for change. The very notions of asset specificity and the fundamental transformation are concepts linked to changes in the system. It is because there is an *ex post* contractual situation, which cannot be fully specified *ex ante*, that there is room for change. "[U]nderlying the central categories in Williamson's analysis . . . is a complex and changing economic reality" (Foss 1993a: 272). Williamson considers transaction cost as the equivalent of friction in classical physics. As he puts it:

> The economic counterpart of friction is transaction cost: do the parties to the exchange operate harmoniously, or are there frequent misunderstandings and conflicts that lead to delays, breakdowns, and other malfunctions? Transaction cost analysis supplants the usual preoccupation with technology and steady-state production (or distribution) expenses with an examination of the *comparative costs of planning, adapting, and monitoring task completion under alternative governance structures*.
>
> Williamson (1985: 2, emphasis in original)

Such an examination is made possible by the use of equilibrium as a foil, i.e. as a method of contrast.

An example of the use of equilibrium as a foil in Williamson can be found in his analysis of territorial restrictions. Williamson writes: "Whereas it was once common to approach customer and territorial restrictions and related forms of non standard contracting as presumptively anticompetitive, transaction costs economics maintains the rebuttable presumption that such practices have the purpose of safeguarding transactions" (Williamson 1985: 39). The approach that sees territorial restrictions as anticompetitive does not use equilibrium as a method of contrast. In other words, Williamson makes use of the equilibrium concept as a foil, which allows him to understand the existence of various contract arrangements as arising from the necessity to economize on transaction costs. The problem is that Williamson's use of the equilibrium concept is not always unambiguous. The fundamental transformation is a good example of his ambiguity.

32

To understand Williamson's concept of the fundamental transformation, it is important to understand his use of the notion of asset specificity. Williamson considers that transactions differ in the strains they put on bounded rationality and in the scope they give for opportunistic behavior. Thus, contractual arrangements will depend on the nature of the transaction, for transaction costs economics asserts that there are economic reasons for organizing transactions in certain ways. Transactions can differ in (a) the specificity of the asset exchanged, (b) the degree of uncertainty of the future and (c) the frequency of transactions.

A digression on asset specificity

Asset specificity "is most important and most distinguishes transaction cost economics from other treatments of economic organization" (Williamson 1985: 52). Asset specificity refers to the fact that resources used in a transaction have a higher value in this transaction than in any other use or to any other user. For instance, "asset specificity arises in an intertemporal context" (Williamson 1985: 54) because durability is a specific characteristic of assets. Asset specificity creates the following problem: the higher the specificity of an asset, the stronger is the possibility for the parties to the transaction to experience "lock-in" effects. "[E]xchanges that are supported by transaction-specific investments are neither faceless nor instantaneous. The study of governance owes its origins to that condition" (Williamson 1985: 56). When two parties sign a contract, the terms are negotiated in a competitive environment in which prices are set by market forces. However, because of the specificity of the asset, at the stage of contract renewal, small-number bargaining is likely. Both parties are locked into the transaction. The asset has become so sufficiently specific to the transacting parties that the asset has no alternative uses in the market. Since there are no equivalent assets in the market, the supplier can take advantage of his or her position to receive a higher quasi-rent from his or her initial investment. Similarly, the buyer can also inflict losses to the supplier by terminating the contract. Both parties are aware that they could experience capital losses in the case of redeployment of their assets during the renewal process[42]. This is Williamson's "fundamental transformation." This type of transaction has implications for governance structures[43].

A window on Williamson's theory of the market

The fundamental transformation has to do with the fact that significant capital losses can be incurred by either party at the time of contract renewal of a transaction involving a specific asset. "Faceless contracting is thereby supplanted by contracting in which the pairwise identity of the parties matters" (Williamson 1985: 62). The fundamental transformation changes the whole nature of the transaction. Since transaction specific investments are made, the identities of the parties matter and protection against capital losses must be devised. As we saw above, the combination of opportunism, bounded rationality (incomplete contracts), asset specificity and uncertainty can transform a situation of a large number competitors into a bilateral monopoly: a specialized governance structure is therefore needed. As Williamson puts it:

> Although both [parties] have a long-term interest in effecting adaptations of a joint profit-maximizing kind, each also has an interest in appropriating as much of the gain as he can on each occasion to adapt. Efficient adaptations that would otherwise be made result in costly haggling or even go unmentioned, lest the gains be dissipated by costly subgoal pursuit. Governance structures that attenuate opportunism and otherwise infuse confidence are evidently needed.
>
> Williamson (1985: 63)

What is important to understand is that the fundamental transformation is in fact a window on Williamson's theory of the market. As he explains, in a market transaction, "[m]onopolistic terms will obtain if there is only a single highly qualified supplier, while competitive terms will result if there are many. Transaction cost economics fully accepts this description of *ex ante* bidding competition but insists that the study of contracting be extended to include *ex post* features" (Williamson 1985: 61). Williamson shows here that he endorses entirely the neoclassical theory of competition in which the notion of "competitive price" will depend on the number of competitors. He also insists that a fundamental transformation will take place if the condition of large numbers bidding at the outset does not prevail thereafter. Indeed, a competitive situation will be transformed into a small-number situation in cases of substantial investments in transaction-specific assets. As he explains: "[W]hat was a large number bidding condition at the outset is effectively transformed into one of bilateral supply thereafter. This fundamental transformation has pervasive contracting consequences" (Williamson 1985: 61).

In most cases, a specialized governance structure will be designed to attenuate opportunism and avoid the effects of the fundamental transformation[44]. It seems, in the fundamental transformation case, that Williamson not only makes use of the equilibrium concept as a description of the world and as a benchmark, but also as a foil. He shows that if the world is in equilibrium at the outset (equilibrium as a benchmark), changes can sometimes occur that lead to small-number situations and which explain the existence of specialized governance structures (equilibrium as a foil). Williamson uses the equilibrium concept in different ways in order to show the existence of adjustments to changes that could take place. He jumps from one view of equilibrium to the other, without realizing that this leap creates methodological problems. Because the world is assumed to be in equilibrium in the benchmark view, it is not possible to proceed from the benchmark view to the foil view without being inconsistent in the use of the equilibrium construct.

Equilibrium as a foil or as a benchmark?

On the one hand, Williamson differentiates himself from neoclassical economics by adopting the comparative institutional view of economic organization. According to Williamson, this approach is the essence of the Coasean research program, it poses the issue of economic organization in very different terms than the neoclassical approach. Williamson's empirical research program is a good example of this: "Empirical research on transaction costs matters almost never attempts to measure such [transaction] costs directly," writes Williamson. "Instead, the question is whether organizational relations (contracting practices; governance structures) line up with the attributes of transactions as predicted by transaction cost reasoning or not" (Williamson 1985: 22).

It is by assessing the relative differences between transaction costs, and not by appraising their absolute magnitude, that such an empirical study can be made. Williamson herein contrasts the world of transaction costs with the equilibrium model. The goal of transaction costs economics consists of the comparative study of alternative costs of planning, adaptation, and control in the implementation of tasks under different governance structures. It is by using this method of comparative study that we can explain the different contractual frameworks.

On the other hand, empirical work in transaction cost economics depends, to a certain extent, on the notion of equilibrium, or what Williamson calls an "efficient sort."[45] It is another use of the natural selection argument (i.e. whatever type of organization exists in the market is efficient). It is the existence of (perfect) competition that allows the selection mechanism to take place and maintains the economy in an "efficient-always world," i.e. an equilibrium-always situation. As Williamson notes himself in a "self-critique":

> [Williamson's] argument relies in a general background way on the efficacy of competition to perform a sort between more and less efficient modes and to shift resources in favor of the former. This seems plausible, especially if the relevant outcomes are those that appear over intervals of five and ten years rather than in the very near term. This situation would nevertheless benefit from a more fully developed theory of the selection process. Transaction cost arguments are thus open to some of the same objections that evolutionary economists [e.g. Nelson and Winter] have made of orthodoxy.
>
> Williamson (1988: 174)

It seems that Williamson emphasizes the use of the equilibrium concept as a method of contrast to show the importance of "frictions" in the real world. In other words, equilibrium provides an *argumentum a contrario* that emphasizes the role of transaction costs and institutions in the market economy. However, as we saw above, in his empirical work, Williamson also uses the equilibrium concept as a description of the world and endorses some kind of an efficiency/natural selection view.

Information and prices: a Hayekian perspective?

An important assumption that Williamson uses in his work is taken from the works of Chester Barnard, Friedrich Hayek and Michael Polanyi. Williamson makes provision for the importance of tacit or personal knowledge in the context of "informal organization." In that sense, he uses Hayek's understanding of the limits of rationality, and Hayek's notion of idiosyncratic knowledge, which depends on people, time and circumstances (Williamson 1975: 5; 1985: 6).

Hayek, he contends, has understood that the economic problem is to explain the adaptive properties of economic systems to new circumstances and, in this respect, knowledge that is tacit or idiosyncratic possesses great economic value even if it cannot be collected under the form of statistical data (Williamson 1985: 8). Williamson seems to understand the contribution of Hayek regarding the nature of knowledge in economic analysis, but in *Markets and Hierarchies* (Williamson 1975) he emphasizes the alleged view of Hayek on the role of prices as "sufficient statistics." As Williamson puts it: "The 'marvel' of the economic system is that prices serve as sufficient statistics, thereby economizing on bounded rationality" (Williamson 1975: 5). This means that prices are seen as conveying sufficient knowledge for agents to act in an efficient way, i.e. to allocate resources to their most valued use.

As Thomsen explains, the problem with this version of Hayek's theory of the role of prices is that we do not know how the prices are arrived at (Thomsen 1992: 48). There is no price setting in this vision of Hayek, which means that if prices are sufficient statistics, then every individual is a price taker and the world is in equilibrium.

However, Williamson does not entirely accept this version of Hayek's theory of the role of prices. "Given bounded rationality, uncertainty, and idiosyncratic knowledge," writes Williamson, "I argue that prices often do not qualify as sufficient statistics and that a substitution of internal organization (hierarchy) for market-mediated exchange often occurs on this account" (Williamson 1975: 5)[46]. The difference between these two views of the role of prices lies in the existence of transaction costs. In that sense, Williamson uses the equilibrium concept as a method of contrast by which he can show that prices are not always sufficient statistics and that the price mechanism must sometimes be superseded by internal organization.

As we will see below, Williamson is still mistaken in this approach, even if he does not adhere to the claim that prices are always sufficient statistics. He confuses the informational role of prices with the bookshelf view of information assumed by equilibrium models (Boettke 1997b: 31). The problem is not to know when prices are sufficient statistics, it is to understand that the nature of the coordinative property of the price system lies in "its ability to communicate information concerning its own faulty information-communication properties" (Kirzner 1985a: 196).

Therefore, Williamson's understanding of the concept of information is, to a certain extent, neoclassical[47]. He endorses Hayek's view

of idiosyncratic knowledge, but he does not entirely grasp the difference between the informational view of prices and the sufficient
statistic approach[48]. These differences, as we shall see below, are
crucial to the market theory one holds.

Uncertainty

Williamson explains that it is especially with regard to *ex post*
contractual arrangements that uncertainty becomes a problem. He
contends that governance structures differ in their capacity to
adapt to uncertainty.

In Williamson's work, uncertainty has, on the one hand, a cognitive origin and, on the other, a behavioral one. It has a cognitive
origin because, in the absence of bounded rationality, the future
would be knowable. As he puts it: "those issues [of adaptation to
uncertainty] would vanish were it not for bounded rationality,
since then it would be feasible to develop a detailed strategy for cross-
ing all possible bridges in advance" (Williamson 1985: 57). He
endorses Tjalling Koopmans's distinction between primary and
secondary uncertainty[49] but he emphasizes that uncertainty also
has a behavioral origin (opportunism), for it arises mainly "because
of strategic non-disclosure, disguise, or distortion of information"
(Williamson 1985: 57). This means that adaptation to uncertainty
through the use of general rules is not sufficient in the presence of
opportunistic behavior (even though it would perhaps solve the
problem of bounded rationality). In other words, there are uncertainties regarding the implementation of contracts (*ex post*) due to
bounded rationality and opportunistic behavior. The parties should
choose a structure of governance that takes these uncertainties into
account.

The question then is: are these two sources of uncertainty compatible with an open-ended ontological view? Williamson *seems* to
endorse an open-ended view of the universe when he writes:
"Events that involve 'novelty' cannot be described by probability dis-
tributions," and "[t]he capacity for novelty in the human mind is
rich beyond imagination" (Williamson 1985: 58). This understanding of uncertainty can be associated with the Knightian view rather
than with the neoclassical approach. But his position is not entirely
clear for two reasons.

First, this view is clearly different from the one he endorsed in
Markets and Hierarchies (Williamson 1975), at which time he was

closer to Simon's approach of uncertainty defined in terms of complexity:

> As Simon indicates, however, and as is maintained here, the distinction between deterministic complexity and uncertainty is inessential. What may be referred to as "uncertainty" in chess is "uncertainty introduced into a perfectly certain environment by inability – computational inability – to ascertain the structure of the environment. But the result of the uncertainty, whatever its source, is the same: approximation must replace exactness in reaching a decision" (Simon 1972: 170). As long as either uncertainty or complexity is present in requisite degree, the bounded rationality problem arises and an interesting comparative institutional choice is often posed.
>
> Williamson (1975: 23)

He even adds in a footnote: "I also point out in this connection that the distinction between risk and uncertainty is not one with which I will be concerned – if indeed it is a truly useful one to employ in any context whatsoever" (Williamson 1975: 23). This is a clear rejection of an open-ended view of the universe and this is consistent with the neoclassical market theory.

Secondly, even if Williamson in *The Economic Institutions of Capitalism* (Williamson 1985) seems to define uncertainty as taking place in an open-ended universe, it looks like he still holds his older view when he writes: "absent the hazards of opportunism, the difficulties would vanish – since then the gaps in long-term, incomplete contracts could be faultlessly filled by recourse to the earlier described general clause device" (Williamson 1985: 63). In that sense, uncertainty is not a general feature of the world, but a consequence of certain (moral) choices made by individuals[50]. Were these choices absent, the world would not be uncertain (and, for instance, comprehensive contracts could be written) and "the main problems of economic organization . . . would vanish or be vastly transformed" (Williamson 1985: 50). Williamson's concept of uncertainty can and ought to be understood in terms of the limitations of the human mind (bounded rationality due to complexity) and hazards of opportunistic behavior (for agents do not necessarily reveal their real self and, even more, have a tendency to make false statements). From that perspective, we can only speak of true uncertainty with respect to the cognitive limitations of individuals (limitations which are rooted into human nature). That is why "[c]omprehensive contracting is not a realistic organizational alternative when provision for bounded rationality is made" (Williamson 1985: 46).

Disequilibrium analysis

"Surely," writes Foss about Williamson, "bounded rationality, complexity, etc. would have little relevance in a setting where all relevant inputs, outputs, technology, etc. were given and unchanging" (Foss 1993a: 272).

Although that statement seems correct, the question is to know whether or not Williamson draws the full implications from the open-ended world he is describing. As Kirzner (1985a, 1992a) shows, the HKP stems from the existence of Knightian uncertainty and genuine ignorance. The real economic problem is not so much the allocation of known resources, but the discovery of dispersed knowledge. As we saw above, even if Williamson's understanding of information is Hayekian to a certain extent, it is, on the whole, quite neoclassical. Informational problems matter because of the idiosyncratic nature of knowledge, not because the problem of knowledge is a problem of discovery. Even if we accept the existence of genuine uncertainty in Williamson's framework, there is no real disequilibrium analysis. Of course, Williamson (1985: 8–9) claims to be concerned with disequilibrium analysis, and he cites Hayek and Arrow on this issue. As he puts it with respect to Hayek: "An equilibrium approach to economics is thus only preliminary to the study of the main issues" (Williamson 1985: 8). However, since he has no Mises–Hayekian understanding of the role of prices, he does not see the essence of the price system in a way Austrian economists understand it. In Williamson's work, prices have no role in providing guidance in error correction and avoidance, because there is no such problem. The fundamental implication of the existence of Knightian uncertainty and genuine ignorance is not addressed in his work. The problem of detecting overlooked profit opportunities and correcting them is simply not there[51].

Adjustment processes

We can therefore question Williamson's dealing with adjustment processes. Williamson explains that his concept of fundamental transformation is part of his concern for "process analysis." As Williamson puts it: "The proposition that process matters is widely resisted and has attracted little concerted research attention from economists" (Williamson 1993 [1988]: 94). He also points out gaps in areas of neoclassical economics. He states: "Although transaction cost economics is underdeveloped in process respects, process arguments nevertheless play a prominent role" (Williamson 1993 [1988]: 94).

However, what Williamson means by process analysis is different from the notion of adjustment processes in the Austrian economic framework. Williamson's intertemporal feature is strictly neo-classical in its essence. He is concerned with *ex ante* and *ex post* situations. Process plays a role to the extent that he discusses contracting in two different situations. His intertemporal feature is linked to the incentive alignment problem that agents can meet *ex post*. This means that transaction cost economics is a comparative study of different states, it is not about disequilibrium analysis, i.e. the role of disequilibrium prices in the discovery of dispersed and not yet known knowledge. Williamson is concerned with the comparative institutional analysis of costs, there is no HKP and therefore no true adjustment in his view. This limited understanding of process analysis leads to a MTP in his work. Although he realizes that a process approach is important to the explanation of the firm, he stays in the neoclassical understanding of the process, and therefore cannot entirely explain the phenomenon[52].

The entrepreneur

The analysis above showed that Williamson's analysis, like that of Coase, has no place for the entrepreneur. Changes are not entrepreneurially driven in his system, they are the result of opportunism and bounded rationality. But does it mean that changes that take place in the system are not entirely genuine? It is difficult to imagine that Williamson's theory is just another Chicagoan descriptive view of the world. However, authors like Sidney Winter are not really sure if Williamson "aspires to a historico-evolutionary mode of explanation or, instead, to something more like the time-less, abstract deduction from presumed 'data' that characterizes general equilibrium theory" (Winter 1993 [1988]: 191). The absence of the entrepreneur creates an inconsistency in modern transaction cost economics. Even if, as we saw above, many features of an open-ended world are used as a background of Williamson's theory, he does not draw all the necessary consequences, because he only demonstrates a partial understanding of the problem of adjustment.

Concluding remarks

We have shown that Williamson's analysis essentially revolves around the understanding of the nature of the transaction, which separates his work from a conventional neoclassical approach. This focus on the transaction (a) sheds light on the nature of the asset transacted and its consequences in terms of investments; and (b) shows that the identity of the parties to a transaction is critical to the nature of the contract. Williamson considers that his transaction cost economics is the first analysis to be able to bridge the key gaps in the neoclassical paradigm. The author provides a taxonomy of transaction costs and shows that his approach can explain the existence of the firm, its efficiency and its structure. The leitmotiv of Williamson's research program is to show that the evolution of organizations can best be understood by the constant search for a decrease of transaction costs.

Even if Williamson makes use, most of the time, of the equilibrium concept as a foil, he does not use the knowledge problem identified by Hayek. The absence of disequilibrium analysis and of entrepreneurship shows the limits of his approach in the development of a theory of the firm based on the fundamental problems identified by Austrian economics. There is a MTP in Williamson's work, for he still makes use of a neoclassical conception of the market, although he wants to cope with the problems implied by the use of this approach. Even if we were to consider Williamson's work as a part of evolutionary economics, as Foss (1993a) seems to argue, this would not change the fact that Williamson does not consider, in the final analysis, the central economic problem.

An Austrian assessment of transaction costs

On the nature of transaction costs

Different authors have different definitions of what transaction costs are. Coase describes the nature of transaction costs as follows:

> In order to carry out a market transaction it is necessary to discover who it is that one wishes to deal with, to inform people that one wishes to deal and on what terms, to conduct

negotiations leading up to a bargain, to draw up the contract, to undertake the inspection needed to make sure that the terms of the contract are being observed, and so on. These operations are often extremely costly.

Coase (1960: 15)

Eggertsson explains that "transaction costs are the costs that arise when individuals exchange ownership rights to economic assets and enforce their exclusive rights" (Eggertsson 1990: 14). It should be noted that Dahlman explains, after having reviewed the different definitions one can give to transaction costs, that "it is really necessary to talk only about one type of transaction cost: resource losses incurred due to imperfect information" (Dahlman 1979: 148). Similarly, Eggertsson writes that "transaction costs are in one way or another associated with the cost of acquiring information about exchange" (Eggertsson 1990: 15). We can therefore consider that transaction costs are information costs arising in situations of exchange of property rights between individuals. More specifically they include:

(1) The search for information about the distribution of price and quality of commodities and labor inputs, and the search for potential buyers and sellers and for relevant information about their behavior and circumstances. (2) The bargaining that is needed to find the true position of buyers and sellers when prices are endogenous. (3) The making of contracts. (4) The monitoring of contractual partners to see whether they abide by the terms of the contracts. (5) The enforcement of a contract and the collection of damages when partners fail to observe their contractual obligations. (6) The protection of property rights against third-party encroachment.

Eggertsson (1990: 15)[53]

It seems that all of these aspects of transaction costs have to do with the search for information in the sense that neoclassical economics understands the notion of search. If we are to include them in the standard perfect competition analysis, we have to realize, following Coase and Dahlman, that perhaps certain "institutions fulfill an economic function by reducing transaction costs and therefore ought to be treated as variables determined inside the economic scheme of things" (Dahlman 1979: 161–2). According to Coase, the firm is such an institution: *it exists in order to reduce the resource losses due to imperfect information associated with exchange.* Indeed, "the costless information that is assumed in the perfect competition model renders the model ineffective for studying the firm" (Demsetz 1993 [1988]: 159).

On the concept of ignorance

Austrian economists agree with transaction costs theorists that there are costs due to imperfect information. There is little doubt that there is imperfect information in the market and that individuals have to obtain information and overcome certain constraints in order to exchange. However the question is: what is the nature of the imperfect information? There is nothing in the transaction cost framework that could allow us to think that imperfections are due to the open-endedness of the world. As we saw above, Coase and Williamson explain that we must take into account the existence of these imperfections. However, it seems that in their views, information is a good like any other good. Therefore, what they mean by imperfect information (transaction costs) is simply the fact that there is an optimal level of information in the economy. Certain activities could be carried out in the market but they are too costly in terms of information to be acquired and constraints to be overcome. The nature of the firm is to reduce these costs (which can be the source of sub-optimalities). This view is consistent with the equilibrium-always approach. As such, the problem with transaction cost economics is not one of internal coherence, it is that it cannot account for a rationale for the existence of the firm in an open-ended universe[54].

Information costs are actually opportunity costs, since they refer to the costs that are incurred in order to obtain information. At any given moment, the economy is likely to be less than fully coordinated with respect to the information in possession of all the actors: there is an optimal level of ignorance, i.e. an optimal level of resources spent in the overcoming of this ignorance, and there is an optimal level of information in the hands of the economic actors[55]. This approach, developed by people such as Downs (1957), Stigler (1957) and more recently refined by Stiglitz (1994), understands ignorance as *known ignorance.* In this world, individuals are assumed to know what they do not know (even if one introduces a probabilistic notion of ignorance).

The existence of transaction costs is compatible with the process view of the market, for this approach incorporates the neoclassical understanding of "ignorance" (which implies that there is an optimal level of information) and the Austrian understanding (which implies that there is a HKP). However, in the process view, ignorance may itself be unknown, in other words, individuals may be ignorant of what it is that they do not know. Therefore, there is no such thing as an optimal level of (unknown) ignorance in the process view because one cannot spend resources to find something that he/she is utterly unaware of. This approach implies an understanding of the economy as an open system, for genuine information might arise in the hands of individuals. This means that individuals are utterly unaware of the fact that others may possess knowledge that could be relevant for them (knowledge is scattered in the economy) or that information (which could become knowledge) is unknown to anyone. As Kirzner explains, while contrasting this view with the closed system:

> For the open-ended universe it is not enough that knowledge is incomplete; it is required that the decisionmaker *be ignorant of the extent of his own ignorance.* He is subject to genuine surprise. One so subject to surprise is not choosing between perceived alternatives about whose outcome he has specifically incomplete information; he is, in important respects, making a choice without knowing what he is selecting, or what he is giving up.
> Kirzner (1988: xvii–xviii, emphasis in original)

The important aspect of the process view is that individuals can *discover* what they were ignorant of. In fact, we can stipulate, following Mises (1966) and Kirzner (1973, 1979, 1985a), that there is a tendency in human beings, by being alert to opportunities, to discover what could help them to reduce or remove felt uneasiness. In the market economy, profit is the incentive for individuals to be alert and to discover what they were utterly ignorant of.

Concluding remarks

There is no HKP in transaction cost economics, for it disregards the process set in motion by entrepreneurs at the two levels of market ignorance (spatial and intertemporal). The analysis above and the concept of ignorance calls for three remarks.

1 The transaction cost school is blind to the real importance of transaction costs. If transaction costs were reduced to zero (costless
   information), then it would still be the case that entrepreneurial
   discoveries would be necessary. In other words, in the case of costless, but not perfect, information, the HKP remains. "[T]he possibility of costlessly acquiring information concerning available
   desirable opportunities is by no means sufficient to ensure that
   these opportunities will ever be grasped. . . . Zero transaction costs
   do not of themselves guarantee that transaction opportunities
   will be discovered" (Kirzner 1973: 227). It is one thing to have
   free information available, it is another to assume that it is
   known to every market participant. A world without transaction
   costs does not preclude sheer ignorance[56].

2 As mentioned earlier, the transaction costs analysis led its propo-
   nents to a comparative approach in which transaction costs are
   assessed and are shown to be the cause of the institutional setting
   under study. The transaction costs view naturally leads to a cost-
   benefit analysis. However, "[as] individuals are not assumed to
   'know what it is that they don't know'," explains Thomsen, "the
   choice between carrying out an activity within an organization or
   leaving it in the market cannot be made in terms of costs and benefits:
   knowing the latter would require individuals to know and evaluate what could or could not be discovered if scope were left for
   entrepreneurship, a logical impossibility" (Thomsen 1992: 110).

3 I contend that the new variations on the transaction cost theme fall
   under the same criticism. Richard Langlois's concept of "dynamic
   transaction costs" (Langlois and Robertson 1995: 35) is, in essence,
   identical to the notion of transaction costs used by Williamson,
   even if there are important differences in degree[57].

Conclusion: MTP and transaction costs economics

The basic conclusion of this section is that it is not enough for a process approach to show, even in a sophisticated way, that there can be
sub-optimalities in the market system due to the costs of transacting,
and that these sub-optimalities can be overcome through integration.
Even if this view is perfectly acceptable in its context (i.e. a neoclassical understanding of the market system), it is only partially
complete from the point of a process theorist. As we will see
below, an entrepreneurial approach sheds a different light on the
importance of transaction costs and emphasizes the discovery
aspect involved in the emergence of a firm.

In this section, I did not deal with the measurement-cost approach, for this view is subject to the same kind of critique as the asset-specificity one. The measurement-cost approach explains that sub-optimalities may arise because of the difficulties of monitoring and controlling the contributions of each individual working in teams or the quality of the output of a stage of production (principal-agent problems). Again, this view is perfectly acceptable in its context, but it represents only part of what process theorists want to explain[58].

The analysis above can also be contrasted with the limits that economists generally find in the transaction costs approach (Milgrom and Roberts 1992: 33–4). One problem is that production and transaction costs both depend on the organization and the technology used in the firm, which makes the conceptual separation between production and transaction costs difficult. This is certainly true as far as empirical studies are concerned, but it does not seem to undermine Coase's insight. Another critique concerns the notion that efficient institutions arise to minimize transaction costs. Why would the suboptimal situation be solved by efficient organizations? It is certainly the case, critics of transaction cost economics say, that transaction costs are not entirely solved in an efficient way within organizations. However, this does not undermine the transaction costs approach if we understand it as a tool to compare institutions. While these criticisms are relevant, they are different in nature from the MTP.

A BRIEF ASSESSMENT OF TWO RELEVANT ALTERNATIVES TO THE TRANSACTION COST VIEW

The MTP and resource-based theories of the firm

Following Peter Lewin (1998b), I would like to assess briefly the core issue of resource-based theories of the firm. I will not deal with capabilities *per se* in this section, since we will explore this issue in relation to the growth of the firm in the next chapter. The resource-based literature asserts that firms possess unique resources (capabilities) that represent their *raison d'être*. From these resources they are able to earn rents. Thus, to understand this body of economics, we must first briefly explore the concept of rent.

As Mises (1966: 635–7) explains, the concept of rent, derived from the Ricardian notion of rent, and as used in standard microeconomic theory does not make much sense. In some ways, economics can do without the notion of rent because this notion was developed to treat problems that have been adequately treated by marginal-utility theory since then. The Ricardian theory of rent was meant to explain differences that could exist among land returns. Some land would provide better returns than others, but all land would earn rent. In Ricardo's model, rent is therefore related to the absolute scarcity of land. However, "[t]he fact that land of different quality and fertility, i.e. yielding different returns per unit of input, is valued differently does not pose any special problem to modern economics," wrote Mises (1966: 635). Land of different quality will yield different returns, and the land with the more suitable quality will tend to be used first. The theory of value and price is not based on classes of goods (land, labor, etc) but on the services each good (whatever its class) will provide. Thus, there is no basis in economics for a theory of rent, except in a restricted definition of the term. A rent can be only be defined as the income stream accruing to an input in payment of its services. In that sense, "the price of the 'whole good,' also known as the capital value of the good, is equal to the sum of the expected future rents discounted by . . . the rate of interest" (Rothbard 1993 [1962]: 418). The rent is the price of a unit of service. This approach was developed by Frank Fetter and refined by Rothbard (Lewin 1998b; Lewin and Phelan 1999).

As Lewin (1998b) and Lewin and Phelan (1999) explain, the concept of rents used in organization theory is convoluted, not clear and therefore hard to pin down. They explain that at least five different concepts of rent can be identified in the literature: Ricardian rent, Marshallian rent, monopoly rent, entrepreneurial rent and quasi-rent. (To which one could add: quasi-Ricardian rent and Pareto rent.) However, no clear definitions of these notions stand out, as they overlap each other. "The sophisticated distinction between 'rents' and 'quasi-rents' is spurious," contends Mises (1966: 635), and so are the other distinctions. Indeed, they either are (a) irrelevant because there are as many distinctions as there are imaginable cases in reality; or (b) useless because they already fall into another category of distribution theory (as in the case of monopoly and entrepreneurial rents).

Most of this confusion over economic rents stems from of the use of the equilibrium concept. In most approaches, the equilibrium concept is used in two ways: (a) as a description of reality, and (b) as an indictment, i.e. as a standard for criticizing reality. In case (a), rents are returns that are attributable to resource heterogeneity.

In the indictment approach, rents are abnormal (excess) returns that have to be attributed to abnormal market situations (monopoly, entrepreneurship). The confusion around the notion of rent in resource-based theories is due to the misuse of the notion of equilibrium (this is a mark of the MTP). In resource-based theories rents are earned by inputs in fixed or quasi-fixed supply, like land in Ricardo's model (Rumelt 1987). From this notion (that supply is fixed), economists derive entrepreneurial rents, monopoly rents, Ricardian rents and the like. In all these cases, the distinguishing mark is the existence of an excess of an asset's value over its salvage value (i.e. its value in its next best use). Again, this stems from the use of the concept of equilibrium as both a description of reality and as a standard. As a result, there is an ongoing internal struggle against the neoclassical paradigm in resource-based theories[59]. However, even if the concept of rent can be useful in some cases (as defined by Fetter and Rothbard), the best solution seems to me to side with Mises and to try to avoid the use of the notion of rent when it is not necessary and when it can be replaced by another, already better understood, notion.

Even if one can find a MTP in resource-based approaches, it is still the case that they are extremely valuable, for they emphasize different phenomena that are, in another context, cherished by Austrian economists. Entrepreneurship and the discovery of profit opportunities are, to some extent, a theme common to resource-based and Austrian views. In other words, competition is understood as a process and not as a state of affairs in both schools. Understanding competition as a process helps explain empirical phenomena that cannot be explained by standard neoclassical theory, such as the persistent dispersion of returns that is wider among firms of the same industry than across industries (Rumelt 1984, 1987) and the different rates of growth among firms of the same industry (Penrose 1995 [1959]). In addition, resource-based and evolutionary theories differ from neoclassical approaches in the sense that they reject the use of the representative firm and they are equipped with various decision-rules systems (Foss 1997b)[60]. A resource-based approach allows us to understand why firms differ and why they must differ in many ways if they are to exist and grow. The problem is that, in the final analysis (Lewin and Phelan 1999), this explanation is still cast into a neoclassical mold, as it does not explain disequilibrium phenomena. The very notion of rent as used in resource-based theories implies a mechanical approach to the existence and development of firms. However, rents come into existence because they are discovered and maintained by entrepreneurial activity. Rents will be derived from a bundle of resources only if entrepreneurial activity constantly makes sure that these assets are allocated in the right direction.

In the rest of this work, I shall adopt an idea that is derived from the resource-based approach: complementary inputs used in a firm may come to be seen as a "resource" in themselves, giving to the whole capital structure of a firm an idiosyncratic property[61]. However, this is not directly related to the idea of rent (or differential rent), as we shall see below.

The notion of rent is a way to try to solve questions that exist only in a disequilibrium world. Rents are an indication of unexploited inefficiencies that cannot exist in an equilibrium-always universe.

The special case of Knight's theory of organizations

Knight is perhaps the economist who has played the most important role as far as an "Austrian approach" to the firm is concerned. According to Boudreaux and Holcombe, the firm, in the Knightian framework, "is a necessary component of the creation of markets. In contrast, the Coasian firm emerges only after markets exist: it engages in management rather than in true entrepreneurship" (Boudreaux and Holcombe 1989: 147). It is true, as we saw above, that even if Knight's work was fairly neoclassical in its tone, he developed a distinctive explanation for the firm. His explanation emphasizes the existence of the entrepreneur who is able to deal with (genuine) uncertainty in the economy. As we saw above, Knight proposed a famous distinction between risk and uncertainty. On the one hand, there is what he calls the "ignorance theory of probability" and, on the other, the "doctrine of real probability."[62] It is in reference to the second epistemological theory that Knight proposes his view of firms. Knight's theory of the firm can be said to take place in real time: genuine knowledge arises over time. Of course, in other parts of his work, he showed a neoclassical understanding of the market, but there is an appreciation of genuine uncertainty in Knight's work that allows for the existence of firms.

The Knightian entrepreneur plays a key role in this picture: he/she bears the uncertainty when the consumer can only handle risk. He/she is the agent in the market who can take advantage of uncertainty and try to obtain profits. Profit is only a residual revenue in Knight's work[63], which is not the case in the work of Kirzner.

The Kirznerian entrepreneur is "alert" to profit opportunities and if he/she discovers one, he/she exploits it: such individuals are at the origin of new knowledge in the market. For Kirzner, genuine surprises go hand in hand with pure profit discoveries made by entrepreneurs. This understanding of the entrepreneur's role and of profit is different from Knight's. One could argue that these differences are epistemological: Knight states that "[i]n so far as there is 'real change' in the Bergsonian (i.e. Heracleitean) sense it seems clear that reasoning is impossible" (Knight 1965 [1921]: 209). For Knight, if genuine uncertainty exists "the universe may not be ultimately knowable" (Knight 1965 [1921]: 210). It is because of a limitation of human consciousness that agents cannot deal with uncertainty, this is beyond all reasoning[64]. Even if Knight considers the fog of uncertainty as unpierceable by human consciousness, it is important to notice that Kirzner considers entrepreneurial alertness as possible under Knightian uncertainty. Indeed, it is because of an individual's alertness that action under uncertainty exists (Kirzner 1985a: 40–67).

To a certain extent, we could put Knight and Coase in the same category, they both have an open-ended approach in their work, but a key difference between the two authors lies in their understanding of the role of the entrepreneur. Coase does not realize what Knight has understood: entrepreneurial judgment cannot be bought and sold, and this requires, in Knight's system, the existence of a firm. However, even if the Knightian view of the firm is based on the entrepreneur, it is not satisfactory for modern Austrian economists. Langlois and Cosgel see Knight's modern followers not in the moral hazard and asymmetric information approach but in the incomplete contracts view of the firm. The reason for this is that the incomplete contracts view offers "a clear interpretation of Knight's notion of guaranteeing" (Langlois and Cosgel 1993: 462). The modern incomplete contract approach, however, takes place in a world without genuine uncertainty, which is incompatible with Knight's view. Indeed, "Knight took the analysis to a higher level of explanation, pointing out not only the effects but also the cause of contractual incompleteness, namely, lack of knowledge of the categories of action and the consequent need for judgment" (Langlois and Cosgel 1993: 462). According to Langlois and Cosgel, it is because of uncertainty that contracts are incomplete in the Knightian framework; whereas it is because of the incompleteness of contracts that moral hazard and hold-up costs arise (and the need of firms) in the approach of authors like Grossman and Hart.

Although Knight's view has an important influence on Austrian economists, it is incomplete in light of modern market process theory.

ARE THE ABOVE APPROACHES SUFFICIENT?

As we saw at the beginning of the chapter, resource-based and transaction cost approaches are the most relevant rationales to explain the phenomenon of the firm. Again, a process view of the problem will shed a new light on the issue of the firm and incorporate the problem of the existence of the firm in the bigger picture of the market process. Yet it is legitimate for an economist to ask the question: why do we need an Austrian version of the solution, when what we have at our disposal has already a powerful explanatory power?

In many instances, Austrian economics is in agreement with neoclassical economics. For instance, transaction costs and the suboptimalities that they can entail are part of the Austrian framework. The same is true with respect to capabilities and many other concepts developed in the field of industrial organization. As White reminds us, "Kirzner has shown that the Coasean view of the firm as 'an island of planning in the sea of the market economy' can be treated as complementary to the Austrian view of the knowledge problems inherent in economy-wide planning" (White 1992: 265). However, it is still the case that certain phenomena require different explanations if we realize the market theory implied and its consequences. Austrian economics aims at giving a much richer, and somewhat different, rationale of market phenomena. The main reason Austrian economists should develop a theory of the firm is analogous to the justification of the Austrian approach to explaining advertising: in equilibrium, firms would not emerge. As I will argue in Chapter 2, in order to understand the emergence of the firm we need explicitly to introduce entrepreneurial activity in a disequilibrium framework. As Kirzner explains with respect to the economics of advertising:

> To be sure these strategies [of the real world advertisers] display features difficult to reconcile with the economics of a closed world. The phenomenon of advertising simply cannot fit a world in which consumers already know what they want. Nor can this phenomenon even fit in a world in which consumers know what information they need to obtain, in order to know what they want. Advertising

exists in a world in which people do not know what information they need to know.

Kirzner (1988: xxi–xxii)[65]

A theory of the firm should be part of a theory of the market process
in an open-ended universe. Therefore, we ought to understand the
existence of the firm in relation to the role of the entrepreneur in
the market. This implies that transaction cost economics (and
resource-based theories) is certainly sufficient in an equilibrium-
always world, but it is not rich enough if one is to make an account
of economic phenomena in a living economy, i.e. a catallaxy. The
phenomenon of the firm can better be understood in a world that
is not only populated by Robbinsian maximizers. For these reasons,
there is a need for an Austrian theory of the firm in economics[66].

CONCLUSION: THE MTP AND BEYOND

One consequence of the MTP in Williamson's work is that the existence of firms is seen as the result of market failures. This is unfortunate, even if the term "market failure" does not carry any normative
content. The economic problem is a knowledge problem, and to state
that markets fail when there is a firm, is to do away with the HKP.
The trick is not to use the equilibrium concept as a foil and to
show that markets fail when firms exist, but to explain why, knowing
the HKP, firms are embedded in markets in the real economy[67].

As Richard Langlois states: "members of this group [new institutional economics] see themselves as going beyond and correcting
deficiencies in the basic neoclassical story" (Langlois 1989: 291). It
is true that Williamson and his followers point out deficiencies,
but the solution provided is still, to a certain extent, within the
original framework. Demsetz (1969) is right when he explains,
like Coase, that economists should not do nirvana economics, but
realize that the world is made of institutions that do not exist in
the perfect competition framework and that we should study these
for what they are. The comparison of feasible alternatives à la
Williamson is therefore a more promising research program than
that of neoclassical economics, but it lacks an identification of the
real economic problem. Williamson is misled by what Kirzner
calls the "allocative paradigm." As Kirzner puts it: "where they
have indeed applied [the allocative paradigm] in such illegitimate
fashion, economists have become trapped in their own paradigm;
they have failed to recognize crucial aspects of socioeconomic

problems that simply do not fit into the allocation framework" (Kirzner 1985a: 153). The MTP is another way of saying that economists have been trapped in their own paradigm, or, in other words, that the neoclassical theory of the market has no room for a causal-genetic explanation of the firm. To explain the emergence of the firm, we cannot retain the neoclassical theory of the market, thus we cannot simply graft the theory of the firm onto the theory of the market.

An Austrian analysis of the firm would incorporate Knightian uncertainty as a feature of the world and genuine ignorance as one of its consequences. As a result, the price mechanism must be considered as a self-corrective system in which disequilibrium relative prices play a fundamental role in the discovery of genuine information. The essence of the mechanism is the existence of profit opportunities that provide the incentives to engage in entrepreneurial activity. As Boudreaux and Holcombe put it: "A fully adequate theory of the firm cannot be developed within a general-equilibrium setting because one of the key characteristics of a firm is decision making under uncertainty" (Boudreaux and Holcombe 1989: 153). This decision making under uncertainty is the subject of the following chapter.

2

THE LACHMANNIAN PROBLEM, THE PROMOTER AND THE EMERGENCE OF THE FIRM

When uncertainty and the task of deciding what to do and how to do it takes the ascendancy over that of execution, the internal organization of the productive group is no longer a matter of indifference or a mechanical detail. Centralization of this deciding and controlling function is imperative, a process of "cephalization," such as has taken place in the evolution of organic life, is inevitable, and for the same reasons as in the case of biological evolution.

Frank Knight (1965 [1921]: 268)

INTRODUCTION

One of the main reasons for the neglect of the firm in modern economic theory is Robbins's emphasis on markets: economics was not meant to be concerned with organizations (as discussed in Chapter 1). Machlup explains, for instance, that a firm is just a "theoretical link, a mental construct helping to explain how one gets from the cause to the effect" (Machlup 1967: 9). It is a way station in the understanding of the allocational role of the market. "As distribution and allocation came increasingly in the forefront of economic analysis," explains McNulty, "production, in the sense of the physical or qualitative transformation of resources, which had been the initial analytical focus of the *Wealth of Nations*, was pushed increasingly in the background, and with it, the role of the firm – the organization through which that transformation had been effected. This was accompanied, as economics developed and aspired to scientific status, by a growing role for the concept of market competition" (McNulty 1984: 239). It is because of their strong focus on markets that economists of the twentieth century, including Austrian economists, have often neglected the firm by giving it an increasingly passive role[1]. Even if we think of Knight's theory of the firm as a contribution to Austrian economics, there still remains a neglect of the firm in the process view. As Witt explains:

> The neglect of the firm as the organizational form of an entrepreneurial venture has a tradition in Austrian economics. It may be traced back to a characteristic of the scientific community in the German language countries. There, economic theory (*Volkswirtschaftslehre*) and business economics (*Betriebswirtschaftslehre*) were institutionally segregated as early as at the turn of the century to a degree still unknown today in the Anglo-Saxon world. As Lachmann once conjectured, Austrian writers therefore considered the organizational form of entrepreneurial activities to be a topic best left to their business economic fellows.
>
> Witt (1995: 12)

Of course, as Foss explains, Austrian economists emphasized the role of institutions in a world of change and realized very early on that "in the absence of the knowledge problems introduced by a changing economic reality there would be no costs of discovering contractual partners, drafting and executing contracts, monitoring production, constructing contractual safeguards" (Foss 1994a: 43). The firm, in this perspective, is an institution that helps people to deal with economic change. Furthermore, the principal-agent concept was implicitly recognized by Hayek in 1940, when he explained that, under socialism, it was not at all clear that plant managers would work in the full interests of the planning authorities. Also, as Foss explains, the Austrian school has always been concerned with property rights (starting with Menger), and Austrian capital theory and business cycle theory contain the concepts of asset specificity and asset complementarity that are crucial in the works of today's theorists of the firm. Foss also shows that even if the economics of the firm was not a distinct subject in the Austrian literature, some, if not many, concepts that are used in contemporary theories were developed by economists in the Austrian approach.

Stavros Ioannides (1997: 2) explains that there are strong relations between an Austrian perspective on the firm and the various theories of the contractual approach. Indeed, many authors have started to explore the link between the capabilities approach and Austrian economics, but the relevance of entrepreneurship to the existence of the firm remains quasi-unexplored[2].

ON THE IMPORTANCE OF THE PRIME
MOVER: THE ENTREPRENEUR

My goal is to develop a theory of the firm that builds on the ideas developed by theorists in the modern Austrian school. The main feature of this approach, of course, is to introduce the entrepreneur as the "prime mover" of the firm. It seems that the entrepreneur is either ignored in the literature on the firm or is seen as a "Robbinsian manager." Kirzner argues that "the conventional theory of the firm tends to mask the purely entrepreneurial element in the decision-making of producers. Yet, the fact that the firm is assumed to make decisions which maximize 'profits' tends to promote the misunderstanding that it is indeed entrepreneurship that is at the core of the theory of the firm" (Kirzner 1973: 54)[3]. Indeed, because of the market theory problem (MTP), there is no element of entrepreneurship in the orthodox view of the firm and in most modern theories (the assumption of maximization of profit – i.e. net revenues – gives, in fact, no room for entrepreneurship). Neoclassical economics has somehow replaced the entrepreneur by the firm, putting great emphasis on its role as a maximizer of profit. "[T]his emphasis has misled many students of price theory," writes Kirzner, "to understand the notion of the entrepreneur as nothing more than the locus of profit-maximizing decision-making within the firm" (Kirzner 1973: 27). Foss (1997a) makes the point that the entrepreneur is seen as a Robbinsian manager: the "job [of the Robbinsian manager] essentially is to shift transactions over the boundaries of the firm under the impact of changing transaction costs. There is no or little recognition of entrepreneurship that relates to the discovery of new types of contracts" (Foss 1997a: 11). This implies that "[s]ome essentially unspecified mechanism is supposed to throw up new types of contracts and essentially unspecified selection forces are presumed to select the fittest/most efficient of these contracts or organizational forms" (Foss 1997a: 11–12). This perspective sharply contrasts with the view of Mises (1966: 303–11), which contends that there is a difference in nature between the entrepreneurial and the managerial functions.

In *The Entrepreneur in Microeconomic Theory*, Humberto Barreto explains that "[n]ot only did the entrepreneur disappear as the firm was integrated into a consistent whole, but as fast as he departed, the modern theory entered. The theory of the firm came in a rush and the entrepreneur was rejected simultaneously, just as quickly" (Barreto 1989: 98). The entrepreneur of classical economics was replaced by the manager. The entrepreneur as a manager is already present in Coase's (1937) article. Coase defines the firm as a "system of relationships which comes into existence when the direction of resources is dependent on an entrepreneur" (Coase 1993a [1937]: 22). The entrepreneur is a resource allocator who decides how to organize transactions within the firm and who makes the make-or-buy decision. In Coase's framework, there are costs and diminishing returns to management: the entrepreneur-manager is a Robbinsian maximizer (a Robbinsian manager) whose work is to carry on an optimal level of make-or-buy decisions.

This view of the Robbinsian manager is "popular" among many authors[4]. According to Alchian and Demsetz (1972), the manager monitors the members of the team and checks their input performance. As we saw earlier, he/she is also in charge of all the contracts (nexus of contract) and receives a residual revenue. Demsetz, more recently, argued that "our understanding of firms can be improved by recognizing that management is a scarce resource employed in a world in which knowledge is incomplete and costly to obtain" (Demsetz 1993 [1988]: 161). The manager is clearly seen as a scarce resource that can be bought and sold on the market. "This is explicitly recognized by Knight and Coase," continues Demsetz, "and it is an important component of theories based on monitoring cost" (Demsetz 1993 [1988]: 161). There is no doubt that Demsetz sees the entrepreneur-manager as a pure resource allocator when he states that, in order to explain the firm, the correct question to ask is "whether the sum of management and transaction cost incurred through in-house production is more or less than the sum of management and transaction cost incurred through purchase across markets" (Demsetz 1993 [1988]: 162). Management costs are the costs attached to the Robbinsian manager whose returns are diminishing. Along the same lines, Sydney Winter wants to develop a theory of the firm "explicitly as a theory about individual entrepreneurs" (Winter 1993 [1988]: 182). However, even if he wants to introduce a strong role for the entrepreneur, it is still a Robbinsian manager that he envisions, for the manager would optimize his/her income–leisure trade-off taking into account the fact that he/she is a utility-maximizer whose work is to manage a firm (Winter 1993 [1988]: 182). The same can be said about Morris Silver (1984) who is eager to find an entrepreneurial theory of vertical integration (he assesses the works of Schumpeter and Kirzner in this respect). The entrepreneur Silver describes has finite managerial resources at his/her disposal, and vertical integration facilitates "the implementation of new ideas by reducing information transmission costs" (Silver 1984: 17). However, Silver does not break away from the optimization view of transaction cost economics, even if he realizes that there is a special function attached to the entrepreneur. Mark Casson (1982) is perhaps the author who went the furthest in seeing the entrepreneur as different from a standard producer[5], but he does not consider entrepreneurship as distinct from other productive factors (Loasby 1982)[6].

Even if Knight's entrepreneur has a lot to do with pure monitoring (as Demsetz reminds us), this is not the only role attributed to the entrepreneur. Indeed, the entrepreneur in Knight bears true uncertainty and therefore is not a pure Robbinsian manager. As Boudreaux and Holcombe say: "The primary function of the Knightian firm is entrepreneurial" (Boudreaux and Holcombe 1989: 147). However, as we saw above, the role of the entrepreneur in Knight's theory is not entirely satisfactory.

"In the beginning there were markets" as Williamson (1985: 87) says. Markets entail the existence of entrepreneurs, in the Austrian framework, but Williamson does not have an entrepreneurial process in mind. "[A] theory of the firm cannot be complete unless it incorporates these entrepreneurial decisions [as proposed in Knight] into firm's activities" (Boudreaux and Holcombe 1989: 153). Boudreaux and Holcombe are perfectly right in saying that the entrepreneur is needed for a more complete understanding of the firm, as the emergence of the firm must be explained with the existence of the entrepreneur. We saw above that we need entrepreneurs to bridge the gaps in knowledge in the economy. In the process view, disequilibrium prices have an important role to play, for they are the source of information and the profits they can bring are rewards for the discovery of unseen (or new) knowledge in the market[7]. The entrepreneur exploits pure profit opportunities that he or she discovers. Understanding this role is fundamental if we are to understand the ever-changing state of the market[8].

Entrepreneurship and the market process

Since 1973, Kirzner has been concerned, among other things, with explaining the "economic problem" which is, as we saw in Chapter 1, not so much the allocation of known resources, but the discovery and use of dispersed (or not yet perceived) knowledge. This Hayekian understanding of the market system led Kirzner to focus his work on a criticism of the equilibrium-always approach of neoclassical economics and to provide a coherent alternative. He showed that the Robbinsian maximizers depicted by mainstream economic theory are only meaningful in a known means–end framework (this is also true if agents are boundedly rational). As such, they cannot be a source of novelty in the system, which, as we saw above, implies that the neoclassical approach takes place in a closed-universe. As Vaughn puts it: "In fact, they [Robbinsian maximizers] could never even be understood to bring about a general equilibrium since all they could do is to operate within the context of what they know" (Vaughn 1994: 141). The situation is therefore twofold. The system is either in equilibrium-always and there is only one thing to study: external shocks to the economy – the use of equilibrium as a description of the world – or the system is not in equilibrium (or in an "unsatisfactory equilibrium" as in Grossman and Stiglitz's paradox) and it stays that way unless we find appropriate policy measures to correct it – the use of equilibrium as a benchmark (a standard for criticizing reality). The problem with these views, as Kirzner shows, is that they do not explain the issue we seek to understand: how is the economic problem solved?

Kirzner, following Mises and Hayek, shows that in order to explain the market process, we need a theory of the use of knowledge in society (and of the division of labor), and this requires introducing the concept of the entrepreneur into the analysis. Entrepreneurial behavior is distinct from the maximizing behavior of neoclassical theory. In Kirzner's theory, the essence of the entrepreneur is "alertness." Alertness is a tendency for an individual to discover what would be profitable to him/her if he/she were to discover it[9]. This is the capacity of human beings to sense that something is likely to be profitable. As Pasteur explains, discoveries do not generally happen by chance, only the prepared mind will notice what has to be noticed[10]. Schumpeter (1989b [1948]: 277) had a similar view when he explained that individuals usually have a pre-scientific hunch, a sense of what it is that they can discover[11]. The entrepreneur notices opportunities that were hitherto ignored. He or she discovers that a demand for a certain good was there, waiting to be discovered, but consumers did not know about it. This demand was implicit in the state of the world, but was not expressed. In that sense, the entrepreneur gives life, so to speak, to an implicit demand on the part of the consumers[12]. This amounts to either noticing a shift in demand curves or noticing the emergence of new demand curves. In other words, the entrepreneur redefines the means–end framework and tends to bring the system closer to equilibrium (this activity tends

60

to increase the coordination of individuals' plans). Entrepreneurial behavior is purposeful[13] and it is brought about by the lure for profit[14].

This view implies that entrepreneurship is not a resource that can be deployed or planned[15]. Alertness cannot be bought and sold and therefore no investment in entrepreneurship is possible. The entrepreneurial function is present in all human action to a certain degree and individuals are alert to different things. The revenue attached to entrepreneurial behavior is profit (whereas labor receives wages and capitalists receive interest) and whenever an individual receives some profit from a trading activity, one can be certain that he/she displayed alertness successfully. Of course, since entrepreneurs operate with disequilibrium prices, profit is a type of revenue that only exists in disequilibrium economies, it disappears in equilibrium. Another fundamental characteristic of entrepreneurial behavior in Kirzner's theory is that it is not dependent on factor ownership[16]. The capitalist is the owner of capital and he/she receives an interest for investing his or her capital in some venture. Kirzner (1992b: 94–6), following Mises, points out that the capitalist will generally be an entrepreneur, but the two categories are analytically distinct.

All entrepreneurship is arbitrage

A first understanding of entrepreneurship is purely "spatialized" and deals only with arbitrage opportunities that were hitherto unnoticed. The entrepreneur bridges the gap of knowledge that exists between individuals by buying low and selling dear. In this view, price discrepancies are only of a geographical character, which means that this approach does not take place in time, for buying and selling are quasi-instantaneous operations.

Another type of entrepreneurial activity involves knowledge that is not currently possessed by anyone in the market. As Kirzner explains, "there presumably exist innumerable useful truths that *might* be known but which, at the moment, are unknown to *anyone* in the market" (Kirzner 1985a: 158, emphasis in original). In this view of entrepreneurship, the entrepreneur does not deal only with knowledge that is scattered in the economy but also with knowledge that is utterly unknown to anyone in the market. This knowledge exists (and may take the form of a property of matter, for instance) but is not present in the economic system. This understanding of entrepreneurial activity allows for the introduction of discovery in time

and shows that the entrepreneur can imagine the future, even if he/
she only discovers one of the underlying future realities. By imagin-
ing the future, the entrepreneur can set the economy in a new path,
and change the pattern of preferences individuals hold at a certain
point in time.

Even if we can find differences in degree between these two kinds
of entrepreneurship, it appears, after a deeper inquiry, that the concept of arbitrage encompasses these two notions of entrepreneurship.
In fact, this view originates with Mises, who saw the function of the
entrepreneur as a pure arbitrageur. As he explains, in *Profit and Loss*:

> What makes profit emerge is the fact that the entrepreneur
> who judges the future prices of the products more correctly
> than other people do buys some or all of the factors of pro-
> duction at prices which, seen from the point of view of the
> future state of the market, are too low. Thus the total costs of
> production – including the interest on the capital invested –
> lag behind the prices which the entrepreneur receives for the
> product. This difference is entrepreneurial profit.
>
> Mises (1980 [1951]: 109)

It is clear from this passage that arbitrage is the essence of all entrepreneurial activity. In other words, the *entrepreneurial function is
arbitrage*[17]. Arbitrage embraces the two notions of entrepreneurship
mentioned above: the "spatialized" and the "inventing the future"
views. In the latter, what is fundamental, from the economist's
point of view, is not the fact that resources are physically transformed, but the fact that an individual decides to speculate over
the use of resources that are undervalued in the present (and this
includes the knowledge necessary for the physical transformation
of the resources). It is the economic function of entrepreneurship
through arbitrage that interests economists.

As Lewin and Phelan (1999) explain, differential (entrepreneurial)
rents are what Austrian economists call profit. Nevertheless, there is
a difference between the two. Rents accrue to resources in the impu-
tation scheme and therefore entrepreneurial rents accrue to entrepreneurial "talent." In other words, this conception of entrepreneurship
involves a resource that can be deployed, just like any other resource.
As we saw above, however, entrepreneurship is not a resource, "it
consists of an alertness in which the decision is embedded rather
than being one of the ingredients deployed in the course of decision
making" (Kirzner 1979: 181). As a result, profit is not a return, i.e.

a rent, it is the result of arbitrage activity, and entrepreneurship is not a class of productive factor.

While arbitrage may involve innovation, innovation always involves arbitrage[18]. Arbitrage in time does not necessarily involve innovation (in the sense of introducing knowledge that was not possessed by anyone in the market). We can find cases of intertemporal arbitrage with production but without innovation. Therefore, the distinction between "spatialized" and "inventing the future" views cannot help us answer the economic question. Instead we will distinguish between two categories: (a) entrepreneurship as an atemporal arbitrage (without production) and (b) entrepreneurship as an intertemporal arbitrage (with production). A subcategory of (b) would be: entrepreneurship as an intertemporal arbitrage with production *and* innovation (but this further distinction is not needed to develop my theory). Henceforth, type I entrepreneurship will correspond to entrepreneurship as an atemporal arbitrage (without production) and type II entrepreneurship will correspond to entrepreneurship as an intertemporal arbitrage with production[19].

A VIEW OF THE LACHMANNIAN PROBLEM

Most market process theorists who share the Kirznerian "middle-ground" view would say that process theory shows that there are equilibrative and coordinative tendencies in the market system. This means that given constant underlying variables (preferences, resource availabilities and technological possibilities) and taking initial induced variables (prices, method of production, quantities and qualities of outputs) as they are, the entrepreneurial market process will tend to adjust induced variables to the underlying ones (Kirzner 1985a, 1992a). Gaps in knowledge that may exist between induced and underlying variables will tend to disappear under the pressure of entrepreneurial competition. In doing so, the market system will integrate the innumerable pieces of information scattered among individuals and will achieve a degree of social integration that would resemble what could have been attained by a single mind that possesses all knowledge (this includes the creation of new information, i.e. information that was not possessed by someone in the market system but that is necessary to satisfy consumer preferences). This process can be seen as coordinative in the sense that (a) individuals' plans will dovetail in accordance with the knowledge currently possessed in society, and (b) exchange opportunities that

63

lie undiscovered at a certain time will tend to be revealed, satisfying ever more consumer preferences. In the long run, the problem is not to allocate resources efficiently in society (i.e. to understand the market as an efficient allocator), but to discover the existence of radically new opportunities for exchange (i.e. to understand market competition as a discovery procedure).

There are equilibrative and coordinative tendencies in the market system that would lead society to a final state of rest. If, however, the constant underlying variables assumption is dropped, then changes in the data of the market will impede the economy from ever reaching a state of rest. Entrepreneurs will constantly be faced with changes in preferences, resource availabilities and technological possibilities, which will produce new induced variables. Thus, no state of rest can ever be reached.

Critics of this Kirznerian view believe that (a) not enough attention has been paid to entrepreneurial mistakes (Vaughn 1994; Salgado 1999); (b) the market process cannot be adequately explained if we maintain underlying variables constant (Lachmann 1976, 1977c [1969]; High, 1986); and (c) even if we keep underlying variables constant, it is not the case that equilibrium can always be derived (Salgado 1999). In order to clarify these issues, we will now turn to the issue of entrepreneurial error.

Entrepreneurial error

If we assume that underlying variables are constant across the market process, entrepreneurs can basically make three types of mistakes.

The first type of error is when an individual misses an opportunity that was available (a "missed opportunity" error). This error is most common in the Kirznerian view, where disequilibrium occurs in the market process because gaps in knowledge are overlooked and profit opportunities have been missed. In other words, some plans are dis-coordinated in the economy and could have dovetailed better had the opportunity been noticed by someone, that is to say, had some people been more alert (depending how far we are from equilibrium). This type of mistake may involve a series of errors on the part of different individuals: none of them noticing the available opportunity. It is a failure to do something that could have been done. This type of mistake can also be seen as involving over-pessimism on the part of entrepreneurs (Kirzner 1997c: 43). However, since this type of error generates pure profit opportunities that attract entrepreneurs, it will tend to be corrected over time (as long as underlying variables are maintained constant). In addition, from a subjectivist perspective, one can reply that if an individual does not notice an opportunity available to him/her, it simply does not exist in his/her mind and therefore there is no error. However, if we consider the underlying reality as being objective – as if there was an omniscient being who could see the discoordinated plans in the economy – one can contend that missed opportunities do exist.

The second type of error is the case where an individual will act as if he/she had discovered something, but in fact there is nothing to be discovered (at least not what he/she believed he/she discovered). This is called a "spurious discovery." As Vaughn (1994) explains, a spurious discovery is an action based on a "faulty perception" of what the underlying variables are. In that case, plans are coordinated (there is no scope for entrepreneurial activity) when the entrepreneur thought they were discoordinated (or they may be coordinated in a way different to that he/she thought). This type of error cannot happen in pure arbitrage, and is therefore possible only in entrepreneurial activity involving production in time.

Entrepreneurs "stick their heads out" and try to seek opportunities, they do not act at random. The market process can only be intelligible if entrepreneurial activity is purposeful and if entrepreneurs know what they are doing. Sometimes, however, entrepreneurs are purely mistaken, and act in the hope of exploiting something that is simply not there. Spurious discoveries are the recognition that an individual can misjudge the data of the market and divert resources into the production of goods that are not demanded. However, it can be the case that the original error becomes a source of new opportunities and creates a new adjustment path along which other entrepreneurs will find new opportunities (Kirzner 1992a; Rizzo 1996b). What the entrepreneur thinks he/she knows about the future use of the inputs in the production process "may differ from what he might have known (without additional resource expenditure) had he been more alert or aware of the true environment" (Kirzner 1992a: 158).

A subcategory of spurious discoveries is when an entrepreneur only partly misreads the data of the market: there is something to discover, but not as much as he/she thought. Errors of over-optimism, for instance, belong to this category. Buyers or sellers who expect too high or too low prices (respectively) make these errors. This kind of error tends to become systematically eliminated as "market experience reveals the unfeasibility of some (hitherto sought after) courses of action and the (hitherto unnoticed) profitability of other courses of action" (Kirzner 1997a: 71).

Salgado (1994, 1999) has theorized the third type of entrepreneurial error: when the objective discoordination of plans (at the level of the underlying variables) that is discovered by an entrepreneur (A) cannot be exploited over time because somebody else (B) steps in. B may have found a better and cheaper product, which makes A's product redundant. It could also be the case that B bids up the prices of (some of) the resources A needs in order to exploit his/her opportunity. As a result, A cannot pursue the exploitation of his/her discovery and is driven out of the market. This is an error due to rivalry. As Mises puts it: "In the market economy the entrepreneurs and capitalists cannot avoid committing serious blunders because they know neither what the consumers want nor what their competitors are doing" (Mises 1966: 676). Entrepreneurs do not (necessarily) know what their competitors are doing, or intend to do. A's discovery was genuine with respect to the (constant) underlying variables at the time before his/her discovery, explains Salgado (1999). Whether B's discovery is genuine or not is not our concern herein, what is important to understand is that the market process itself may generate coordination failures that are not the result of spurious discoveries. The activities of other entrepreneurs affect the exploitation of already discovered opportunities[20]. The Kirznerian approach seems to contend that gaps in knowledge are closed once they are discovered. What Salgado shows is that the exploitation of simultaneous gaps, because of the interdependence of entrepreneurs' activities, may lead to the emergence of new gaps.

If we drop the assumption that underlying variables are constant, the typology of errors becomes more complex. Basically, the case of rivalry, as described above, is amplified many times. A discovery can be genuine at the beginning and appear spurious over time because of a change in the underlying variables. This change occurs because the activities of other entrepreneurs may change the ends–means framework of many people in the marketplace. However, in order to show that there is no need to drop the assumption of constant underlying variables, it is sufficient to know that errors due to rivalry may exist under these circumstances. Following Salgado (1999), we can now see why it may be difficult to use profits and losses as a criterion for measuring equilibration. Even though A's discovery is genuine and A should have cashed in profits, the fact that B's discovery took place afterwards, puts A in a situation where he/she has to incur losses (if he/she does not make a new discovery).

The Lachmannian problem

The driving force of the system in the Mises/Kirzner theory is the entrepreneur who discovers profit opportunities that had been over-looked, and whose activity brings individuals' plans into greater coordination. The constant-underlying-variables assumption allows Kirzner to show that the marketplace has built-in tendencies towards equilibration, which is why a certain degree of order prevails. However, in a living economy, constant changes in the underlying variables derail the tendency towards equilibration and push the system onto an unpredictable path. It is still the case, however, that the forces at work make sure that, at every moment, previous gaps in knowledge are discovered and coordination is improved.

Lachmann sees the workings of the marketplace differently. He does not account for the entrepreneur in the same way as Kirzner. To Lachmann, the radical uncertainty of the future prevails at every moment and existing patterns are always bound to be dis-rupted. Lachmann insists that any use of the equilibrium construct is almost useless for the study of a world in which continuous changes in the pattern of knowledge take place. Besides, as High (1986: 115) explains, we cannot try to explain the phenomena of the market process by keeping underlying variables constant, because these changing variables are the source of the phenomena we want to explain[21]. According to the Lachmannian problem there is a flaw in the Kirznerian theory (which assumes that entrepreneurs act most of the time in accordance with the underlying reality and bring the system closer to equilibrium (even if errors are sometimes made)) because individuals' plans change and preferences are not con-stant over time. Lachmann, following Shackle, describes the market economy as a *kaleidic world*, that is to say "a world of flux in which the ceaseless flow of news daily impinges on human choice and the making of decisions" (Lachmann 1976: 56). The idea that entrepre-neurs tend to perform an equilibrating role is misleading. The market process cannot be determinate: equilibrating and disequili-brating forces take place at the same moment (Lachmann 1977c [1969]). In a world in which change is genuine and knowledge is affected by the passage of time, individuals' plans must be con-tinuously revised. Prices do not tend towards equilibrium when the future is unknowable (although not unimaginable, as he explains) to market participants. As Lachmann puts it himself, the market is a:

The future is unknowable
≠ the future is unimaginable.

67

> particular kind of process, a continuous process without
> beginning or end, propelled by the interaction between
> the forces of equilibrium and the forces of change. . . .
> A model in which individual plans, each consistent in
> itself, never have time to become consistent with each
> other before new change supervenes has its uses for elucidat-
> ing some striking features of our world.
>
> Lachmann (1976: 61)

Lachmann is at the confluence of recent market process theory,
which contends that, even if we can observe order in the world, we
must strongly acknowledge the existence of disequilibrating forces
in the economy (High 1986; Rizzo 1996b). In Lachmann's view
the world is kaleidic and the market process cannot be seen as a
deterministic phenomenon. This means that we cannot know, in
the course of events, whether individuals' activities are equilibrating
or not, for the market is an endless flow of counteracting forces: this
is the Lachmannian problem.

As Rizzo explains in the new introduction of *The Economics of Time
and Ignorance* (Rizzo 1996b), it is now widely recognized amongst
Austrian economists that not all market adjustments are equilibrating and that disequilibration is a more common feature of the market
economy than was believed before (in the 1970s).

Disequilibrating tendencies in the market system are not simply
the result of exogenous changes (like changes in preferences), but
also of endogenous changes (emerging from the equilibrating
forces themselves). In that sense, it is more difficult to sustain, in
the light of recent controversies, that there is a tendency towards
equilibrium in a market economy. As we saw above in the case of
errors due to rivalry (Salgado 1999), disequilibrium tendencies
emerge from the market process itself (even if we maintain the underlying variables constant). In fact, "[w]hat is at stake is whether the
market, to a greater or lesser extent, generates its own equilibria
or, in other words, whether equilibrium is 'defined in the process
of its emergence'" (James Buchanan, quoted in Rizzo 1996b: xx).
The equilibrium point changes in the course of the market process
because data change irreversibly (see Kaldor 1934b). (Thus, there
is no use for equilibrium as a description of the world in economics.)
Data change constantly and, as Hayek (1948 [1937]) explains, the
economic problem arises because of changes in the data.

The debate between the Kirznerian view and the Lachmannian
approach revolves around the meaning of the "Austrian tradition."

Both approaches try to explain the consequences of uncertainty on the economic system and the existence of observed order in the real world. Nevertheless, Kirzner believes that "the more pressing immediate task is not to further elaborate on how genuine uncertainty *might* derail all systematic processes altogether, but to explicate the extent to which, *despite* genuine uncertainty, systematic processes (the empirical existence of which, after all, is so often obvious even to the most superficial observer) can be understood" (Kirzner 1985b: 44). It is the search for a theory that explains order in the marketplace that is the driving force of contemporary Austrian economics. What remains to be understood are the reasons for firms in the market process (what role do firms fulfill?). Why entrepreneurs need firms is not adequately addressed in the current market process theory. Thus, to create a more complete market theory, we have to show how firms are part of the market process. The central problem is that economists need to explain how the existence of firms is linked to the ceaseless operation of the market[22].

THE LIMITS OF THE TRANSACTION COST PERSPECTIVE

In the case of general equilibrium (i.e. complete coordination) with perfect information, there is no Hayekian Knowledge Problem (HKP): all the necessary knowledge about other people's plans is in the hands of every individual in the economy. In such an economy, nobody will overlook an opportunity for profit, because everyone knows what other people want and everyone knows what everyone knows. Such an economy is in a state of final rest, there is no coordination problem. In this economy, entrepreneurs are unnecessary, for there is no knowledge to be discovered. Also, individuals have perfect knowledge as there are no transaction costs and no uncertainty. Therefore, the problem of production in a firm does not exist. In this situation, individuals can perfectly use the marketplace in order to use complementary inputs in the production of goods. With perfect information there is no ignorance whatsoever regarding consumers' wants, the methods of production, the enforcement of market contracts, and the like. Firms are unnecessary in such a world as all the production can be carried out in the market.

Consider a world where the economy is in a state of equilibrium (there is no HKP), but information is not perfect (individuals do not possess all the necessary information available in the market to carry on their activities (the use of means to achieve ends) because of the existence of transaction costs). As Coase showed, we can find in such a situation a rationale for the firm. The economy is in equilibrium: there is an optimal amount of information in the hands of every individual. This equilibrium is obtained with the existence of firms as institutions that economize on transaction costs. As we saw earlier, Coase (and his followers) shows that because transacting is costly, the market does not always adequately organize transactions. Thus, firms are used to economize on costs of exchange. As we also saw above, there are some problems with this approach. Mainly, however, it implies the following alternative: (a) transaction costs and firms have somehow always existed or (b) the emergence of the firm can only be explained in terms of external shocks to the system (it emanates from outside), which increase the costs of transacting[23].

This view also implies a cost-benefit analysis on the part of the manager. When a manager needs to use inputs in the production of a good, the manager has to appraise the information costs attached to the use of these inputs in the market and within the firm. The manager knows that he/she needs these inputs in the production of his product but, at the same time, he/she is ignorant of information that is relevant to these transactions (for it is too costly to be obtained). In other words, the manager is aware of his/her ignorance. The transaction cost view specifies that the firm facilitates economizing on the amount of resources spent in order to overcome *known* ignorance.

Let us now assume that the economy is not in equilibrium and that information is not perfect and is costly. There is a HKP and there are information (especially transaction) costs. We know that the case has been made by Coase, and more recently by the advocates of transaction cost economics, that transaction costs in themselves are sufficient for the explanation of the firm. Including Demsetz's (1993 [1988]) criticism of transaction costs into the picture simply shifts the debate to information costs in general (especially production costs), instead of transaction costs in particular (in a narrow sense of the term). The question is, to what extent are information costs important to the issue of existence of the firm or, in other words, to what extent is a cost-benefit analysis relevant in the setting of a firm? In order to provide an answer to that question, we have to assume a state of discoordination with perfect information.

The problem with Coase's analysis is, again, the discovery problem. In order to assume that information costs (i.e. management, production and transaction costs) are present at the origin of the firm, it is necessary to assume that there is only known ignorance in the market, which is not the case in the Austrian approach. Unless we remove all true ignorance there is a discovery problem. Theories on the emergence of the firm must take this aspect of the problem into account. For instance, while a cost-benefit approach can be used in an open-ended economy, it only depicts part of the picture. In order to solve the puzzle of the firm, one cannot make assumptions about what is not entirely yet known to (some) market participants, for "cost occurs," as Thirlby explains, "only when decisions are made, that is, in planning stages" (Thirlby 1973 [1946]: 174). The Coasean case for transaction costs leads, in the context of a disequilibrium economy, to an impossibility: it cannot explain the coming into existence of firms. One has to assume away the HKP in order to solve the puzzle of the existence of the firm in the transaction cost approach. In other words all individuals already know what the entrepreneur is supposed to discover. Although a world without transaction costs does not preclude sheer ignorance, it appears that transaction costs are not necessary for the existence of the firm, even if in the Coasean framework, they are sufficient[24].

A THEORY OF THE EMERGENCE OF THE FIRM: THE EXPLOITABILITY THESIS

The question central to the development of a process view of the firm is what would the market process be like if there were no firms? This amounts to a use of the *argumentum a contrario* method, described in Chapter 1, which shows that the emergence of the firm can be understood through a pure process perspective and without reference to any kind of transaction costs. Thus, I developed a model based on the following assumptions.

- Underlying variables are constant over time. Induced variables may change.
- There are no transaction costs (as defined in Chapter 1).
- The economy is in disequilibrium in the sense that there are unexploited opportunities for profit (whether plans are "compatible" or not is not the problem here)[25].
- There are no firms (by definition): individuals do not set up long term contracts and hierarchies to allocate resources.
- There is type II entrepreneurship: intertemporal arbitrage with production.

In this economy, individuals do not incur cost to shed light on their ignorance, they know everything they can know (given the underlying variables and the existence of radical ignorance, i.e. "they don't know what it is that they don't know") at a certain point in time. As we saw in the assumptions above, in such an economy, there is an objective discoordination: opportunities for profit, corresponding to gaps in knowledge, can be seized and entrepreneurs can make mistakes, especially of the third type (as developed by Salgado 1999). Let us use again the example given in the above section on error. An entrepreneur (A) discovers an opportunity for profit that involves production in time (it is type II entrepreneurship). It is perfectly possible to imagine that another (or more) entrepreneur (B) interferes with the process of exploitation in many ways, rendering the exploitation difficult, if not impossible. B might have found another opportunity for profit that utilizes some of the resources of A or he/she may have found a better way to extract the same opportunity for profit (by using the same inputs in different ways). As a result of the rivalrous market process, A might be driven out of the market (whether B's discovery was genuine or not). The prices paid by entrepreneur A to obtain his/her resources are not independent of the activities of entrepreneur B (and of many other entrepreneurs). As Lachmann explains, the capital structure of the economy is a gigantic web of interconnected interests that is never in equilibrium, since the activities of the multitude influence the situation of everyone.

The entrepreneur, resource owners and the unexploitability thesis

As we assume above, over time and in a rivalrous market a price discrepancy discovered by an entrepreneur can disappear (due to the activities of other entrepreneurs). It is important to understand what exactly the rivalrous process taking place in the market system means. Let us suppose (a) that the entrepreneur must employ different inputs in coordination in time (a multiperiod plan) – i.e. in a specific capital structure – in order to exploit his/her opportunity; and (b) this scheme involves the decisions of other individuals as input owners (of themselves – i.e. labor – or of other goods). As assumed above, there are no firms in the economy. As a result, A will not set up a firm in order to exploit his/her profit.

The entrepreneur does not know what other entrepreneurs may discover over time, but he/she sees that there is a discrepancy between current input prices and the price of the product that the factors will contribute to produce. In order to exploit the gap, he/she needs to obtain the inputs needed at their current market price. The entrepreneur ignores what might be the availability and the prices of inputs over time (for this is partly dependent on the behavior of other individuals), as a result, he/she must engage in the exploitation of the opportunity as soon as possible.

In the process of gathering the necessary inputs for production, the entrepreneur buys the services of input owners. In an uncertain world, "entrepreneurial behavior" is a synonym for exposing oneself to the uncertainty of a loss. When a resource owner sells an asset, he/she becomes exposed to the uncertainty of a loss for this may entail missing better opportunities elsewhere. He/she displays entrepreneurial activity. As Kirzner puts it:

> When a resource owner announces his willingness to sell quantities of resource services for specified amounts of money, under specified conditions of employment, he is taking a daring entrepreneurial gamble. He has no guarantee that his offer will be accepted. Perhaps he has priced himself out of the market. And, on the assumption that his offer to sell *is* accepted, he has no guarantee that he is obtaining the "true" market value of his resource service. Perhaps his resource could have displayed far greater productivity in a different industry, or in the hands of manufacturers other than those to whom he is making his offer. Had these other potential employers been made aware of the availability of his stock of resources, they would be prepared to offer higher prices. So that his present offer may be the expression of error, of sheer ignorance; it may be, in an entrepreneurial sense, an embarkation on a *losing* venture, since it will yield less than the true value of what he is surrendering.
>
> Kirzner (1989: 116)

Factor owners, in our world in disequilibrium in which transaction costs are zero, are acting, at least to a certain extent, in the nature of an entrepreneurial gamble when they engage in the selling of assets with buyers.

Rivalry among entrepreneurs in the marketplace implies that "[e]ach entrepreneur is eager to buy all the kinds of specific labor he needs for the realization of his plans at the cheapest price. But the wages must be high enough to take the workers away from competing entrepreneurs" (Mises 1966: 594). In other words, the possibility that B will step in and drive away some of the labor that A needs is part of the market process. Since we assume that entrepreneurs cannot set up long-term market contracts among input owners, B may drive away at any moment the labor force A needs for the exploitation of the profit opportunity. In fact it is the particular place of labor that makes the problem acute. Indeed, if all factors of production were absolutely specific, entrepreneurs could only use what is compatible with their type of production and nothing else, and this would reduce rivalrous competition. However, the "fact that *one* factor, labor, is on the one hand required for every kind of production and on the other hand is, within the limits defined, non-specific, brings about the general connexity of all human activities. It integrates the pricing process into a whole in which all gears work on one another. It makes the market a concatenation of mutually interdependent phenomena" (Mises 1966: 392, emphasis in the original). Because of this property of labor, A might not be able to exploit his/her opportunity, for, in the absence of firms (as assumed above) B could bid away A's labor force. This is the unexploitability thesis: in the absence of firms, the exploitation of the opportunity discovered cannot take place. This thesis is based on the relative non-specificity of many factors, especially labor. The implementation of a plan requires that the inputs be at the disposal of the planner for the duration of the plan; if this is not the case, no plan can ever be fulfilled[26].

If the entrepreneur cannot secure the use of the necessary inputs for the exploitation of his/her plan, no production can take place. As a result, the *argumentum a contrario* method shows that, without firms, many types of production processes are not possible: type II entrepreneurship *cannot take place* in the economy[27]. Thus, the assumption that there are no firms must be dropped. In many cases, an entrepreneur will need to secure the use of his/her inputs by setting up a series of long-term contracts, which supersede the price mechanism. I shall name this entrepreneur – following Mises (1966: 255) – the *entrepreneur–promoter*[28].

My thesis has some similarities with the views of Klein *et al.* (1978) and with the analysis of Williamson (1985: 48). These views basically sustain that the existence of quasi-rents implies strategies of integration in order to guard against *ex-post* opportunistic behavior that could appropriate the quasi-rents at stake. This resemblance is limited though, for the role of the firm is not (only) to protect against opportunistic behavior on the part of others, but

74

to secure the use of inputs that could be used elsewhere by other entrepreneurs in the course of the market process. My thesis is not related to the existence of opportunistic behavior but to the existence of type II entrepreneurship under structural uncertainty. The fundamental difference between these two views can only be captured through the entrepreneurial understanding of the market process, which, due to the existence of radical ignorance, accounts for the kaleidic nature of the marketplace.

The emergence of the firm: the exploitability thesis

At the moment of his/her discovery, the entrepreneur–promoter knows which factors (at which prices) he/she needs in order to exploit his/her opportunity over time (in a multiperiod plan). Moreover, the use of inputs in the implementation of a plan may give birth to another phenomenon: factors used in common will become specific to each other over time (Penrose 1995 [1959]; Lachmann 1977b [1947]). In other words, these separate factors may become a resource as a whole. This is especially true of labor, which can be at the same time the least and the most specific factor of production. Indeed, entrepreneur B might compete with entrepreneur A for the same labor inputs, and B could "withdraw these specialists from the employments in which they happen to work at the moment. The only means he [B] has to achieve this is to offer them higher pay. . . . The entrepreneurs are not merely faced with a shortage of 'labor in general,' but with a shortage of those specific types of labor they need for their plants" (Mises 1966: 597). In other words, it is because labor can be unspecific that the unexploitability thesis can be sustained (under the assumption that no firms exist). Moreover, it is because labor can become – at the same time – specific that inputs used in common become a resource as a whole (and that other entrepreneurs' activities may be a threat). The problem is not only an issue of shielding oneself against the rivalrous activity of other entrepreneurs, but also to secure the capabilities of the inputs that will come into existence when they are used in common[29]. Inputs, because of their specificity when used in common, are not easily replaceable. The only way the entrepreneur–promoter can exploit his/her discovered opportunity is by the implementation of a firm.

In order to fulfill his/her plan, the entrepreneur–promoter needs to convince input owners of his/her superior foresight and that if they bet on him/her, they will not regret it for they will obtain a better return on their assets than they could earn elsewhere. When factor owners sell their services (either their labor or their assets) to the entrepreneur–promoter, they discover that if they engage in a long term contract with him/her they will capture a pure profit. Exploitation of the discovery made by the entrepreneur–promoter requires resource owners to take entrepreneurial gambles as well[30]. Therefore, the firm results in simultaneous discoveries made by all the parties to the contracts. As a result, capabilities will emerge over time. The input-owners discover that what the entrepreneur–promoter offers is a good alternative. The entrepreneur–promoter can exploit his/her discovery having only seen through some parts of the fog of uncertainty and relying on resource owners to see through other parts of the fog. The emergence of the firm can be seen as the simultaneous exploitation of profits by different entrepreneurs. Most of these entrepreneurs are within the firm, they have been hired (this is fundamental), and others are outside the firm (they previously owned assets outside the firm that are now used in the firm).

It is only because the entrepreneur–promoter is able to pull entrepreneurial alertness together that he/she can exploit the profit over time as he/she discovers it (unless he/she is in error). The firm can be seen as a pulling together of entrepreneurial alertness and becomes the locus of exploitation of a profit discovery made by the entrepreneur–promoter where capabilities develop[31].

Thus, the firm is a non-price planned coordination over time between complementary inputs in which market errors due to the ignorance of other individuals' plans do not exist. The entrepreneur–promoter coordinates all the inputs. He/she has brought different parts of the market into coordination with each other under a common decision-making system. The firm is an island of planning and it serves as the locus of exploitation of a discovered profit. By pulling together entrepreneurial alertness and allowing for simultaneous discoveries, the promoter coordinates knowledge possessed by the input owners. Planning is necessary to coordinate knowledge that could not otherwise be coordinated[32]. That is why we must understand the problem of the firm as linked to the coordination issue.

In this concept of the firm, those who have sold the services of their factors of production and who are part of the vertical integration do not act as entrepreneurs anymore. They have "surrendered their alertness" to the entrepreneur–promoter and they follow his/her plan[33]. "A firm, carrying out a plan extending over a period of time," writes Lachmann, "is during that period in equilibrium, as equilibrium means essentially consistency of a number of acts by different individuals" (Lachmann 1977b [1947]: 202).

Another essential aspect of the firm is the possibility for the entrepreneur–promoter to assess, at any time, the use of his/her inputs and the value of his/her output through economic calculation. Economic calculation, especially the system of double-entry bookkeeping, makes the managerial system possible (Mises 1966: 304). Economic calculation, in the case of the firm, is the tool that allows the entrepreneur–promoter to evaluate his/her own perception of reality and tells him/her how good his/her foresight was. It is also the tool that allows the assessment of the alternative arrangements that are possible, especially with respect to the capital structure of the economy and the level of the interest rate. Vertical integration is not necessarily the only response available, long term contracting is also possible. The choice between these two options will depend on how specific is the input in question to the growth of capabilities of the firm[34].

This thesis has to be distinguished from the resource-based approach. In the resource-based view, "[t]he performance of firms is tied to the earnings (rents) that can be attributed to these resources and the ability to sustain such a competitive advantage is linked to the ability of the firm to identify and protect (and perhaps extend) that essential heterogeneity" (Lewin 1998b: 16). In the exploitability thesis, pure profits seized through the development of capabilities, not rents, are the driving forces behind the emergence of firms. Inputs used in common are likely to become specific to each other, but this is not (only) because of quasi-rents, it is because these inputs are linked in the exploitation of a profit opportunity.

Concluding remarks

Two aspects have been put forward in the theory of the emergence of the firm developed above. In the absence of transaction costs and when type II entrepreneurship is present, a firm may be necessary to the exploitation of a profit opportunity because of: (a) the truly unpredictable evolution of the market process and (b) the specificity of inputs used in common in the exploitation of a profit. These two aspects are the two faces of the same coin[35]. In this approach, the emergence of the firm is not linked to a rent differential, but to the discovery of a profit opportunity that has to be exploited in spite of the continuous market process.

TOWARDS A SOLUTION TO THE LACHMANNIAN PROBLEM

It appears that this entrepreneurial theory of the firm may be part of a solution to the Lachmannian problem. It may also be part of a solution to an ongoing debate in Austrian economics: how can one explain the existence of a certain degree of order in the marketplace? Indeed, as Salgado (1999) points out, if one admits the existence of the third type of error (mistake due to rivalry), and even if one assumes that underlying variables are constant, there are no reasons to believe why order rather than chaos should prevail in the market. However, since a certain degree of order is observable, one must conclude that there exist forces in the market system that push towards coordination rather than discoordination of plans. The emergence of firms can be viewed as such a force. Indeed, instead of having many individuals exercising their entrepreneurial propensity, a firm aligns entrepreneurial alertness along one vector: that of the promoter. Within a firm, a series of acts by different individuals are consistent with one another under the guidance of the promoter. The existence of firms therefore permits the exploitation of many opportunities for profit, which could not have been exploited otherwise. By committing resources to the exploitation of opportunities in a firm, promoters create islands of stability and order within the market. However, this has a cost: some opportunities will never be exploited because resources have already been committed to other uses (even if the alternative opportunities could have been superior). However, firms are a necessary condition for production and, as a consequence, for consumption.

It is because the economy is (at every moment) set onto a specific path by the organizational and production choices made by entrepreneur–promoters that a certain degree of order can be observed. In other words, it is the commitment of resources within firms that (a) solves the exploitation (of profit opportunities) problem (i.e. the unexploitability thesis) and (b) produces institutional stability within the market place that permits individuals to coordinate their plans (at the cost of better opportunities) because they know that the exploitation of opportunities is possible (Lachmann 1977b [1947]; Loasby 1976, 1991)[36]. The path taken (at any moment) by the economy (i.e. the capital structure) is not optimal, as other paths could lead to greater satisfaction of human needs, but it creates the environment that allows for future discoveries to take place and better ways of serving the consumers to come into existence.

The exploitability thesis is important to our understanding of the role of firms because it takes place in an economy that is not in equilibrium and in which information is costless. In such a world, there is a HKP and there are no transaction costs. This view emphasizes that the firm has a role to play in the institutional structure of the market system beyond the existence of transaction costs. By aligning entrepreneurial alertness along one vector, the firm is a locus of exploitation of a profit opportunity that could not have been exploited otherwise. This is the way the increasing complexity of the capital structure is managed (Lewin 1997: 77). To explain that firms, in my theory, provide some answers to the Lachmannian problem is not to say that there is a persistent movement towards the final state of rest in the economy. All we are saying is that dis-equilibrating forces can be controlled to some extent, which is why a certain degree of order prevails in the marketplace[37]. As Hayek explains: "The persistence of an order through continuous change is based on a division of knowledge among different persons, an aggregate of different sorts of knowledge the whole of which no single person can command" (Hayek 1977 [1958]: 271). Thus, the business firm in the market economy can be viewed as an *institution*, in which a certain division and combination of knowledge takes place under the command of a single individual (or group of individuals). Without the existence of this institution, the greater unplanned division of knowledge in society would not be possible. For these reasons, firms are as essential to the existence of plan coordination among individuals as money or property rights.

The firm as a specific capital structure

We know that one of Williamson's favorite themes is the issue of asset specificity as a main factor for internalization. In his approach, Williamson shows that considering capital as just a homogeneous good (K) is not helpful when it comes to the understanding of the specific contractual nature of the firm. Without a heterogeneous concept of capital, one cannot account for the main characteristics of the firm: long term contracts, hierarchical structures and residual claims. Austrian economists have never understood the concept of capital as a homogeneous good, for them capital has always been a *structure* "in which each capital good has a definite function and in which all such goods are complements" (Lachmann 1977b [1947]: 199). As Vaughn puts it: "a theory of capital should . . . examine how individuals choose to create particular kinds of intermediate goods at particular times and how these intermediary goods lead to the eventual production of consumer goods" (Vaughn 1994: 150)[38]. Foss (1994a) also remarks that Austrian economists have used the concept of asset specificity for decades. This use of the concept of asset specificity is due to their concern with the economic calculation issue. On the one hand, if capital is considered as homogeneous then there is no economic calculation problem since alternative uses are known immediately. However, if there is no calculation problem there is no economic problem. On the other hand, if capital is considered as purely specific, these assets have no alternative uses, and there is no calculation problem either[39]. By dismissing the economic problem, this approach cannot illuminate economic inquiry. This is why Austrian economists, especially Hayek and Lachmann, emphasized that capital goods are capital "not by virtue of their physical properties but by virtue of their economic function" (Lachmann 1978: xv)[40].

The particular combination of inputs that an entrepreneur needs in order to exploit a discovery constitutes a specific capital structure. The capital structure of the firm is determined by the expectations of the entrepreneur with regard to the complementarity of the assets over a multiperiod plan: it is a combination of assets employed for the same end. Because the entrepreneur chooses how to combine certain assets, the capital structure of a firm is always specific regarding the plan of the entrepreneur: capital goods are complementary in the exploitation of a discovery[41]. A certain asset employed in the exploitation of a profit is economically relevant to the entrepreneur only in combination with other well-defined assets, that is to say, only if it is part of a certain capital structure. Capital goods are therefore *always* specific, to the extent that they are employed in a plan, by an entrepreneur, for the same end[42]. As Lachmann writes, "[f]actor complementarity presupposes a plan within the framework of which each factor has a function" (Lachmann 1977b [1947]: 200). The function of the asset shapes its specificity. The degree of specificity will of course vary, and the difficulty of shifting inputs to more urgent uses will be uneven. This indicates that complementarity of factors, not substitution (which may play a different role), is the source of the firm[43].

As we saw above, the notion of homogeneity implies perfect substitution. The understanding of capital as a structure expresses the fact that, in order to·produce, the entrepreneur needs factors that are complementary in his/her plan and among which substitution is generally impossible[44]. In this view, each factor has a function (i.e. is specific) and "function, where a number of factors is involved, implies coordination and complementarity" (Lachmann 1977b [1947]: 205). When an entrepreneur sees a discrepancy between current input prices and the price of the product that the factors will produce, this discrepancy allows him/her to find complementarity (between capital goods) that was hitherto overlooked. This complementarity exists only because of the disequilibrium prices of the inputs. Had the prices been different, complementarity between the goods would not have been discovered. Therefore, this complementarity makes the capital structure specific to the exploitation of the discovered opportunity[45].

Williamson understood that the concept of capital homogeneity was useless for the firm, but he retained it as a benchmark. The bottom line of his analysis is that certain assets are very specific as a result of a market failure. Capital goods are always specific to a plan and sometimes cannot be re-employed elsewhere and therefore have no market value. Williamson's analysis assumes that the price of an asset is in equilibrium in the first place (equilibrium as a tool), which cannot be the case in an Austrian approach to capital structure. His fundamental transformation can be reinterpreted in terms of disequilibrium markets. Because the price of the asset is in disequilibrium, the asset's owner accepts the offer made by the entrepreneur to buy and integrate the asset in his/her firm. In the price offered, the asset's owner sees a new opportunity and seizes it. When an entrepreneur pulls together different assets into a firm, he/she creates a new capital structure that will be assessed as a whole (by the stock market for instance). In the eyes of the promoter, the value of the firm is given by the profit opportunity that can now be exploited.

THE DISTINCTIVE NATURE OF THE FIRM

"Is the firm different by nature from the market?" is one of the questions of modern economics. Some economists state that there are no basic differences between firms and markets, they are of the same nature, only the form of contracting differs (Cheung 1983; Cowen and Parker 1997). In contrast, the entrepreneurial theory of the firm stands in the Coasean tradition: the firm is, by nature, different from the market. However, the firm is indeed part of the market and must use the market both to obtain inputs and to sell outputs; that is to say, without the market system there would be no tool for economic calculation and no firms. Thus, the firm is a market phenomenon and it is not comparable to a socialist economy (Mathews 1998).

Contending that the firm is different in essence from the market means the following. As shown above, the emergence of the firm is linked to the entrepreneurial activity taking place in the market. Therefore, the firm can be defined as a set of long term contracts among input owners under the guidance of the entrepreneur–promoter. He/she is the one who knows what the plan is, and even if he/she uses managers to implement it, it is under his/her direction that things are organized. As Lachmann puts it: "The revision of plans is the function of the entrepreneur, the carrying out of existing plans is the function of the manager" (Lachmann 1977b [1947]: 212).

As a result, the distinctive nature of the firm does not rest on the existence of transaction costs, but on the fact that a firm is an organization, that is to say, a division of labor that serves only one goal: that of the entrepreneur. Hayek (1976: 107–32) makes the distinction between an economy, on the one hand, and a catallaxy, on the other. An economy, in the strict sense of the word, is an organization. It is a set of means allocated in order to implement a single plan (or a series of ends). By contrast, the marketplace is not governed by a single unitary plan. In a catallaxy the means are not allocated in order to achieve a single scale of ends, but are allocated according the myriad of plans of the acting individuals. "While within an organization the several members will assist each other to the extent that they are made to aim at the same purposes," writes Hayek, "in a catallaxy they are induced to contribute to the needs of others without caring or even knowing about them" (Hayek 1976: 109). In other words, in an organization, individuals are ends-connected, whereas they are merely means-connected in a catallaxy. In the marketplace plans can be discoordinated, while in an organization they are coordinated (this is what Lachmann means when he explains that the firm is in equilibrium).

Thus, the essence of the firm is different from the essence of the market system. Although, as stated above, a firm is unlike a socialist economy because it emerges from the market and uses the market as a compass for development, a firm is like a socialist economy because inputs are ends-related and are under the guidance of a promoter. For this reason alone, the essence of the firm is different from that of a catallaxy. Williamson is correct when he explains that hierarchy is a distinctive mark of the firm. The existence of some sort of hierarchy (even if it is very flat) is a reflection that individuals within a firm are pursuing a common purpose.

CONCLUSION

The purpose of this analysis of the firm is not to provide a comprehensive theory of the firm. The entrepreneurial theory of the firm emphasizes one aspect of the problem of the existence of organizations. The model employed in this analysis assumes that:

- underlying variables are constant;
- there are no transaction costs;
- the economy is in disequilibrium, there is a knowledge problem;
- entrepreneurship is the driving discovery force in the economy;
- there is arbitrage with production in time: type II entrepreneurship; and
- complementarity of inputs is essential to the exploitation of a profit opportunity.

These assumptions allowed us to see that *the firm plays a role in solving the coordination problem in the market*. In certain cases, the entrepreneur alone cannot fulfill this coordination role. The entrepreneurial theory of the firm is a causal-genetic explanation of the emergence of the firm in the market system[46].

The analysis in this chapter emphasizes that the firm is not only a solution to a problem of cost, as many economists have already shown, but also a solution to a problem of true ignorance and co-ordination[47]. While the transaction cost approach is sufficient and necessary for the existence of the firm in an equilibrium-always world, it only explains the emergence of the firm as an exogenous phenomenon. An entrepreneurial analysis is necessary to develop an endogenous explanation of the emergence of the firm. Firms exist because promoters have visions of what the future could be like, the market process is an ongoing rivalrous process, and labor can be at the same time non-specific and specific. This is not to say that the transaction cost approach does not provide useful insights, it just means that if we are to give a market process (i.e. causal-genetic and endogenous) explanation of the emergence of the firm, a transaction cost view is not sufficient.

The firm is a pulling together of entrepreneurial activity by a central entrepreneur: the promoter. The firm is entrepreneurially centered, to use Thomsen's terminology. The entrepreneur–promoter needs to rely on the entrepreneurial insights of other individuals in order to exploit the profit he/she has discovered. This theory gives a social dimension to entrepreneurship that is not present in type I entrepreneurship.

3

CAPABILITIES, ENTREPRENEURSHIP, CENTRAL PLANNING AND THE GROWTH OF THE FIRM

Un général en chef n'est pas à couvert de ses fautes à la guerre par un ordre de son ministre ou de son souverain quand celui qui le donne est éloigné du champ d'opérations et qu'il connaît mal ou ne connaît pas du tout le dernier état des choses. D'où il résulte que tout général en chef qui se décharge d'exécuter un plan qu'il trouve mauvais est coupable; il doit représenter ses motifs, insister pour que le plan soit changé, enfin donner sa démission plutôt que d'être l'instrument de la ruine de son armée[1].

Napoléon Bonaparte
(*Maximes de guerre et pensées*)

INTRODUCTION

The model of the entrepreneurial firm developed in Chapter 2 contained a restrictive assumption: input owners (labor) would surrender their alertness to the promoter (this is the "simple firm"). This is only a heuristic that has no counterpart in reality, but it is helpful in showing the entrepreneurial origin of the business firm. Chapter 2 also showed that the firm is a locus of exploitation of a profit opportunity (this is the firm's function). The firm is also a non-price planned coordination over time between complementary inputs in which market errors due to the ignorance of other individuals' plans do not exist (this is the firm's form).

In a living economy, new profit opportunities constantly emerge and the entrepreneurial process is never at rest. However, is it the case that once a profit opportunity has been exploited, the simple firm must cease to exist, for it has fulfilled its role? The answer to this question will depend on the nature of the business and the views of the promoter. The pure profit will be exploited after some time and then disappear because of the competitive process, but it could be the case that returns are left to be exploited for an open-ended period. In most cases, the market process will force the entrepreneur frequently to adjust his/her plan (Harper 1996). In fact, the issues of existence and growth (of the firm) are different to a large extent and call for a different analytical treatment. As Langlois explains: "the matter of origin [of the firm] is logically quite distinct from the issue of ongoing functionality – that is, from the question of how, once established, a system of rules maintains itself" (Langlois, 1995: 255).

"Planning, from an entrepreneurial perspective," writes Thomsen, "has the disadvantage of not providing a framework stimulating a discovery process the way a market system does" (Thomsen 1992: 110). This is true by the very nature of planning. However, casual experience shows that many firms last, grow and are the source of many innovations – and inventions – in the marketplace. In this chapter, I would like to show that the firm is not only a locus of exploitation of a profit opportunity but is also a locus of discovery that is essential to the working of the market economy. This will involve addressing the issue of innovation and the growth of the firm, which has concerned economists since the work of Edith Penrose (1995 [1959]) at the end of the 1950s, and which still continues to attract and puzzle many economists. As Williamson has said: "The introduction of innovation, plainly complicates the earlier-described assignment of transactions to markets or hierarchies based entirely on an examination of their asset specificity qualities. Indeed, the study of economic organization in a regime of rapid innovation poses much more difficult issues than those addressed here" (Williamson 1985: 143). A few economists have tried to examine these issues in relation to entrepreneurship, but their answers are incomplete. It is true, as Schumpeter explains, that this question has proven difficult for economics to answer. "In the large-scale corporation of today," writes Schumpeter, "the question that is never quite absent arises with vengeance, namely, who should be considered as the entrepreneur" (Schumpeter 1989a [1947]: 226). The notion of the "entrepreneurial firm" refers to the fact that entrepreneurial activity takes place within the firm and not to the fact that the growth of the "entrepreneurial enterprise" (to use Chandler's 1977: 381 term) is an internally financed endeavour (i.e. no issuance of stock to raise capital).

In the entrepreneurial theory of the firm, the concept of growth regarding the firm is defined as the never-ending discovery and exploitation of profit opportunities by the individuals (managers and employees) in the firm. This involves addressing the problem in entrepreneurial terms and exploring the related issues of knowledge and central planning, in order to assess the notion of the "complex firm" (the firm that grows over time because it is a locus of exploitation of profit opportunities). In this approach, employees do not surrender their alertness (the entrepreneurial aspect of human action is carefully examined in the context of the organization) and the economy is in disequilibrium (there is a HKP)[2].

AN AUSTRIAN VIEW OF CAPABILITIES THEORY

Edith Penrose's approach to the growth of the firm

Introductory remarks

Economists can trace back current discussions on the evolution of the firm in terms of growth of the firm to the work of Edith Penrose (1995 [1959]). Her work laid the foundations of the "resource-based" theory of the firm, and she was probably the first economist to move away from viewing firms as a "black box." In *The Theory of the Growth of the Firm* (Penrose 1995 [1959]), she analyses the importance of managerial activity and organizational structure in the growth of the firm. After Penrose and G. B. Richardson[3], there was a weakening in the claim that the firm was just a theoretical link, a mental construct or a way-station in the understanding of the allocational role of the market.

In her book, Penrose aims to show that the growth of the firm is not merely a mechanical reaction to changes in prices, costs and the extent of the market[4]. There is an "internal process of development" that is worth studying because it provides insights into the adjustment processes taking place in a market system and the organization of industry. In order to develop a meaningful theory of the growth of the firm, she focused on the "internal resources" of a firm – especially with respect to the management and the experience it acquires over time. She emphasized that the entrepreneurial aspect of a firm is essential to growth. As she puts it: "For a firm, enterprising management is the one identifiable condition without which continued growth is precluded" (Penrose 1995 [1959]: 8)[5].

Penrose deals with a concept of the firm which, for 1959, was new in economics. She saw the firm as a (growing) organization that possesses a collection of productive resources, the disposal of which is determined by hierarchy and in which individuals make judgments and acquire knowledge in order to outdo their competitors[6]. However, most economists, in interpreting her work, do not emphasize one important aspect of Penrose's view: the entrepreneurial element within enterprise management.

The enterprising management, capacities and the expansion of the firm

Penrose studies, in the third chapter of *The Theory of the Growth of the Firm*, the issues of productive opportunity, the firm and entrepreneurship. The problem of the firm, as Penrose (1995 [1959]: 31) sees it, is to organize the use of both internal and external resources for the production of goods in order to make a profit. Production is directed according to "productive opportunities" that the entrepreneur sees. Penrose has a clear understanding that the entrepreneur (in the firm) plays a fundamental role and that this role must be distinguished from the purely managerial role. As she puts it: "This extremely personal aspect of the growth of individual firms [the entrepreneurial aspect] has undoubtedly been one of the obstacles in the way of the development of a general theory of the growth of firms" (Penrose 1995 [1959]: 33). It is because one (or many) individual in a firm has the "spirit of enterprise" that a firm will grow over time, i.e. there is no growth without the entrepreneur. Indeed, a firm that loses productive opportunities ceases to expand and eventually declines (Penrose 1995 [1959]: 34). It is only if the management is entrepreneurial that a firm can find productive opportunities. "[T]he managerial competence of a firm," she writes, "is to a large extent a function of the quality of the entrepreneurial services available to it" (Penrose 1995 [1959]: 35).

Penrose's understanding of the firm as a set of resources – including entrepreneurial resources – has led her and her followers to develop the notion of capacities (or capabilities, in Richardson's terminology). Capabilities can be, at the same time, a source of and a limit to expansion. At any given period of time a firm's resources are finite. Importantly, both managerial services and entrepreneurial services are limited (Penrose 1995 [1959]: 44–56). By using the term "capacities" to describe the resources of a firm, Penrose gave managerial and entrepreneurial services almost a physical content. The firm possesses certain capacities that set a limit to its expansion. Just as entrepreneurial search is limited, so is the planning of new activities. This is true for the present, and is also true for the past and the future: a firm "inherits" certain capacities from its past (its capabilities are path-dependent) and this limits the amount of activity that can be planned and absorbed in the future (Penrose 1995 [1959]: 65–6). The experience thus gained increases the possibilities for action and translates into new capacities for the firm. This is why Penrose is able to argue in favor of managerial economies, and to show, in very Marshallian terms, that the firm can increase its capacities and extend its boundaries from within by improving its management practices[7].

As a result of this view in terms of capacities, the management's "goal" is to try constantly to increase the capacities of the firm in order to capture more productive opportunities. Many new capacities will be found within the firm in the form of currently unused capabilities[8]. Capacities are never fully used, they are partly idle because the management is cognitively limited. As the experience of the management increases, managers find new ways to exploit the firm's idle capacities[9]. Exploiting new capacities is only a matter of experience (inherited resources) and time. Without unused capacity, there is no potential for growth. Growth is therefore the result of the potential for a capacity to change. This potential is partially left dormant until the right amount of experience and knowledge is reached. The underlying assumption herein is the idleness of certain capabilities within the firm, i.e. the ever-existing capacity to change.

New accounts of the Penrosian theory: the knowledge-based theories of the firm, organizational learning and capabilities

The core issue is knowledge

Industrial organization economics is mainly based on problems that arise because of information. The contractual theories of the firm (or measurement–cost approach), which explain the existence of firms on the basis of moral hazard, adverse selection and various agency problems, are a direct extension of the neoclassical understanding of the economic problem. In this tradition, the firm can be understood from a pure optimization perspective and knowledge problems (as understood by Austrian economists) are ultimately irrelevant[10].

Capabilities theories take a different view of the problem of information and knowledge. In this approach, various types of economic organization are understood in terms of their function as a repository of knowledge and a seedbed of learning (Conner and Prahalad 1996; Grant 1996; Libeskind 1996). The firm, as a nexus of incomplete contracts, is able to coordinate collective learning and adapt to unforeseen changes in a more effective way than markets (Foss 1996c). In this perspective, *tacit* and *social* knowledge are fundamental keys to the understanding of the firm (Penrose 1995 [1959]: 53–4). The concept of capabilities cannot be understood without these two notions[11]. As Foss puts it:

> productive activities are not best understood as a matter of applying commonly accessible explicit knowledge ("blueprints") in the instantaneous and profit-maximizing combination of factors of production. Rather, such activities involve the processes of accumulation of partly tacit knowledge through various largely incremental learning-processes (learning by doing, learning by using, and learning by searching).
>
> Foss (1996b: 17–18)[12]

The Penrosian notion of the firm as a pool of resources that permits the management to establish one or more "impregnable bases" (Penrose 1995 [1959]: 137), for instance, is very similar to the more modern notions of "core competence" (Prahalad and Hamel 1990)[13] or "intrinsic core of idiosyncratic resources" (Langlois and Robertson 1995) as all these concepts emphasize the tacit and social nature of knowledge[14].

The notion of routines developed by Nelson and Winter is also related to the same issue. As Nelson and Winter (1982) explain, routines are the memory of the organization. Individuals remember a routine by exercising it and, in turn, the routine becomes actual when individuals learn what is being done in the organization. Part of this knowledge is, by nature, tacit and social. Routines constitute a subset of a firm's capabilities in the sense that they refer to what an organization actually does and not to what it could also do if certain capacities were put into use (Langlois and Robertson 1995: 16).

Capabilities are heterogeneous and, because of their nature, they are difficult to trade and to imitate in the short run (and sometimes in the long run as well). The complex nature of capabilities explains why they may indeed be central to theories of the boundaries of the firm. Clearly, the capabilities approach is fundamentally different from the measurement–cost view and is not based on incentive considerations (Foss 1993b).

Organizational learning

There is a current trend in capabilities theories that views the firm as a nexus of incomplete contracts that can be interpreted, not in conjunction with the measurement approach (incentive alignment problems), but as structures dedicated to *problem solving* (Demsetz 1993 [1988]; Foss 1996c, 1997a; Loasby 1991; O'Driscoll and Rizzo 1996 [1985]). Dividing problems into sub-problems can help solve problems. Once sub-problems are solved, solutions can either fit into an overall solution or they have to be discarded. A trial and error process takes place, and the firm, with its hierarchical structure, is, in fact, like a locus of conjectural processes where it is necessary first to find the right decomposition of a problem, and then eventually the right overall solution (see Harper 1996). The firm's capabilities are employed to solve problems and learn from these solutions. Because contracts are incomplete, the firm can be seen as a seedbed of knowledge in which individuals and teams learn and improve the routines of the firm. Without incompleteness of contracts, there is no individual and organizational learning.

This is why Demsetz (1993 [1988]) saw the rationale for the firm in terms of the knowledge and learning that is provided for by hierarchical structures. "Direction substitutes for education (that is for the transfer of knowledge)," explains Demsetz (1993 [1988]: 172). This is the "knowledge substitution effect" which takes place through the firm's hierarchical structure. This effect can also take place in the market, but since production and information costs are lower in an organization, the knowledge substitution effect is most likely in a firm. This knowledge substitution effect is closely related to the "flexibility effect." The flexibility effect refers to the greater adaptability of the firm (relative to market contracting) to unforeseen contingencies. The flexibility effect derives directly from the existence of incomplete contracts and hierarchical structures. The firm is required when strongly interdependent learning processes must be coordinated because this coordination cannot take place unless there is room for knowledge accumulation and for experimentation (Foss 1996c: 23–5). Foss shows that the coordination problem within the firm can be addressed by using the notion of a "firm-specific mental construct" (Foss 1997a: 28). In other words, intra-firm learning processes take place because of a shared mental construct that characterizes the firm.

Corporate coherence

The notion of "corporate coherence" refers to the ability of an organization (especially, as shown below, the firm in its M-form) to generate and explore synergies within its own structure. This is primarily related to the notion of economies of scope (economies obtained from sharing given assets (Silver 1984)), but it can also be seen in relation to the stock of knowledge (capabilities, routines and interconnectedness between assets) or related diversification (Teece *et al.* 1994; Foss and Christensen 1996). In this approach the firm is seen as "an integrated cluster of capabilities and supporting complementary assets, and coherence is a quality of the relations between the constituent competencies and assets" (Foss and Christensen 1996: 8). Foss and Christensen refer to the work of Luigi Marengo (1992), who shows that the coordination of learning processes inside the firm leads to the emergence and exploitation of organizational knowledge. Marengo emphasizes the fact that there is a trade-off between exploitation (of new knowledge) and its exploration.

Inspired by Austrian economics and post-Marshallian evolutionary economics (see, for example, Marengo), Foss and Christensen (1996: 20) define corporate coherence as the capacity for a firm (a) to integrate existing dispersed knowledge (i.e. deal with what they call the HKP 1) and (b) to generate new knowledge and exploit novelty (i.e. deal with what they call the HKP 2). Corporate coherence refers to the capacity for generating and exploiting "economies of diversity."[15] In order to obtain these economies, a firm must have a powerful learning code that enhances the cohesion of the various individual learning processes: this is corporate coherence.

Towards an integration of capabilities and contractual approaches

As some economists have argued (Langlois and Robertson 1995; Foss 1996b), there is ground today for combining the capabilities approach and the contractual theories of the firm into one common view[16]. From a certain perspective, many issues of the measurement–cost and asset-specificity approaches can be restated in terms that fit the mold of the capabilities view (Foss 1996b: 14–15). The dynamics of changes in the division of labor within the firm (and its limits) are rooted in changes within transaction costs, which themselves depend on the capabilities available. As Langlois and Robertson put it: "Whether there is continuity, merger, or dis-integration is a function of the cost structure at that time, which in turn depends on the existing distribution of capabilities and the degree of efficiency of markets" (Langlois and Robertson 1995: 45). This modern Marshallian–Penrosian approach to the growth of the firm suggests that the boundaries of the business organization are determined by transaction costs in the short run and by capabilities in the long run, the former depending on the latter in the final analysis. It also points out that *production costs* and *communication costs* (which are extremely specific to individual firms) are key concepts in understanding the firm.

Is the entrepreneur missing again?

Is Penrose's "enterprising management" really entrepreneurial?

As Penrose admits, defining the nature of the entrepreneurial func-tion is difficult[17]. The entrepreneur is the one who introduces, on behalf of the firm, innovation in every possible way (with respect to products, location, technology, personnel, administrative organi-zation, etc). This is to be contrasted with managerial services, which relate to the implementation of entrepreneurial innovation. Further-more, enterprising is "a psychological disposition on the part of individuals to take a chance in the hope of gain, and, in particular, to commit effort and resources to speculative activity" (Penrose 1995 [1959]: 33). Presented in those terms, entrepreneurship, as Penrose understands it, seems to be in accordance with an entrepre-neurial theory of the firm. Penrose even evokes the notion of specu-lative activity, which can be linked to Kirzner's notion of arbitrage[18].

Nevertheless, Penrose equates entrepreneurship with the *search* for opportunities: "The decision on the part of a firm to investigate the prospective profitability of expansion is an enterprising decision" (Penrose 1995 [1959]: 33). Entrepreneurship is one of the resources of the firm and as such it can be deployed. As she puts it: "we include 'entrepreneurs' among the resources of the firm and the range of ideas of entrepreneurs among the services rendered" (Penrose 1995 [1959]: 86). She also writes that "[t]here is no supply curve or production function into which such [entrepreneurial] services can be fitted, but they are nevertheless inputs in production" (Penrose 1995 [1959]: 75). The enterprising management decides to search for opportunities, in other words, entrepreneurship is like R&D. Penrose's notion of entrepreneurship is, in essence, a variation of the Robbinsian maximizer[19].

Alfred Chandler (1990a [1962]) has also developed a view of management that is entrepreneurial. It is worth noting here his contribution, for, like Penrose, he views the firm as a set of capabilities and gives a significant role to the entrepreneurial aspect in the organization. His view of the entrepreneur can also be understood as a variation on the Robbinsian maximizer theme, even if, like Penrose, he emphasizes that novelty in the organization (and certainly in the market system) can be traced back to the entrepreneurial function. He makes the same distinction as Penrose between entrepreneurial activity and managerial activity. As he puts it: "*entrepreneurial* decisions and actions will refer to those which affect the allocation or reallocation of resources for the enterprise as a whole, and *operating* decisions and actions will refer to those which are carried out by using the resources already allocated" (Chandler 1990a [1962]: 11). However, entrepreneurship, defined in such a way, is purely neoclassical and is therefore not different, in nature, from operational activity[20].

Capabilities: how do firms acquire them?

As we saw above, economists in the capabilities approach emphasize the social and tacit nature of knowledge. They explain that teams almost always have greater problem-solving skills than individuals, and part of the knowledge acquired is non-transmissible and cannot be made explicit. Although this view of knowledge seems accurate, it gives more emphasis on the transmission of knowledge than on its emergence. The emphasis is on learning by doing, by using and by searching, which, one would certainly concede, fits into the knowledge-seen-as-a-commodity mold. Although the tacit and social nature of knowledge is very important, it is not the whole story. It is also necessary to investigate the consequences of ignorance (tacit and social knowledge may be linked with unknown ignorance). In other words, what also matters is *learning by discovering*.

The firm must be a locus of discoveries if capabilities are to grow over time.

As mentioned above, Penrose dedicates a chapter in *The Theory of the Growth of the Firm* to enterprising management and how it affects the growth of the firm. However, more recent works on capabilities theory generally do not deal with the concept of enterprising management[21]. The capabilities of a firm are supposed to change over time. Firms *and* markets are supposed to become more "capable" in the long run. Therefore, the boundaries of a firm will be determined by the cost of capabilities in the market, relative to the cost of capabilities in the firm. Disintegration or integration will depend on the evolution of these relative capabilities. This is what Langlois and Robertson have named "dynamic transaction costs" (Langlois and Robertson 1995: 35)[22].

The question then is how do capabilities change and increase over time? Capabilities theorists would respond that the entrepreneur is at the origin of these changes without specifying the nature of entrepreneurship. As we saw above, one of the answers provided by theorists is to introduce into the analysis the notion of organizational learning and corporate coherence. The firm provides an institutional setting that solves coordination problems (Foss 1993b, 1997c, 1997d). In this view, as the following quotation shows, the entrepreneur is assigned a role: "Corporate intrapreneurs may act in a basically Kirznerian way by demonstrating alertness to opportunities for integrating hitherto dispersed knowledge [within the firm]" (Foss 1997a: 28)[23]. Yet the question of just how the "corporate intrapreneur" operates within the firm is not really addressed. While Foss (1997a) deals with the notion of a "specific-mental construct," he does not clearly relate it to the corporate intrapreneur.

The corporate coherence path does not address the issue of entrepreneurship clearly either. Indeed, if corporate coherence is taken to mean the capacity to solve HKP 1 and 2 (Foss and Christensen 1996: 20), why does it imply the capacity to generate and exploit "economies of diversity" (Foss and Christensen 1996: 20)? Or, to put it differently, how can firms engage in "asset creation" in order to obtain "economies of diversity"? If economizing is the issue at stake, then entrepreneurship cannot be addressed in Kirznerian terms. Moreover, if corporate coherence implies that there is a trade-off between "exploitation" and "exploration" of new knowledge (Foss and Christensen 1996: 16), then pure discovery is not the issue. If we are to be concerned with learning by discovering, we must admit, as Marengo seems to say, that an organization is not entirely limited by such a trade-off (Foss and Christensen 1996: 16).

Concluding remarks: is the capabilities approach sufficient?

The question that one must ask is, do existing explanations account adequately for the phenomenon they seek to explain? In the above assessment of Penrose's work and modern capabilities theories, we saw that the phenomenon this analysis seeks to explain is the growth of the firm. This phenomenon is rooted in the use of excess capacities, the building up of capabilities and the existence of dynamic transaction costs. It is true that these explanations, in a way, account for the growth of the firm, but these views can be seen as insufficient with respect to the general explanation of the market process that is put forward in Austrian economics. They only account for the facts in ways that are compatible with Robbinsian maximizing, and they fail to see the deeper phenomenon that is at the origin of the workings of the market system: entrepreneurship.

In a way, the existing explanation could be set in an equilibrium-always world, in which "entrepreneurship" can indeed be defined as the search and allocation of unused resources in the firm. It is conceivable that in equilibrium the capabilities approach, as understood by non-Austrian economists, would be sufficient. However, in a disequilibrium world, in which entrepreneurial activity is essential to the functioning of the market process, one cannot explain the firm in terms of capabilities without the entrepreneurial function. Therefore, even if the capabilities approach accounts for the phenomenon it seeks to explain, it is not sufficient to explain the growth of the firm in the context of an economy in disequilibrium[24]. In this context, it is implausible that firms would acquire and develop capabilities without Kirznerian entrepreneurial activity and without being confronted with a HKP.

The Penrosian account is another form of the MTP, for there is an inconsistency involved in trying to answer questions that would not exist in a world without entrepreneurs. The equilibrium approach cannot tell us why there are unused capacities. If capabilities spread in an automatic fashion, then one has to show how the evolution of capabilities is similar to the emergence of money or law. In other words, one has to show that there is a Mengerian process at stake (Menger 1985; Kirzner 1992a: 163–79). However, there are good reasons to believe that the growth of a firm and its increase in capabilities is not only a spontaneous order of that kind, but also a phenomenon that can be traced back to entrepreneurial discoveries. Of course the development of unused capabilities may lead to new routines and this process can take place sometimes in a tacit fashion, but this is not the only relevant aspect of the growth of a firm. When Foss (1997a) tries to introduce Austrian insights in the capabilities and problem solving approaches to the firm, he reduces the issue to a coordination problem (the firm is seen as a problem-solving institution, i.e. as a cognitive entity that promotes the coordination of plans of input-owners in the face of change) without specifying how discoveries take place, which is the explanation the entrepreneurial approach tries to provide.

It seems that the Penrosian approach had two consequences. On the one hand it has kept the theory of the firm within the walls of neoclassical economics, for it maintained a certain concern for pure optimizing problems in the economics of organization (the entrepreneur is neoclassical). On the other hand it led to a theory of change and growth of the firm that was inconsistent with the standard analysis. It shows, for instance, that the way the management uses and organizes various resources is crucial to the growth of the organization; and that new services can become available from already existing resources[25]. In other words, the capabilities view sustains, to a certain extent, an open-ended approach. However, the entrepreneurial aspect of Penrose's view has never been really developed and it seems that capabilities theorists take for granted part of the process of the growth of the firm. Therefore, the capabilities approach is not sufficient. However, a theory of the growth of the firm is necessary if we consider, as we see below, that the building up of capabilities by firms is a vital aspect of their entrepreneurial activity.

This chapter shows that there is a need for a distinctive capabilities approach to organization, one that does not boil down to a purely contractual issue, but which is entrepreneurial. As Foss puts it: "it is possible to construct propositions about economic organization that do not directly turn on considerations of morally hazardous behavior and incentive alignment" (Foss 1996b: 24). But we cannot agree with Foss when he concludes: "Instead, economic organization is fundamentally a matter of economizing with knowledge costs" (Foss 1996b: 24). Economic organization problems emerge because of the existence of a HKP, and not only because of knowledge costs as Foss (1996b) and Demsetz (1993 [1988]) argue.

KNOWLEDGE PROBLEMS, INCENTIVES, CAPABILITIES AND THE COMPLEX FIRM

Introductory remarks

In my model of the "simple firm" in Chapter 2, the firm is a tool for the exploitation of a discovered profit opportunity. The question that arises then is what happens once the profit has been exploited. In a living economy, if a firm has no other role than exploiting the discovered profit opportunity, it will cease to exist once the profit has been exploited. The fact that a firm ceases to produce and to exist is not, in itself, a concern of ours. Indeed, it is part of the market process that some firms stop their activity while others are founded. Nevertheless, it is a historical fact that many firms persist, continually produce new products and are, therefore, a source of novelty in the marketplace.

As I explained in the introduction of this chapter, we need to understand how a firm not only exploits the initial profit that is discovered, but how it also serves as a locus for further discoveries and, in the process, grows. In other words, the question is: in a living economy, how does the firm stay in existence and how does it grow? In the section above we saw that although Penrose emphasized the link between the growth of the firm and entrepreneurship, modern capabilities theorists' treatment of the growth of the firm is incomplete. The remaining parts of this chapter develop a capabilities view that is more consistent with the existence of entrepreneurship in the economy (Sautet and Foss 1999).

The Hayekian Knowledge Problem in the context of the organization

As I argued in Chapter 2, this analysis of the firm aims to show the interconnectedness between the market process and the firm. Firms play a role in solving the coordination problem in the market.

Hayek (1973) distinguished between rules (in relation to spontaneous orders) and commands (in relation to the organization). Rules need not be known to the individuals who are following them (they can be tacit), and they may be of spontaneous origin (Hayek 1973: 43–5). In the complex firm, individuals are alert, on the one hand, and possess knowledge that can be local, tacit and social in nature, on the other. In that sense, the complex firm cannot function like a simple firm, for the employees' knowledge cannot be entirely centralized. There will always be knowledge possessed by the employees that will depend on the particular circumstances of time and place and which the promoter cannot know (even if this would be valuable to him/her). This knowledge could be about the internal allocation of resources or about a profit opportunity in the marketplace. In other words, there is a HKP in the complex firm: the entrepreneur–promoter can be ignorant of his/her ignorance with respect to the knowledge possessed by some of his/her employees (and this knowledge could be crucial to the firm). This is in addition to the HKP in the marketplace. Therefore, the entrepreneur–promoter may not only be ignorant of his/her ignorance with respect to profit opportunities in the market, but also with respect to what his/her employees know. Because of this *double Hayekian Knowledge Problem*, the complex firm encounters:

> [t]he problem which any attempt to bring order into com-
> plex human activities meets: the organizer must wish the
> individuals who are to cooperate to make use of knowledge
> that he himself does not possess.
>
> Hayek (1973: 49)[26]

For this reason, the complex firm must·"rely also on rules and not only on specific commands. The reason here is the same as that which makes it necessary for a spontaneous order to rely solely on rules: namely that by guiding the actions of individuals by rules rather than by specific commands it is possible to make use of knowledge which nobody possesses as a whole" (Hayek 1973: 48–9)[27].

As well as relying upon commands *and* rules to function, the complex firm is, to some limited extent, a spontaneous order. This combination of commands, rules and spontaneous order is beneficial to the growth of the firm.

> [B]y relying on the spontaneous ordering forces, we can
> extend the scope or range of the order which we may
> induce to form, precisely because its particular manifestation
> will depend on many more circumstances than can be known
> to us.
>
> Hayek (1973: 41)

This entrepreneurial theory of the firm aims to understand the reasons behind Hayek's contention and to develop an entrepreneurial view of the complex firm. The complex firm can be defined as a production process taking place over time through a semi-planned coordination between complementary inputs, under the guidance of a promoter and of a system of rules and commands, and in which alert (and partly truly ignorant) individuals possess knowledge that may be local, tacit and social. Unlike the simple firm, the complex firm is not entirely entrepreneurially centered but, like the simple firm, its purpose is given to it by the entrepreneur–promoter.

Incentives for discovery: can entrepreneurship be channeled in the organization?

The complex firm provides the individuals in the organization with the power to act upon the knowledge they possess or discover, without the promoter being aware of it. In other words, the rules and the structure of the complex firm make room for entrepreneurial discovery.

However, entrepreneurial process analysis allows us to see that the complex firm can only be a locus of discovery if it is a structure in which the discoverers are the gainers. In order to induce individuals in the organization to make use of knowledge that only they possess, the incentive system must be carefully designed.

Robbinsian incentives

As we saw above, incentive alignment is one of the rationales for the firm in the transaction costs view. In this approach, incentives are "called for to motivate an agent to engage in some costly activity" (Kirzner 1985a: 86). Indeed, "[e]conomists treat the concept of an incentive as referring to the provision of an encouragement for a decision maker to select a particular one out of an array of already perceived alternatives" (Kirzner 1985a: 94). In order to obtain the desired planned coordination, the manager motivates his/her employees with (high enough) wages. He/she is in general the residual claimant (Alchian and Demsetz 1972), he/she rewards the different employees and he/she has the power to enforce the different contracts. These incentives are "Robbinsian incentives." They are based on the fact that the reward must compensate the cost of acting: the salary must exceed the disutility of work. (For a complete account of this subject, in connection with the principal–agent problem, see Milgrom and Roberts 1992: 214–39.) These incentives are present in the simple firm.

Williamson (1985: 131–62) makes the distinction between "high-powered incentives" and "low-powered incentives". The former characterizes markets and the latter characterizes firms. In markets, one can appropriate all of the net receipts, which provides incentives to exhaust them (exchanges will take place until there are no gains to trade left), whereas in the firm, an individual receives a specified salary, which lowers the incentive to do well. The manager, as a residual claimant, will have high-powered incentives, whereas the employees will have low-powered ones. Williamson explains that corporations try to use high-powered incentives, especially between two divisions when one supplies the other, but this does not come without problems. First, "firms cannot mimic the high-powered incentives of markets without experiencing added cost" and second, "although recourse by firms to low-powered incentives is thereby indicated, that too comes at a cost" (Williamson 1985: 140). In fact, high-powered incentives in firms are "inherently subject to corruption." That is to say, "[t]he assets of the supply stage are not utilized with due care, and the net revenue stream of the supply stage is subject to manipulation" (Williamson 1985: 140)[28].

The problem with this view is that it takes place in a world without entrepreneurship[29]. As a consequence, Williamson does not see any other way to introduce high-powered incentives in the organization except through the relationship among various divisions. It is certainly true that when one division supplies another with intermediary goods, there can be problems with the level of transfer prices, accounting procedures and so forth[30]. However, these problems do not rule out high-powered incentives within an organization, as we shall see below.

Entrepreneurial incentives

Another kind of incentive "operates to encourage the adoption of A by making A more likely to be noticed by the decision-maker," explains Kirzner. "The incentive to undertake A operates, under the specified assumptions, through its inducement to discover the possibility and/or the attractiveness of A" (Kirzner 1985a: 96). The goal is to induce the individual to be alert to discoveries for net profit, and not only to gains that are already known (wages, for instance). In the marketplace, entrepreneurs tend to notice what is in their interest, because of the sheer lure of money. This type of incentive can exist in the complex firm. Many corporations function with incentive compensation systems that reward personal achievement (i.e. profit discovery for the company) by measuring it through profit centers (see below).

This is what Robert Townsend, while discussing the effectiveness of an incentive compensation system of profit sharing, explained in his book *Further Up the Organization* (Townsend 1984). Such a system should include the following characteristics:

1. It should be related as directly as possible to performance. Therefore, wherever a participant has primary responsibility for a profit center, his incentive compensation is directly related on a percentage basis to the profits of that center. Where his relationship is more remote, or where his judgments are of a staff type, evaluation is based on the judgment of his boss, but this is far less desirable. Spend company time and effort on the preparation of profit-and-loss statements for profit centers to enable as many people as practicable to be measured that way. . . . For maximum effectiveness, no ceiling should be put on a profit-measured bonus merely because it has become substantial. . . . [D]on't let any paternalistic feeling ameliorate the situation of a manager whose business has turned bad and who, for the first time, may receive no bonus at all.

2. . . . Incentive compensation is to measure variations in performance [i.e. employees should obtain a minimum salary irrespective of performance].

3. Get your board of directors to establish in perpetuity (a moral binder) that 15 percent of total pre-tax profit will be available for those eligible for incentive compensation. The perpetuity is important. . . .

4. Bonuses measured by profit centers are handled by formula. Changes in formula should be resisted. . . . Fairness and full disclosure are the two keys to making the system work.

Townsend's compensation system does not have the following characteristics built into it:

1. No "thirteenth month" type of bonus or profit sharing by which every employee simply gets an extra pay period during the year, unrelated to performance. . . .

2. No incentive compensation is paid to an employee who does not otherwise merit it because "he is counting on it." Such a payment is always injurious to the organization and its employees, since it tends to reinforce the meritless one in the practices which justified an unsatisfactory rating.

3. No penalizing an employee – who has conducted himself well and shown tangible results – because of others either above him or elsewhere in the organization. . . .

4. No reducing the percentage of participation of a manager because his bonus is "getting too high," since such fudging corrupts the entire system. . . .

5. There are no secrets. No private payroll, for example. Since at least 15 percent of your employees should share in incentive compensation, it is very difficult to keep them in the dark about any expenditure with which they are unfairly burdened.

Townsend (1984: 95–103, italics removed)[31]

Townsend gives more than the usual incentive-alignment story. He says that the management can devise a plan that would induce individuals to work for profit and not only for their salary[32]. In other words, if the management is to set profit centers within the organization, it can directly reward individuals with the profits they have made[33].

In the same vein, Townsend also believes that stock-options should be given more often, so that more than the top management (especially salesforce) can own stocks in the company. He also explains that promotion should be carefully done and that the management should try to avoid filling up positions with people from outside the organization as much as possible[34]. (See Milgrom and Roberts 1992: 423–45 for a complete account of the executive and managerial compensation issue.)

A similar idea can be found in Penrose when she writes on the profit motive: "The profits of a firm do not confer such advantages on individuals unless they are paid out as income to individuals" (Penrose 1995 [1959]: 27). The key is to relate the profit received to the discovery made[35]. Rules within the organization are, in this respect, fundamental[36]. From this perspective, even if the rationale for the firm is not the pure alignment of incentives, as in the measurement view, it is still the case that incentives are fundamental to promote the discovery of profit opportunities and the growth of firms.

It is of course difficult to establish the connection between entrepreneurial behavior and the incentive system in the firm. This comes from the fact that the *same* behavior can be interpreted, on the one hand, as displaying an entrepreneurial component, or, on the other hand, as the result of pure optimization (Shmanske 1994). Austrian economists believe that it is only by taking into account the entrepreneurial function in human behavior that one can understand and solve the economic problem (Kirzner 1994). Of course, the burden of proof lies on the shoulders of process theorists who introduce another dimension of human action. I believe that this entrepreneurial theory of the firm will contribute to a better understanding of the role of entrepreneurship in the marketplace.

Rules as a form of entrepreneurial incentives

In a sense, Townsend illustrates Hayek's contention about the use of rules in the organization. "What distinguishes the rules which will govern action within an organization," writes Hayek, "is that they must be rules for the performance of assigned tasks" (Hayek 1973: 49)[37]. The assigned task is, for example, to name a certain person as the manager of a profit center (and give him/her a goal) and the rules are expressed, for instance, as in Townsend's compensation system. The notion of rules could also be taken in the sense of habit or custom: this is the route followed by many organization theorists[38]. In the Great Society, as Hayek explains, only general abstract rules are needed to allow for the possibility of correct foresight (Hayek 1977 [1958]). It is because individuals are ignorant that rules must be sufficiently abstract and general to permit adjustment. By analogy, rules within an organization will permit the completion of an assigned task and the possibility of adjustment to unforeseen contingencies. The greater the chances that adjustment to future conditions will be required, the more rules will be preferred over command. As Langlois (1995: 258) explains, organizations that rely more on abstract rules will be able to adapt better to changing circumstances[39]. It is only by allowing individuals to use the knowledge they possess that the promoter will be able to rely on the knowledge possessed by his/her employees. As Hayek puts it: "we cannot improve the results by specific commands that deprive its members of the possibility of using their knowledge for their purposes" (Hayek 1973: 51)[40].

104

In his book *Bureaucracy*, Mises (1983 [1944]) argues that a rigid system of social organization – a bureaucracy – cannot bring about change and improvement. Such an organizational system is necessary in certain cases – the State or the Roman Catholic Church, for instance – but it cannot be conducive to adaptation and change in the case of "profit management." This argument is similar to the Hayekian distinction between rules and commands. State bureaucracies function according to a set of very rigid principles that must be followed, for what is sought is not discovery of profit (like in a firm), but the establishment of certain procedures that will form the institutional framework of society. In a firm, on the other hand, individuals are seeking new profit opportunities and only general rules can be conducive to novelty in such a case[41].

The Hayekian notion of rules within the organization can also be connected to the concept of "shared mental construct" that we saw above, or to views of the firm as a constitutional system (Vanberg 1992)[42]. These rules help to coordinate knowledge within the firm in the sense that they induce individuals to act upon the knowledge they possess and which is not shared by anyone else in the firm. Therefore, rules promote intra-firm learning processes and local discoveries (Foss 1997a: 29)[43].

Firms as a nesting of entrepreneurs

Kirzner particularly emphasizes the origin of the entrepreneurial insight. As he puts it:

> The entrepreneur is the person who hires the services of factors of production. Among these factors may be persons with superior knowledge of market information, but the very fact that these hired possessors of information have not *themselves* exploited it shows that, in perhaps the truest sense, their knowledge is possessed not by them but by the one who is hiring them. It is the latter who "knows" whom to hire, who "knows" where to find those with the market information needed to locate profit opportunities.
>
> Kirzner (1973: 68)

Kirzner sometimes gives the example of a taxicab company that would give enough freedom to its employees to act upon their knowledge of time and place and to be alert to profit opportunities (taxi drivers will get a good tip if they drive safely and quickly, and if they speak nicely to the client, for instance[44]). It is still the case, though, that drivers work for their employer (who could be the initial promoter or his/her successor) and not for themselves. Drivers are limited in the type of discoveries they can make and, in the final analysis, resources are allocated by the management only.

It is also the case that in the "complex firm," entrepreneurial incentives are deployed throughout the organization. This complex firm is different from the simple firm in the sense that it is not entrepreneurially centered and planning is limited. In fact, the view of the complex firm as a nesting of entrepreneurs becomes a reality with the multidivisional firm (the M-form).

Langlois (1995), following ideas developed by Menger, Hayek and Vanberg, established a typology of made and spontaneous orders (see Table 3.1). As I argued above, the simple firm, as defined in Chapter 2, is a heuristic and would fall in the "pragmatic organizations" box. The complex firm is in the "organic organizations" box. This means that, following Langlois, we move beyond the familiar dichotomy between organic orders (the market system) and purely pragmatic ones (the Coasean firm). As argued below, this does not mean that planning is absent in the complex firm, it just means that there is more than pure central planning.

Table 3.1 Typology of made and spontaneous orders

Organic orders	Organic organizations
Pragmatic orders	Pragmatic organizations

Source: From 'Do firms plan?' by R. Langlois in *Constitutional Political Economy* 6(3): 249, © 1995. Reprinted by permission of Kluwer Academic Publishers.

Are capabilities necessary for the existence of entrepreneurship in the firm?

In the complex firm, discoveries of new profit opportunities add to the experience of individuals and make capabilities grow over time. As mentioned above, a key aspect of entrepreneurship is the notion of alertness. An entrepreneur is alert to profit opportunities that he/she might discover in his/her environment. We know that entrepreneurial discovery is costless and that rather than depending on the amount of search individuals engage in, it depends on what individuals are alert to. From that perspective, alertness will depend on what individuals know at some point in time and the individual's capabilities. Capabilities and alertness are therefore related in the sense that capabilities make people more alert to certain aspects of their environment[45]. Consequently, while one cannot search for discoveries, alertness means that people will thus tend to discover what is in their interest to discover. Alertness (and therefore discoveries) will depend on capabilities and capabilities will depend on discoveries: this is *learning by discovering*.

Capabilities are necessary for the existence of entrepreneurial activity within the firm. A taxi driver in a cab company will be more alert if he/she has strong capabilities; that is to say, if he/she knows the area well and has experience in dealing with clients. Chandler (1990a [1962]) provides another example of this link between discoveries and capabilities. He explains, with respect to the innovation of the M-form organization at du Pont, that "the initial awareness of the structural inadequacies caused by the new complexity came from executives close to top management, but who were not themselves in a position to make organizational changes. . . . The innovators appear to have been the executives closest to the problem who were given or took time away from operating duties" (Chandler 1990a [1962]: 303–4). It was the particular position in the firm of certain managers – and their experience and capabilities – that made them more aware of a certain problem (and its solution) than others.

Chandler also mentions the case of the committee of young executives at du Pont that was at the origin of structural innovations. This case illustrates that capabilities can also be embedded and developed in a team and that discoveries can take place as a result of teamwork. It is only when a particular team (young executives who held responsible positions in divisions at du Pont, for instance) is put together that discoveries can be made: this is team entrepreneurship[46]. The discoveries made by the team could not have been planned by the initial entrepreneur, he/she just discovered that putting certain people together in a team can lead to discoveries. This is spontaneous undeliberate team learning that would not have come into existence otherwise. Team entrepreneurship is an important component of explanations of social knowledge in the firm (Penrose 1995 [1959]; Foss 1996b)[47].

Thus, the capabilities approach is necessary if we are to understand the growth of the firm. It is difficult to imagine the growth of the firm without analyzing the growth of capabilities. However, the capabilities approach – as it is understood in the modern literature on organizations – does not provide a full answer to the question of the growth of the firm[48].

THE MULTIDIVISIONAL CORPORATION AS THE ARCHETYPE OF THE COMPLEX FIRM

Introductory remarks

The importance of knowledge in the firm is not a new subject. Ghoshal *et al*. (1995) emphasize the decentralized nature of knowledge in the corporation and quote the work of Hayek. They realize that what they call "local entrepreneurship" in the firm has to do with a knowledge problem and that this shows that strict hierarchy is not always suited to the problem of production in the corporation. Instead, they conceptualize the firm as a distinct coherent institutional context, which goes beyond the mainstream issues of governance. As they put it, the firm enables individuals to:

> chart a different path, one that actually *defies* (albeit, and importantly, for only a limited time) the relentless gale of the market forces and, in that process, creates a social environment with a combination of its own unique mix of incentives and *muted* market incentives which encourages the development, assimilation, transfer and combination of local knowledge in ways that are difficult to do under alternative institutional contexts of the market or of other institutions.
>
> Ghoshal *et al*. (1995: 757)[49]

As I argue above, although this view is similar to the entrepreneurial view of the firm in certain respects, it lacks the benefit of a comprehensive economic theory. The definition of the HKP is incomplete and, therefore, their theory misunderstands the implications of the HKP for (a) the notion and role of entrepreneurship[50] and (b) the problem of planning in the firm. Austrian economics provides more powerful tools to understand the problem of knowledge and the growth of the firm. This will be shown by dealing with the notion of separation of ownership and control.

The separation of ownership and control

There have been many disputes among economists on the modern corporation and the separation of ownership and control[51]. The separation of ownership and control is a problem because managers can fail to do their proper job: they can try to maximize their own satisfaction instead of that of the owners – i.e. the monetary receipts that should accrue to the stockholders. Managers can divert the firm's resources (i.e. owners' resources) from their "optimal allocation." As some theoreticians have shown, there are many contractual devices (the market for corporations and control, see Manne 1966) that provide incentives that align the interests of the owners and managers and make the corporation viable.

Following Kirzner, we should stress that this separation may have some virtues. It can be understood as a separation that allows for entrepreneurial discretionary behavior to take place within the firm. In other words, it is an essential feature of the complex firm. As Kirzner puts it:

> where the corporate form of business organization permits a measure of independence and discretion to corporate managers, this is an ingenious, unplanned device that eases the access of entrepreneurial talent to sources of large-scale financing. Instead of the entrepreneur having to borrow capital – with all the transaction costs we have seen this to involve – the corporate form of organization permits would-be entrepreneurs to hire themselves out to owners of capital as corporate executives. The capitalists retain formal ownership, permitting them, if they choose, to divest themselves easily of their shares in badly managed firms or, in the last resort, to oust incompetent management. Yet the executives, to the limited extent that they do possess discretionary freedom of action, are able to act as entrepreneurs and implement their ideas without themselves becoming owners at all.
>
> Kirzner (1979: 104)

The separation of ownership and control implies incompleteness of contracts. We saw above that incompleteness of contracts can be seen as an instrument for adaptation that is necessary for learning to take place (Foss 1996c). It is also necessary for entrepreneurial activity, so that would-be entrepreneurs can hire themselves out to the owners of capital. This separation is one of the distinguishing marks of the multidivisional form. A division is, with respect to the central management, like a manager with respect to the stockholders: to a limited extent, there is a separation of ownership and control. Central management retains the power to rule in the last resort (i.e. to solve conflicts and to decide the long-term policy), but local managers are in control of the division. However, the separation of ownership and control is not of the same degree as the separation of managers and stockholders. This is why Williamson explains that "even if middle managers [i.e. division managers] are 'ostensibly' free from oversight during the operating interval, the absence of oversight should not be implied if (1) strategic management can and does intervene when a crisis occurs . . . and (2) the operating plans are periodically renegotiated" (Williamson 1985: 146). Yet, even if there is a difference in degree, the relationship is of the same nature: division managers have access to internal capital markets and may hire themselves out to the central management which makes the final decision regarding the use of capital[52].

A presentation of Chandler's historical analysis in *Strategy and Structure*

The emergence of the departmental structure

In *Strategy and Structure* Alfred Chandler (1990a [1962]) presented a historical analysis of the evolution (in terms of structure and strategy) of four major companies (du Pont, General Motors, Standard Oil NJ and Sears Roebuck & Co) between the end of the nineteenth century and the late 1950s. I would like briefly to summarize the context in which these companies (especially du Pont) underwent major changes in their structure, so that this analysis can used to illustrate the entrepreneurial understanding of the firm.

Before 1850, firms in the USA had little systematic organizational structure, there were no departments and full-time administration. When the railroad business became geographically important (with the growth of the urban population in the second part of the nineteenth century) for instance, new informational needs arose within railroad companies (detailed reports on daily and weekly activity for instance). This encouraged railroads (especially the Erie Railroad Company) to create departments with full-time administrative units (Chandler 1990a [1962]: 20–4). Additionally, new legal dispositions came into existence. At the end of the 1880s, New Jersey changed its incorporation law to permit a corporation to buy the stock of another (Chandler 1990a [1962]: 30)[53].

By the turn of the century, many firms had a departmental structure, which usually reflected the types of products they produced (depending on the number of factories, salesmen, etc). Each major function the firm had to deal with came to be managed by a separate department. However, firms, on the whole, would still produce one major product or line of products and would operate over a relatively small area. Firms were organized in departments, each having its headquarters, with a general office in which the president and the board of directors (of the departments) took managerial and long-run decisions.

This type of structure is also called the unitary form (U-form). Du Pont's structure, prior to the First World War is a good example of a firm with a departmental structure. This mode of organization was progressively adopted by most companies and, by the end of the First World War, the "centralized structure" was the dominant organizational structure (see Figure 3.1).

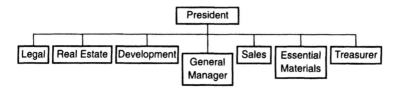

Figure 3.1 Du Pont structure, *circa* 1911.
Source: From *Strategy and Structure* by A. Chandler, © 1990. Reprinted by permission of MIT Press.

Growth and the emergence of the multidivisional form

Sources of economic growth in firms became more diverse, especially with the growth of urban populations, at the turn of the century. Firms were faced with three choices: (a) continue to expand along existing lines, (b) try to reach new markets and new sources of supplies in more distant places, or (c) try to develop new types of products for new customers and enlarge their capabilities (Chandler 1990a [1962]: 42).

Most metals companies and agricultural processing companies continued to develop, in the first quarter of the twentieth century, along their existing lines. Metals companies continued with the production of traditional metals such as copper, zinc, iron or steel, and sold this production to the same type of users. Of course, the technology used to produce steel products evolved and new demands for steel came into existence during that period, but expansion was driven by changes in the costs of production (better services, cheaper products, etc) not through developing new products or moving into new geographical areas. The same pattern of development occurred in tobacco, sugar, liquor and banana companies. Expansion of these firms did not really bring new types of administrative problems; and as Chandler explains, by the early 1960s, most of these companies were still run through the centralized form (Chandler 1990a [1962]: 42).

In other industries, growth was driven by the movement into overseas markets and the multiplication of products. Many chemical companies followed the path opened by du Pont at the end of the 1920s, and grew through diversification into new lines of products. This occurred in the power machinery, electrical and automobile industries[54]. For instance, automobile companies started to produce a wide range of products (tractors, diesels, trucks, airplane engines and even electrical equipment), which were mostly based on the internal combustion engine. In those cases, the unitary form – like that at du Pont – started to resemble the growing departmentalized firm (Figure 3.2).

Most firms that began to grow through diversification and territorial expansion eventually changed their organizational structures. They went from the departmental to the multidivisional form[55], as if their structure was related to the nature of their business. As Chandler puts it: "The historical record certainly does suggest that structure does follow strategy" (Chandler 1990a [1962]: 49). The multidivisional structure, with its divisions and departments within each division, is shown in Figure 3.3. The following analysis of the multidivisional structure will not aim to explain historically what took place at what moment, it will simply be a theoretical account of the growth of the firm in the marketplace through the use of Chandler's case studies.

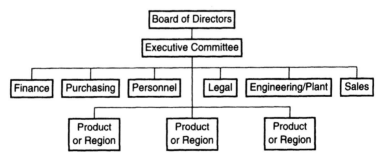

Figure 3.2 The growing departmentalized firm.

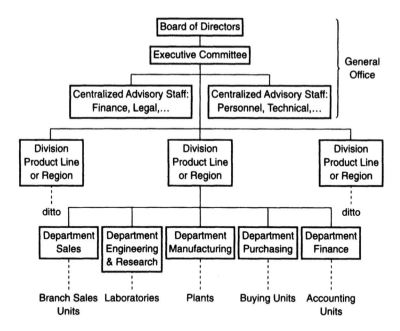

Figure 3.3 The multidivisional structure.

Rationales for the metamorphosis

Chandler and Williamson: complexity, opportunism and bounded rationality

Williamson views the modern corporation as the product of a series of organizational innovations that economize on transaction costs (Williamson 1985: 273). Among these innovations, the most significant of all is the development of the multidivisional structure (M-form).

Chandler's position with respect to the explanation of the M-form has perhaps evolved over the last two decades (see his account of organizational capabilities in *Scale and Scope*, Chandler 1990b). Nevertheless, he and Williamson have shared a common understanding of the problem for some time[56]. In his 1962 book, Chandler emphasizes the importance of the complexity of the tasks involved and the limitations of managers to achieve administrative and operating goals. As he puts it with respect to the departmental firm, for instance:

Yet the dominant centralized structure had one basic weakness. A very few men were still entrusted with a great number of *complex* decisions. The executives in the central office were usually the president with one or two assistants, sometimes the chairman of the board, and the vicepresidents who headed the several departments. The latter were often too busy with the administration of the particular function to devote much time to the affairs of the enterprise as a whole. Their training proved a still more serious defect. Because these administrators had spent most of their business careers within a single functional activity, they had little experience or interest in understanding the needs and problems of other departments or of the corporation as a whole. As long as an enterprise belonged in an industry whose markets, sources of raw materials, and production processes remained relatively unchanged, few entrepreneurial decisions had to be reached. In that situation such a weakness was not critical, but where technology, markets, and sources of supply were changing rapidly, the defects of such a structure became more obvious.

> Chandler (1990a [1962]: 41, emphasis added)

Chandler also explains that growth by diversification and geographical expansion led to serious new administrative problems. As he puts it:

Growth through diversification into several lines increased the number and *complexity* of both operational and entrepreneurial activities even more than a world-wide expansion of one line. The problems of obtaining materials and supplies, of manufacturing and of marketing a number of product lines for different types of customers or in different parts of the world made the tasks of departmental headquarters *exceedingly difficult to administer systematically and rationally.* The coordination of product flows through the several departments proved even more formidable. Appraisal came to involve not only a constant intelligent analysis of the operating performance in the different economic functions, including engineering and research as well as production, distribution, transportation, the procurement of supplies, and finance, but the making of these appraisals in several very different industries or lines of business.

Chandler (1990a [1962]: 44, emphasis added)

The language of Williamson is very similar, and following Chandler (and certainly Simon), he emphasizes complexity and managers' cognitive limitations:

> The ability of the management to handle volume and complexity of the demands placed upon it became strained and even collapsed. Unable meaningfully to identify with or contribute to the realization of global goals, managers in each of the functional parts attended to what they perceived to be operational subgoals instead . . . In the language of transaction costs economics, bounds on rationality were reached as the U-form structure labored under a communication overload while the pursuit of subgoals by the functional parts (sales, engineering, production) was partly a manifestation of opportunism.
>
> Williamson (1985: 280–1)

According to Williamson, the M-form structure economizes on the bounded rationality of the management and safeguards the internal resource allocation process against the hazards of opportunism. He points out that the internal structure shapes how the firm can cope with the problems identified by transaction cost economics (bounded rationality and opportunism). In the M-form, the central management is composed of an elite staff with the capacity to evaluate divisional performance and give rewards and penalties (Williamson 1985: 284)[57].

As we saw above, Williamson's theory does not fully address the issue of the growth of the firm in a living economy. Nevertheless, it is clear that central management can be confronted with complexity and experience cognitive limitations. Moreover, this theory is true and sufficient in an equilibrium-always world. However, as we saw above regarding capabilities theories, a theory of the growth of the firm must be entrepreneurial if it is to explain a phenomenon of a world in constant disequilibrium. Thus, there is more to the M-form structure than economizing on bounded rationality and reducing opportunism. The M-form is a structure that fosters entrepreneurial discoveries.

The M-form as an answer to the double Hayekian
Knowledge Problem: the limits of central planning in
the firm

The story described by Chandler and Williamson can, in fact, be understood as another version of the problem of central planning. The issue of central planning becomes clear once we emphasize the double HKP. As we saw above, when a firm grows – that is to say, when it tries to exploit new profit opportunities by diversifying into new products and by expanding in new geographical areas – it has to confront a double HKP: the entrepreneur–promoter is not only ignorant of his/her ignorance with respect to profit opportunities in the market, but also with respect to what his/her employees might know.

The problem of central planning in economics is very similar[58]. As Kirzner (1992a) explains, central planners, because of the HKP, may be unaware of their own ignorance regarding the relevance of their plan for each individual in society, especially regarding the circumstances of time and place. The planner will be unable to gather and discover all the necessary information to make his/her social plan "successful," for he/she would have to know what he/she truly ignores[59]. The knowledge problem can only be solved (or partially solved at any moment) through the existence and role of the entrepreneurial function. As Kirzner puts it, "what renders the Hayekian knowledge problem critique of central planning so devastating is the circumstance that in a market system, with decentralized decision making, *the insoluble knowledge problem confronted by central planners tends to dissolve through the entrepreneurial-competitive discovery procedure*" (Kirzner 1992a: 159, emphasis in original). In other words, since no one knows what the overall order should look like, only decentralized decision-making through entrepreneurial activity is likely to discover what will make individuals' plans mesh.

By analogy, I contend that the central office in the departmental firm becomes, in certain circumstances, more and more confronted with the HKP. Not only do problems of informational and computational complexity emerge, as Williamson shows, but epistemological problems also arise: how can central managers mobilize and utilize the knowledge necessary for the development of the firm when they do not possess it? In order to discover new profit opportunities, the promoter must rely on his/her employees to make use of knowledge that he/she does not possess (Hayek 1973: 49). It is because of this limitation that the firm, if it is to grow in related but diversified areas, cannot rely on complete central planning. As with central planners in a socialist economy, the central management must rely on the entrepreneurial process to discover new profit opportunities: *the multidivisional structure is an answer to the impossibility of complete central planning beyond a certain limit within the firm*[60].

As we saw above, according to Chandler, organizational changes in the 1920s occurred in certain circumstances only: when firms started to develop new and different lines of products (diversification) and/or when they began to expand in remote geographical areas. The HKP is more important in cases of diversification and expansion than in cases where firms try to grow along their existing line of products and markets[61] – like Ford before the Second World War. In the case of Ford, the promoter exploited a discovered profit and found new profit opportunities, but there was only a very limited double HKP. It is only when the strategic decision is made to diversify and/or to reach new areas, that the HKP becomes a double HKP, and that central planning cannot obtain the necessary knowledge for economic calculation[62].

I contend that one way firms can solve the knowledge problems encountered through expansion is by changing the organizational structure and implementing a multidivisional form that fosters entrepreneurial discoveries. Even if Chandler's concept of entre-preneurial activity basically means long term planning, it is still the case that he sees that the multidivisional structure enhances entrepreneurship. As he puts it:

> The inherent weakness in the centralized, functionally departmentalized operating company . . . became critical only when the administrative load on the senior executives increased to such an extent that they were unable to handle their entrepreneurial responsibilities efficiently. This situation arose when the operations of the enterprise became too complex and the problems of coordination, appraisal, and policy formulation too intricate for a small number of top officers to handle both long-run, entre-preneurial, and short-run operational administrative activities. To meet these new needs, the innovators built the multi-divisional structure with a general office whose executives would concentrate on entrepreneurial activities and with autonomous, fairly self-contained operating divisions whose managers handle operational ones.
>
> Chandler (1990a [1962]: 299)

One *could* interpret this passage as transaction cost theorists do and explain that the management's ability to handle the complexity of their task became so strained that it collapsed, and thus bounded rationality is indeed the major reason for organizational innovation. However, as we saw above, the transaction cost approach is not sufficient in a living economy and, even if it is sufficient in equilibrium, transaction cost economics leaves part of the problem unexplained. It is preferable simply to point out what Chandler partially explains: in the centralized structure senior executives became unable to handle their entrepreneurial responsibilities efficiently, that is why the multidivisional form emerged. In that sense, my view of the complex firm is an explanation of the entrepreneurial aspect of the theories of Chandler and Penrose.

Does strategy imply planning?

In his paper "Do firms plan?", Langlois (1995) argues that firms must generally be considered as organic organizations that do not plan or, more exactly, which plan in a quite different sense from the usual meaning. I subscribe to this general view about planning and, as I contend above, see complex firms as organic organizations.

Nevertheless, I do not share Langlois's understanding of the role of the entrepreneur. As he explains, he sees the entrepreneur as a visionary in the Schumpeterian sense and considers, like Penrose or Chandler, entrepreneurship as an economic capability (Langlois 1995: 255). Langlois also subscribes to a more or less evolutionary view of institutions, where *ex post* adaptedness is more important than foresight. Langlois obviously does not share a Kirznerian understanding of entrepreneurship, where the alert entrepreneur sees through the fog of uncertainty and discovers a profit opportunity[63]. From that perspective, "the firm is less a matter of planning than it is of coherent conjecture, of hypothesis" (Langlois 1995: 255). I do not deny that there is a dose of trial and error in the growth of the firm, and one could surely understand the firm as a locus for testing conjectures (Harper 1996; Loasby 1976, 1991). But it is the case that if one understands entrepreneurship as alertness to profit opportunities, the firm cannot be seen (only) in evolutionary terms. The complex firm is a locus of exploitation and discovery of profit opportunities that are discovered by entrepreneurs.

Therefore, there is some planning in the firm. Planning is present because of the fact that a firm's *raison d'être* is the exploitation of a profit opportunity and this requires some form of planning. In that sense, and as we saw in Chapter 2, I see the nature of the firm as different from the nature of the market. As the example of the M-form shows, a strategy to exploit newly discovered opportunities (like the expansion in new geographical areas) is part of a planned scheme that will lead to subsequent unplanned developments (entrepreneurial discoveries in the divisions). Even if this planning leads to spontaneous (i.e. unplanned) subsequent developments (i.e. the initial structure is planned, the subsequent discoveries are not), this planning is not the result of a trial and error process, it is the result of entrepreneurial activity. Incentives that are, at some point, necessary to induce entrepreneurial discoveries, are also the result of some sort of planning, but this is due more to the design of rules than to planning (Townsend's approach is a good example of that sort of design). This designed aspect could, and generally will, later on become part of the set of accepted rules in the firm and not be a designed element anymore (and therefore will participate in the growth of routines and capabilities)[64].

In that sense, the complex firm is an organic organization and, for reasons we saw above, central planning is limited and must rely on yet-to-come knowledge. The complex firm is an organic organization that results mainly from entrepreneurial discoveries and not only from a Mengerian (Menger 1985) process of evolution (even if, as Langlois 1995 points out, an evolutionary process also takes place in the firm). The overall development of the complex firm is unintended because entrepreneurial discoveries cannot be planned, but since their exploitation is planned, planning is, in one form or another, a distinguishing mark of the firm that is non-existent in the marketplace[65]. As Hewlett-Packard co-founder David Packard has explained:

> Early in the history of the company, while thinking about how a company like this should be managed, I kept getting back to one concept: if we could simply get everybody to agree on what our objectives were and to understand what we were trying to do, then we could turn everybody loose and they would move along in a common direction.
>
> Quoted in Milgrom and Roberts (1992: 116)

Thus, if the firm is to grow it will eventually become an organic organization. However, its nature will be different from an organic order.

The limits of central planning and the institutional context

This analysis of the M-form clarifies the fundamental issue of incentives in the firm. As we saw in Chapter 1, transaction costs economics (especially its measurement approach) sees incentive problems as crucial to the existence of the firm. As shown above, a case can be made where the existence of the firm is not related to incentives. This does not mean that incentives are not an important aspect of the analysis of organizations. On the contrary, the fact that structure follows strategy shows that one cannot dissociate the structure of the firm from incentives. It is because managers are confronted by informational and epistemological problems that the growth of the firm becomes problematic. However, these problems are due more to the absence of the structure in which incentives can operate fully than to missing incentives (it is still the case that managers supervise employees). In order to find ways to develop the firm, the *institutional context of the firm itself* must be considered: the limitations of central planning can be overcome only if a structure conducive to discovery and the full working of incentives is in place. The M-form provides the various managers and employees with the knowledge necessary for monetary calculation and assessment of the activities of the firm as a whole. The M-form is the institutional context of the firm in which incentives operate and discoveries are made (see also Vanberg 1992). In that sense, structure follows strategy.

We now understand the nature of the parallel made between central planning within the firm and central planning in the marketplace. As Kirzner (1992a: 159) explains, the HKP within the market system "tends to dissolve through the entrepreneurial-competitive discovery procedure." In the same way, the HKP within the firm tends to be solved by the various structural changes that the firm undergoes.

The definition of divisions' boundaries is the definition of the institutional structure of the firm itself, which will help to solve the internal HKP. However, given all this, the problem of finding the right institutional structure for a firm is difficult. There are many ways to divide up a business, and it is often difficult to find the structure that will: (a) minimize coordination problems (among divisions, customers and suppliers) and, (b) enhance entrepreneurial discoveries. Divisions can be defined, for instance, geographically, technologically, by the products produced or by the market segments being served. Hewlett-Packard had to face a problem of this kind when the company entered into the personal computer business in the 1980s. No division was big enough to design and produce a whole computer system, various parts had to be handled by various divisions. This, however, led to serious co-ordination difficulties as no single individual was in charge of the whole operation. As a result, Hewlett-Packard decided gradually to centralize the production of personal computers and redesigned its divisions (Milgrom and Roberts 1992: 547).

Another solution to the problem of finding the right institutional structure is to maintain relatively small divisions and to marshal together those that might need coordination among them: these are division groupings. "The individual division managers in the group then all report to one senior executive, who is responsible for the group and rewarded for its performance," write Milgrom and Roberts. "The largest firms may even have a number of groups, with their presidents reporting to another level of executive below the top levels of the firm" (Milgrom and Roberts 1992: 547–8). Division groupings are shown in Figure 3.4.

The issue of incentives and information cannot be divorced from the structure of the firm, because the problem is not only the performance of an assigned task, but also the discovery of new profit opportunities. Just as it is not possible to dissociate the issue of central planning from its institutional context, it is also not possible to separate the firm's structure from the epistemological problem it confronts.

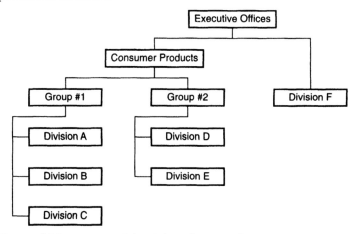

Figure 3.4 The structure of the M-form firm with division groupings.
Source: From *Economics, Organization and Management* by Milgrom and Roberts, ©1992. Reprinted by permission of Prentice-Hall, Inc., Upper Saddle River, NJ.

Discovery mechanisms in the firm

This section considers whether there is a mechanism analogous to the price system within the firm that makes individuals discover that organizational restructuring is necessary.

The M-form is an *entrepreneurial innovation within the firm* that helps to solve the double HKP encountered by the top management. As we saw above, the simple firm's growth is entrepreneurially centered, therefore the exploitation of new profit opportunities depends largely on their discovery by the promoter. In other words, the simple firm as a nesting of entrepreneurs, even if it remains entrepreneurially centered, gives room for individual discovery that allows for organizational learning and capabilities to grow. Capabilities make people more alert to certain aspects of their environment and, in that sense, they are necessary to the growth of the firm.

There is no price system within the firm that would allow for market arbitrages as described in Chapter 2. Therefore, any organizational innovation is in fact the result of phenomena external to the firm to which it must adapt (like the geographical distance of new markets). If we follow Chandler in his analysis, it is a fact that managers are confronted with new organizational problems when the firm grows along certain dimensions. The inner HKP emerges because the firm grows: structure must follow strategy. In the cases studied by Chandler, growth by diversification and by geographical expansion was the new strategy. This strategy put the structure of the firm under new constraints: the managers were no longer aware of all the information necessary for the management of the organization. This was not a problem of complexity *per se*, as bounded rationality was not the main source of ignorance. The HKP originated because of the nature of knowledge itself. What managers need to make the firm grow is local, social and tacit knowledge, which is not in their possession. Managers require knowledge that has not been discovered yet, and that may not even be suspected to exist: a knowledge of time and place. As Hayek (1973: 49) emphasized, managers in the central office need to rely on knowledge they do not possess in order to make the firm grow. Thus, a new structure is required that will allow for more knowledge to be discovered and exploited. This implies that some administrators in the firm became aware of the problem.

At du Pont, General Motors and Jersey Standard, explains Chandler, the necessity for structural reorganization was not discovered by the respective presidents of the companies, but by executives who were close to the top management and not in a position to make those changes themselves (Chandler 1990a [1962]: 303)[66]. Coordination difficulties among the various departments were certainly the major problem that emerged in those firms when they tried to implement new strategies. There were also marketing problems which, in fact, resulted from the coordination difficulties. This explains why the people who first became aware of the structural issue were not the top managers, but the individuals (such as those in charge of departments) who had local knowledge about the coordination problems that the president of the company did not possess[67]. It was the case at du Pont, for instance, where "a committee of young executives who held responsible posts in each of the major functional departments . . . became conscious of the inadequacies in their own units and particularly of the difficulties of interdepartmental coordination" (Chandler 1990a [1962]: 304). Alfred P. Sloan (with Donaldson Brown) played a similar role at General Motors. "He was currently managing a number of operating units and attempting to coordinate the activities of these units, not only with each other, but with the major car assembling and marketing divisions" (Chandler 1990a [1962]: 304) when he realized that the structure of the organization required change[68].

To make the new strategy for the growth of the firm possible, certain executives (those who had the knowledge of time and place and who were alert to coordination issues) had to change the structure of the firm to address internal coordination problems[69]. In fact, internal coordination problems were a symptom of the inner HKP that confronted general managers. That is why the most important discovery made by the committee of young executives at du Pont (or by Sloan at General Motors) was related to management issues. They found out that day-to-day operations had to be separated out from central office functions (by the creation of the general office), so that general officers could dedicate themselves to the business of the company as a whole (solve any coordination problems that could arise and handle long term decision making), and operating managers could focus on their day-to-day management. This discovery was made by individuals who were alert to structural problems in the organization, but the decision to change the structure was made by the president and the board of directors[70].

A more recent development is the "flattening" of organizational structures in certain companies (see the example of ABB below). In these situations, employees have to make more decisions themselves because the middle-management layer has been removed. With an increasing level of human capital, delegation of authority (team-based operations) becomes increasingly possible, and this delegation diminishes the inner HKP (provided new coordination problems are under control). However, delegation is just one of the ways to solve the inner HKP. As the above Hewlett-Packard example shows, some future developments may involve a redefinition of divisions' boundaries and more centralized decision making.

Executives are not the only people who can make discoveries in the firm. More and more firms are adopting the Japanese approach, which consists of making employees participate in the ever-improving production process (Deming 1986). Alanson Minkler (1993), quoting the works of various scholars, gives many examples of firms in which dispersed knowledge – knowledge of time and place – is used to induce discoveries that could not have been made otherwise. As he puts it:

> Pepsi's Riverside plant [Lang 1990] and Harley-Davidson's entire operations [Reid 1990] were constructed using employee ideas and have incorporated management systems that involve employees in decision-making and problem-solving. Womack, Jones, and Roos [1990] attribute Toyota's success largely to its policy of allowing workers to make decisions based upon their on-the-spot knowledge. In fact, the use of just-in-time supply systems intentionally forces employees to use their knowledge to solve problems.
> Minkler (1993: 575)[71]

Within the firm there is no mechanism that is analogous to the price system. Transfer prices, for instance, are crucial to economic calculation in (and among) each profit center (especially regarding the computation of costs), but they are not market prices (even if divisions managers have the autonomy to deal with outsiders, see Milgrom and Roberts 1992: 80). Therefore, discoveries will not take place in the same way within the firm as they do in the market-place. Nevertheless, the implementation of a new strategy changes the informational landscape of the firm and makes the top managers in the central office ignorant of information that would be necessary for them to discover and exploit new profit opportunities. In that sense they need to rely on the alertness of others (the committees of young executives at du Pont or Sloan and Brown at General Motors) to become aware of the problem[72]. Thus, the view held by the advocates of the market-process approach to management, which basically says that firms *should* "mimic" the market in order to enhance its adaptive capacities, seems flawed[73]. Discoveries cannot take place in the firm in the way they take place in the market, for the reason that what individuals in the firms may discover is related to ignorance in the marketplace and not to ignorance in the firm itself. The fact that managers confront an inner HKP does not mean that some entrepreneurial profit can be made in the firm, it simply means that the exploitation of new profit opportunities might lead to informational problems that could be an impediment to the exploitation of the profit itself and to future profit discoveries. Moreover, when Cowen and Parker discuss the use of decentralized methods of management, especially the M-form, they see the creation of markets in the firm when there is, in fact, the use of entrepreneurial incentives (Cowen and Parker 1997: 27–8). There are no markets inside the firm, there is only an accounting system – which can be based on some shadow prices – which gives information to the managers about the use of inputs by the various departments and divisions of the firm. The shadow prices are internal rates of trade-offs that are ultimately justified by external markets, i.e. through the profit and loss made by the entire firm[74]. Thus, firms and markets are fundamentally different.

This discussion can be related to Langlois's hypothesis: "The more radical the change – the more radical the deviation from the customary path – the more abstract will be the institutions necessary to change, create, or otherwise redirect concrete capabilities in an effective direction" (Langlois 1995: 258, emphasis removed). Moreover, Langlois states that, in the multidivisional firm, because day-to-day managers have to deal with concrete details, they will certainly follow more concrete rules than strategic managers. Following Hayek – who stated that the more abstract the rules of a system, the better able the system is to coordinate a diversity of concrete purposes – Langlois explains that strategic managers will be able to deal with more severe variations in their environment than day-to-day managers.

While Langlois's contention seems accurate, it is not obvious that rules followed by operating managers are less abstract than rules followed by general managers. For example, in the M-form, operational managers are also able to display entrepreneurial alertness. The initial discovery of the new structure at du Pont, for instance, came from executives who were in charge of day-to-day operations and had to deal with coordination problems. However, it is the case, as we saw above, that there is a need for abstract general rules in the organization if entrepreneurial incentives are to be implemented. Abstract general rules are required to emulate a certain degree of spontaneous order in the firm. Our interpretation of Langlois's hypothesis is that the M-form, in fact, generalizes the use of abstract rules in the organization in such a way that division managers can act as entrepreneurs.

The role of the general office and the nature of information flows between the divisions and the headquarters

The importance of a steady flow of information

In the M-form, the management (in the general office) relies on rules as well as specific commands, and induces entrepreneurial discoveries in the divisions. As we saw above, the corporate form allows much discretionary behavior by division managers. In a sense, division managers hire themselves out to the general office and this allows them to implement their ideas without requiring them to take responsibility for the entire company: they can be entrepreneurial and act upon the knowledge they possess and exploit the profit opportunities they discover[75]. In this form of organization, it is thus possible to make use of knowledge that nobody possesses as a whole, for the growth of the firm depends on many minds. As Foss (1995) explains, corporate headquarters enhance the firm's capabilities by performing "knowledge direction," exploiting the flexibility of incomplete contracts and promoting "organizational learning by combining hitherto separately developed knowledge and insights" (Foss 1995: 18). This is the parenting function of the central management.

The central management performs a long-run entrepreneurial task: to discover how to allocate the resources of the firm to the most promising entrepreneurs in the organization, and to coordinate the various activities so that it promotes organizational learning and the growth of the firm's capabilities. Nonaka and Takeuchi (1995) explain that for organizational learning to take place and to be exploited as a capability, knowledge acquired by various individuals must be disseminated. It is the role of the central management to ensure the dissemination of knowledge in order to take advantage of the various local discoveries.

That is why the channels of communication between the various divisions and the central office are vital to the existence of the firm. The M-form can be superior to the centralized structure only if decentralization creates new knowledge and if this knowledge is used; in other words, if profit opportunities are exploited. Sloan and Brown, for instance, spent a lot of time in 1921 devising an informational system that would provide both the division managers and the central office with a picture of their respective performances (Chandler 1990a [1962]: 307)[76]. Within the M-form, the divisions can discover knowledge that was hitherto non-existent, and they can provide the final decision-makers with more and better data. Conversely, the general office will supply information of all kinds to the various divisions in order to solve any coordination problems. Each operating unit could then be closely checked and their past and present performance could be monitored more closely[77].

This flow of information is possible not because the general management can dedicate its time to long term planning as central planners would do in a socialist economy or in a simple firm, but because they can rely on knowledge that they do not possess to plan the destiny of the firm. There is still some central planning in the M-form, as Chandler explains, but it relies on decentralization to function, that is to say, it relies on the fact that the knowledge necessary for the plan will be discovered during the implementation of the plan itself. Again, the knowledge that general managers obtain in the M-form is different from what would be obtained in the case of the U-form. *The decentralized structure produces knowledge that would be impossible to produce in a different organizational structure*[78]. It is only when there are managers in charge of operational activities that this knowledge can be produced. Division managers build capabilities, become more alert to profit opportunities essential to the growth of the firm as a whole and provide the general management with information that is otherwise unobtainable. That is how the "epistemological problem of the firm" gets progressively managed.

In such a situation, general managers can use new knowledge that would not have existed otherwise. They can also use (or comprehend) more of the knowledge available to them than would be possible in a different context. However, the information-overload problem described by Williamson is not reduced because division managers treat and filter out information, it is reduced because division managers produce new knowledge that can be used by central managers in their discovery of long term profit opportunities. The M-form is a new division of labor in the firm (and, therefore, a new division of knowledge); a division that is necessary to bring about knowledge that would be undiscoverable in a centralized structure.

On accounting and profits

"[F]rom the point of view of investment policy," writes Penrose, *"growth and profits become equivalent as the criteria for the selection of investment programmes"* (Penrose 1995 [1959]: 30, emphasis in original). If division managers have the discretionary power to exploit the profit opportunities they discover, then can we say that the accounting profits made by the various divisions (and also by the profit centers) are pure economic profit? In other words, do accounting profits measure pure economic profit?

Accounting profits are an important tool for general managers, but economists cannot really say that they measure pure economic profit. Essentially, accounting profits compute returns on investments. Part of the returns on investments may be pure economic profit. However, there is no way to know to what extent this is the case, and, in any case, managers do not really care. Although managers aim to make as much profit as possible, i.e. to make more profit than they could have made had they invested their capital elsewhere, it is empirically difficult to say to what extent any additional profit they make represents pure economic profit and not a return on some previous investment[79].

As long as the general management obtains measures of accounting profit from the various divisions, it can determine which line of business is more profitable and should be expanded, even without knowing if there is any pure economic profit being made. The same logic applies to incentives. As we saw above, to obtain entrepreneurial incentives in the firm, individuals must be able to retain a share of the accounting profits. In this way, if any pure profit has been made, the discoverers can capture it. Therefore, accounting profits are a necessary tool as they reveal entrepreneurial error. Assuming that the profit and loss mechanism works (i.e. it reveals to some extent the current state of underlying variables), which is what economists usually assume, accounting profit provides an objective measure of success, without which entrepreneurship is meaningless. Accounting measures of profits allow the multidivisional structure to reduce the effects of entrepreneurial error on the corporation. If a division starts to lose money, the central management can reallocate the capital to some other use.

However, accounting profits are not the only tool that managers require. For instance, the notion of profit centers is not always useful in an entrepreneurial perspective[80]. Williamson's criticism of "accounting chicanery" seems relevant here as profit centers are

often just an accounting device that gives the management information regarding the cost of production of certain units, they are not
necessarily relevant to a discussion on pure profit. Nevertheless, it
could still be the case that profit centers act like autonomous
divisions in which the decision-maker can exercise discretionary
entrepreneurial behavior. For instance, certain firms have recently
developed the notion of "clusters," where largely autonomous teams
of employees of undifferentiated rank work together on a certain
task[81]. It could surely be the case that these forms of decentralized
management enhance entrepreneurial activity, like divisions in a
multidivisional firm.

The case of Asea Brown Boveri

An interesting example of the complex firm (M-form) is Asea Brown
Boveri (*The Economist* 1996). Asea Brown Boveri (ABB) consists of
1300 legally separate units subdivided into 5000 profit centers,
each with an average of 50 employees, and with a total of 200 000
individuals. Percy Barnevik, the Swedish CEO of ABB is the father
of the "multicultural multinational." Indeed, since 1988, he has
established a corporation that is diverse enough to operate in many
countries and to respond to local tastes while providing a certain
unity behind the products. The company has only a small layer of
managers (about 100 people work at the headquarters in Zurich)
to supervise a myriad of profit centers, but employs about 500
"global managers" who are regularly shifted from one country to
another to "knit the organization together, to transfer expertise
around the world and to expose the company's leadership to differing
perspectives" (*The Economist* 1996: 56)[82]. Divisions retain one third
of their net profits[83].

ABB is an interesting example of the complex firm as a nesting of
simple firms[84]. The structure of the organization was designed by a
promoter – Percy Barnevik – who made a series of organizational
innovations (1300 divisions; 5000 profit centers; internal bench-
marking; centers of excellence; and corporate parenting) which can
be interpreted as entrepreneurial discoveries that solved part of the
HKP confronting the central management of a firm with 200 000
employees in many different countries. Through these innovations,
the firm was able to take advantage of local knowledge and to discover profit opportunities that would have otherwise been ignored
by the headquarters. The central management and the CEO promoted
organizational learning by connecting the different profit centers

together through the use of common rules (for example, every employee must read Barnevik's booklet about the company's aims and values).

Ghoshal et al. (1995) explore, in their discussion of ABB, the paradoxes that the firm is supposed to solve[85]. They argue that rational control and blunt incentives (i.e. strict hierarchy) are not conducive to the development and use of local knowledge and that market incentives (what Williamson calls high-powered incentives) limit the sharing of local knowledge. In other words, the authors state that the internal governance required for firms like ABB to function facilitates "(i) distributed initiatives to exploit the benefits of local resources and knowledge within each of its constituent parts, (ii) lateral sharing and integration of such distributed resources and knowledge to achieve economies of scale and scope, and (iii) central monitoring and administrative authority to prevent misuse of the system by any individual and to resolve conflicts" (Ghoshal et al. 1995: 753). Thus, what is required for the development of ABB is "shared context," not structural hierarchy.

Ghoshal et al. are accurate in their treatment of many issues, especially the limitations of the incentive–alignment view[86]. Indeed, much modern organization theory dwells around the notion that a firm is, by necessity, a hierarchy because the fundamental problem that has to be overcome is the misalignment of incentives. As Ghoshal et al. show, following J. S. Coleman, it has become increasingly difficult to apply the concept of agency to the employment relationship in the corporation because the separation of the functions of each party is not always clear cut. However, while Ghoshal et al. have identified the correct problems they have not identified all their causes. For instance, it is interesting to see that Ghoshal et al. (1995: 753) relate the element of "central reporting and control" at ABB to the transactional economies emphasized by Williamson, and not to the flows of information that are necessary for the management of the firm but which could not have been discovered with central planning.

As we saw above, the fundamental reason for the structure of ABB is the HKP and the necessity of fostering entrepreneurship to overcome the knowledge problem that central planning must confront. The reason ABB is multidivisional is due more to the knowledge limitations of central planning than to bounded rationality and opportunistic behavior. Indeed, the way ABB will evolve in the future will depend on how its managers discover new ways of structuring the firm in order to respond to the nature of its business and the need to solve epistemic problems.

CONCLUDING REMARKS

I argued in this chapter that while capabilities theories are necessary for explanations of the growth of the firm, they are limited in their explanation of the processes of growth in reality. Indeed, they do not make room for an entrepreneurial discovery procedure, which, I claim, is the source of the growth of capabilities. As a consequence, these theories do not entirely account for the problem of the discovery of knowledge and they overlook the issue of central planning.

I do not deny that there is an incentive–alignment problem in the firm and that the internal governance mechanism that solves this problem is hierarchy. However, instead of focusing on the pure Robbinsian incentive–alignment problems that have been described intensively in the literature, I prefer to focus on the issue of entrepreneurial incentives that are conducive to the discoveries of profit opportunities, to the growth of knowledge and, as a result, to innovation. In that sense, my approach lies more in the domain of production than in the domain of transaction (Langlois 1995). In fact, I focus more on the "generating" aspect of knowledge instead of its processing and integrating components (which are the subjects of many articles and books in organization theory). I see the rationale for the growth of the firm in terms of the division of labor and the discovery of knowledge, and my focus on entrepreneurship directs us to the main problem: how does a firm come to produce what it produces?

I contend that one of the ways for a firm to grow is by becoming multidivisional. Chandler (1990a [1962]) and Williamson (1985) are correct when they argue that the emergence of the M-form has been fundamental. However, the M-form is not only important for the reasons Williamson provides. I see the main function of the M-form as solving the inner HKP (with which the general managers are confronted) and, at the same time, as overcoming the impossibility of planning (completely) the growth of the firm (in a diversified and geographically dispersed way) from the central office. The complex firm, like the simple one, is a locus of exploitation of discovered profit opportunities (genuine uncertainty and type II entrepreneurship play the same role). However, the complex firm is also a locus of growth, and, for that reason, planning does not play the same role in the complex firm as it does in the simple firm. In the complex firm, planning is decentralized to the level where dispersed entrepreneurial discoveries are possible (within the limits of economic calculation).

My approach is a new interpretation of Chandler's conclusion on the revolution that took place in the American corporate world between the First World War and the Second World War. As he puts it regarding the M-form:

> The basic reason for its success was simply that it clearly removed the executives responsible for the destiny of the entire enterprise from the more routine operational activities and so gave them the time, information, and even psychological commitment for long-term planning and appraisal. Conversely, it placed the responsibility and the necessary authority for the operational administration in the hands of the general managers of the multifunction divisions.
>
> Chandler (1990a [1962]: 309)

What Chandler describes is the fact that the decentralized structure is a locus of discovery and of exploitation of profit opportunities. This is possible, not simply because bounded rationality problems were overcome (even if this is certainly true), but rather because the knowledge necessary for the growth of the firm could be discovered only through a decentralized structure that is conducive to entrepreneurial discovery. The M-form allows for the discovery of knowledge that would not have been discovered otherwise. It solves the inner HKP by easing the coordination problems that the centralized firm encounters in certain types of growth. My view is based on the idea of the market as a discovery procedure, which allows me to understand the problem in entrepreneurial terms and to develop a new interpretation of Chandler's historical account of the growth of the modern corporation. I believe that this chapter is the first development of a more general theory of the entrepreneurial capabilities of the firm[87].

GENERAL CONCLUSION

The profit motive through the instrumentality of which the entrepreneurs are driven to serve the consumers to the best of their ability is at the same time the first principle of any commercial and industrial aggregate's internal organization. It joins together utmost centralization of the whole concern with almost complete autonomy of the parts, it brings into agreement full responsibility of the central management with a high degree of interest and incentive of the subordinate managers of sections, departments, and auxiliaries. It gives to the system of free enterprise that versatility and adaptability which result in an unswerving tendency toward improvement.

Ludwig von Mises (1983 [1944]: 36)

I have come to three conclusions in the three previous chapters. First, the neoclassical theory of the market has no room for a true endogenous explanation of the emergence of the firm. That is why most of what strict neoclassical theory has produced is limited to cost-benefit analysis and relies heavily on incentive–alignment considerations to develop a rationale for the firm. This led me to understand that there is a "market theory problem" – i.e. an inconsistency involved in trying to answer questions that would not exist in an equilibrium-always world – in the modern economics of the firm, and that even transaction cost economics suffers from this MTP. Thus, one needs to provide a richer and deeper explanation of the existence of the firm. This explanation needs to be based on entrepreneurial market process theory and to account for the firm as a disequilibrium phenomenon.

In the second chapter, I developed a model of the emergence of the firm in the market process. In this model, I showed that the

133

emergence of the firm could be explained in a disequilibrium economy with zero transaction costs and where underlying variables are maintained constant. In such a world, and because of the nature of labor, the firm emerges because it plays a role in solving coordination problems in the market. The firm can be seen as a pulling together of entrepreneurial activity by a central entrepreneur. It is not, however, as some authors have argued (Kirzner 1973: 52), necessarily related to the notion of ownership: the essence of the firm, in that context, is coordination rather than ownership.

The question of the growth of the firm is the subject of the third chapter. Therein, I argued that capabilities theories are perhaps sufficient to account for the phenomenon they seek to explain in a neoclassical framework, but they cannot explain the growth of the firm in a living economy. A firm must induce entrepreneurial activity if it is to grow. However, other types of problem appear during its development. Basically, managers in a firm may have to face an internal Hayekian knowledge problem and, as a result, may become limited in their capacity to plan the development of the organization (in addition to the informational asymmetries and behavioral problems pointed out by Williamson and others). An entrepreneurial response is to divide the firm into various divisions, in other words, to give the firm a new institutional structure that will be more conducive to entrepreneurial discoveries and will help to solve the internal knowledge problem. The multidivisional form is a response to the limits of central planning in the firm. In fact, the "institutional context" of the firm, i.e. the structure of the firm itself, is the prerequisite to the workings of incentives in the firm. There is no incentive–alignment issue unless the framework in which incentives operate is in place.

Although the issue of the complex firm can be analyzed through the grid of complexity, I chose to address it in terms of entrepreneurial discovery. The entrepreneurial approach does not replace alternative views of the firm, it complements these views by adding a deeper understanding of the phenomenon of the firm in a living economy. While the entrepreneurial approach leaves room for an evolutionary theory of the firm, it emphasizes the fact that organizations, even if they are organic to a certain extent, are the result of human actions *and* human design.

I contend, in this entrepreneurial theory of the firm, that the nature of the firm is different from the nature of the market for the reason that, if one understands the firm as a locus of exploitation of a profit opportunity, then a certain amount of central planning is required to exploit the discovery of profit opportunities. The concept of the firm is distinct from the concept of the market in the sense that it necessarily embodies central planning in order to exploit a profit – a phenomenon absent from the unhampered market system as such (if we consider the marketplace as a pure system of exchange among individuals). However, I do not agree with Cowen and Parker when they say that "[t]he alternative to the use of market principles within firms is a continuation of the command and control or Taylorist paradigm" (Cowen and Parker 1997: 75). One should not confuse the issue of discovery that can take place in a firm (as I show in Chapter 3) with the issue of exploitation, which is why entrepreneurs set up firms in the first place. The Taylorist view can be seen as: (a) a normative principle in the organization of the firm (and not as an account of how firms function in the marketplace), and (b) a way to exploit a profit opportunity (and not as a recipe for innovation).

"In a competitive and technologically progressive industry," writes Penrose, "a firm specializing in given products can maintain its position with respect to those products only if it is able to develop an expertise in technology and marketing sufficient to enable it to keep up with and to participate in the introduction of innovation affecting its products" (Penrose 1995 [1959]: 132). Following Penrose, most theorists would now say that the problem of the growth of the firm relates to the development of expertise and participation in the introduction of innovation. The question I have raised in this work is how does this phenomenon take place? In this entrepreneurial theory of the firm, I have developed a deeper and fuller understanding of the source of (true) innovation, and this source is the entrepreneurial activity that a firm can induce.

NOTES

GENERAL INTRODUCTION

1 Ronald Coase himself has developed his "own view" of economics in order to establish a theory that could include (and explain) firms and institutions. See his introduction to *The Firm, the Market and the Law* (Coase 1990).

1 THE ECONOMICS OF THE FIRM, THE MARKET THEORY PROBLEM AND TRANSACTION COST ECONOMICS

1 *Gedankenexperiment* in German.

2 I use the concept of "ideal-type" in its Weberian sense (Boettke 1997b). Fritz Machlup gave a slightly different meaning to the concept of ideal-type, for he used it as a representation, in a positive way, of the essential features of a phenomenon. For the sake of clarity, in the remainder of this work, I will only use the term foil (see also Koppl 1994).

3 Fink and Cowen (1985) explain that Austrian economists have used the equilibrium concept in four different ways: (a) to explain the market economy's direction of change, (b) as a building block in the analysis of complex phenomena, (c) as a starting point in the analysis of change, and (d) as a foil against which to compare a complex order (see also High 1986). The predominant use of the notion of equilibrium in Austrian economics is the *argumentum a contrario*, i.e. equilibrium used as a foil against which the market process is evaluated. (This also implies the use of equilibrium as an explanation of the direction of change, but this understanding is included in the foil use.)

4 As Cowan and Rizzo put it: "Many of those who disagree with this position and call these situations 'disequilibria' really think of them as simply non-market-clearing or non-Walrasian equilibria. . . . In neither view, however, is there any question of endogenous change; there is simply disagreement over the nature of the equilibrium state" (Cowan and Rizzo 1996: 287).

5 See also Lucas (1981) on this issue, in which he makes a more sophisticated, but similar, argument about the use of equilibrium.

6 This view implies a bookshelf approach to information. As Boettke puts it: "Both the laissez faire Stigler and the interventionist Stiglitz (*et al.*) treat

136

knowledge "as if" it exists on a bookshelf, so that the only question is whether it is in one's interest to pull it off the shelf or communicate it accurately to others" (Boettke 1997b: 31).

7 As Boettke puts it (while considering the Chicago use of equilibrium as a description of reality):

> By collapsing the gap between the model and reality, the Chicago school in its purest form does away with the need for intervention of the sort advocated by Samuelson *et al*. Hence the current reputation of laissez-faire as a wildly unrealistic economist's dogma. . . . The Chicago school's use of equilibrium to describe reality conflates with the mental and empirical worlds. And while those who use equilibrium to indict reality recognize that the world is not perfect, their ignorance of the ways imperfect institutions do produce a semblance of economic order gives them an unduly pessimistic view of the market, and an unrealistically optimistic tendency to rely on legal fiat to bring reality up to a par. *In both cases, the heuristic value of equilibrium is sacrificed.*
> Boettke (1997b: 24, emphasis in original)

8 Arrow's (1974) view of uncertainty cannot account for his later understanding of the problem of economic growth: "While dissemination of existing information can certainly account for some of the gains in productivity," writes Arrow, "it is clearly necessary for sustained growth to have information new to the entire system, not merely learned from others" (Arrow 1994: 7). This view of new information seems to imply the existence of genuine uncertainty.

9 "The impossibility of prediction in economics," writes Ludwig Lachmann, "follows from the fact that economic change is linked to change in knowledge, and future knowledge cannot be gained before its time" (Lachmann 1977a [1959]: 90).

10 For a brief presentation of realism and the ontological issue of open-endedness in economics see Foss (1994b: 39–45) and Kirzner (1988: xvi–xvii). For a defense of indeterminism in physics and metaphysics, see Karl Popper (1982: 41–113).

11 Some Austrian economists, like Rothbard, have criticized the use of objective probability theory in the world of human action. "In the real world of human action," writes Rothbard, "virtually all historical events are unique and heterogeneous, though often similar, to all other historical events. Since each event is unique and nonreproducible, it is impermissible to apply objective probability theory; expectations and forecasting become a matter of subjective estimates of future events, estimates that cannot be reduced to an objective or 'scientific' formula" (Rothbard 1979: 93–4).

12 Langlois explains that "[Knight's] category of uncertainty blurs the distinction between situations of structural uncertainty and situations in which there are well-defined states of the world but simply no objective probabilities to assign to those states. Since the so-called Bayesian revolution, we have learned that the absence of objective probabilities is no bar to conceiving of uncertainty along the lines of Arrow's definition" (Langlois 1986: 228). See also Langlois (1994).

13 The same view can be found in Langlois and Cosgel (1993). Uncertainty is a situation in which no judgment can be made with regards to the classification of instances. In other words, the individual cannot even estimate the possible outcomes because "novel possibilities are always emerging and these cannot be easily categorized" (Langlois and Cosgel 1993: 462).

14 Mises (1966: 244–50) is very specific with respect to the tools used to study change. He distinguishes two concepts: the state of rest and the evenly rotating economy.

15 A good example of the classical view of the economic problem is in Oskar Lange's (1938) famous essay "On the Economic Theory of Socialism." As Lange puts it: "The economic problem is a problem of choice between alternatives. To solve the problem three data are needed: (1) a preference scale which guides the acts of choice; (2) knowledge of the 'terms on which the alternatives are offered'; and (3) knowledge of the amount of resources available. Those three data being given, the problem of choice is soluble" (Lange 1938: 60). In this approach, knowledge is understood as a commodity (i.e. the preference scales of individuals and the amount of resources available) and the only problem is to make sure that it is efficiently used in the allocation of resources (i.e. that exchanges are made according to the terms of the alternatives). For Lange, the problem is not to discover knowledge, but to allocate it. This is similar to Robbins's (1932) definition of the economic problem.

16 I subscribe to the distinction between information and knowledge which considers knowledge as information perceived by individuals. As a result, knowledge is necessarily theory laden. Such a distinction may be problematic for economists (it rests on perception), however it is possible to conduct economic enquiry without a specific theory of perception if it is assumed that individuals act on the information they perceive, whether this is correct or not.

17 See also Baumol (1968: 67) in which he explains that the mathematical relationships that define the activity of the firm exclude entrepreneurship.

18 Another consequence is the absence of Bergsonian time. As O'Driscoll and Rizzo put it: "Time, in this sense [duration], is not the static subjectivist concept used in planning or reflection. Instead, it is a dynamically continuous flow of novel experiences. This flow is not in time, as would be the case from a Newtonian perspective; rather it is or constitutes time. We cannot experience the passage of time except as a flow: something new must happen, or real time will cease to be" (O'Driscoll and Rizzo 1996 [1985]: 59–60). "The Newtonian conception of time is spatialized; that is, its passage is represented or symbolized by "movements" along a line. Different dates are then portrayed as a succession of line segments (discrete time) or points (continuous time). In either case, time is fully analogized to space, and what is true of the latter becomes true of the former" (O'Driscoll and Rizzo 1996 [1985]: 53). The equilibrium-always view generally implies a Newtonian understanding of time, which limits our analysis of the growth of knowledge in the market process. "Time and knowledge belong together" said Lachmann (1977a [1959]: 85) and so do action and time. The passage of real time is inseparable from the action of men. In economics, the time that elapses between the short and the long run is referred to as "operational time." As Langlois and

Robertson (1995: 27) explain, the adoption of a "learning-and-organization view" implies a different conception of time regarding the long run. Operational time is replaced by real time in order to account for the growth of knowledge and change. Nevertheless, I do not view the use of real time as necessary in my work, for I just need to use time in the sense of more than one period. On that issue, see also Vaughn (1994: Chapter 7), and the new introduction in O'Driscoll and Rizzo (1996).

19 Transaction cost economics, for instance, is one of the approaches in the broad category of "industrial organization" which stands against various alternatives (especially technological ones).

20 This organizational principle applies for even those theories that try to break away from the neoclassical approach (capabilities and evolutionary theories, for instance).

21 The emphasis on pure competition encouraged the economics of anti-trust (and pro-regulation) as the main field of application of industrial organization over the past 40 years, at least until comparative institutionalism (i.e. transaction cost economics) started to tell the economic profession a slightly different story.

22 As Coase puts it: "The economic system 'works itself.' This does not mean that there is no planning by individuals. These exercise foresight and choose between alternatives. This is necessarily so if there is to be order in the system. But this theory assumes that the direction of resources is dependent directly on the price mechanism" (Coase 1993a [1937]: 19).

23 "In view of the fact that while economists treat the price mechanism as a co-ordinating instrument, they also admit the co-ordinating function of the 'entrepreneur,' it is surely important to inquire why co-ordination is the work of the price mechanism in one case and of the entrepreneur in another" (Coase 1993a [1937]: 20).

24 "A factor of production (or the owner thereof) does not have to make a series of contract with the factors with whom he is co-operating within the firm, as would be necessary, of course, if this co-operation were as a direct result of the working of the price mechanism. For this series of contracts is substituted one" (Coase 1993a [1937]: 21).

25 "For Coase insists that many of the contracts constituting the firm are open-ended, or, in modern terminology, 'incomplete'" (Foss 1993a: 271).

26 Tyler Cowen and David Parker make the following remark with respect to the use of the term "transaction costs": "Coase did not use the term 'transaction costs' in his 1937 paper. Kenneth Arrow appears to have been the first to use the term, in 1969, to describe the 'costs of running the economic system' (Arrow 1969: 84)" (Cowen and Parker 1997: 33).

27 Of course this type of analysis is fundamental, for, as Boettke explains, "Coase was able to link the nature of economic organization to marginal cost-marginal benefit calculus" (Boettke 1997c: 3). However, it is not sufficient, in my view, to describe the process at stake (if we accept the Hayekian understanding of the economic problem).

28 It is interesting to realize that many references that are made today to Coase's concept of transaction cost almost never mention transaction cost as that of discovering prices. Hart writes for instance: "According to Coase, the main cost of transacting in the market is that of learning and haggling over the terms of the trade" (Hart 1995 [1989]: 156).

NOTES

The terms of trade could include the price of the transaction, but modern economists, like Hart, are uncomfortable with this idea.

29 Coase thinks that "[t]he concept of transaction costs has not been incorporated into a general theory" (Coase 1992: 718). Moreover, "incorporating transaction costs into standard economic theory, which has been based on the assumption that they are zero, would be very difficult" (Coase 1992: 718). Coasean economics is based on the "equilibrium as a foil approach" and therefore is not suited to be incorporated into general theory.

30 As I show below, this aspect of Coase's work will become, under the influence of Williamson, one of the pillars of transaction costs economics.

31 The subject of "entrepreneurial failure" or, more exactly, "management failure" is perhaps related to a missing theory of bureaucracy in transaction costs economics. As Williamson explains: "As compared with the market failure literature, the study of bureaucratic failure is very primitive. What are the biases and distortions to which internal organization is given? Why do they arise? How do they vary with organization form?" (Williamson 1985: 392).

32 It is an ongoing theme in Williamson's work. "Rather than focusing on technology and production costs, attention is focused on transaction cost economizing" (Williamson 1975: ix). "I argue in this connection that, but for a few conspicuous exceptions, neither the indivisibilities nor technological nonseparabilities on which received theory relies to explain nonmarket organization are sufficient to explain any but very simple types of hierarchies" (Williamson 1975: 2). "Transaction cost analysis supplants the usual preoccupation with technology and steady-state production (or distribution) expenses with an examination of the comparative costs of planning, adapting, and monitoring task completion under alternative governance structures" (Williamson 1985: 2). In this sense, he also rejects the approach in terms of production function which does not make any room for the subtle economizing purposes that are served by organizational variety (Williamson 1985: 7).

33 Williamson adds in the appendix of Chapter 2: "I do not insist that every individual is continuously or even largely given to opportunism. To the contrary, I merely assume that some individuals are opportunistic some of the time and that differential trustworthiness is rarely transparent ex ante" (Williamson 1985: 64).

34 It is interesting to notice that Coase does not address the issue of opportunism as central to a theory of the firm. In his discussion of fraud (Coase 1993c [1988]: 57–8), he writes "that avoidance of fraud was not [when he wrote in 1937] an important factor in promoting integration" (Coase 1993c [1988]: 58). With respect to the existence of opportunism, Williamson writes: "The efficacy of alternative modes of contracting will thus vary among cultures because of differences in trust" (Williamson 1985: 9).

35 As Williamson puts it: "Organize transactions so as to economize on bounded rationality while simultaneously safeguarding them against the hazards of opportunism. Such a statement supports a different and larger conception of the economic problem than does the imperative 'Maximize profits!'" (Williamson 1985: 32).

36 This difference is perhaps not so important after all, depending on how

we understand the cognitive problem involved here. Herbert Simon is a cognitive psychologist and has done a lot of work in problem solving, which explains his approach to rationality. On the issue of cognitive limitation and the firm, March and Simon write: "[M]embers of organizations have wants, motives and drives, and are limited in their knowledge and in their capacities to learn and to solve problems" (March and Simon 1958: 136).

37 It is not certain that cognitive capacity limitation is the reason why comprehensive contracts are unrealistic for followers of Williamson, like Hart for instance. As Hart puts it: "[I]n practice transaction costs are pervasive and large. A consequence of the presence of such costs is that the parties to a relationship will not write a contract that anticipates all the events that may occur and the various actions that are appropriate in these events. Rather they will write a contract that is incomplete, in the sense that it contains gaps on missing provisions" (Hart 1993 [1988]: 141). In Hart's view there is an optimal level of ignorance (due to transaction costs) that the parties have to bear. In that situation, "it is no longer the case that any rights conferred by ownership can necessarily be contracted away . . . since it may be impossible to describe these rights unambiguously" (Hart 1993 [1988]: 141). The incomplete contracts approach identifies ownership of an asset "with the possession of residual rights of control over that asset, that is, the rights to use the asset in any way except to the extent that specific rights have been given away in an initial contract" (Hart 1993 [1988]: 142). Hart concludes: "in a world of incomplete contracts there is an optimal allocation of residual rights of control." In other words, there is an optimal level of incompleteness, and this is due to an optimal level of ignorance for the parties. Hart's analysis is, in this respect, more neoclassical than Williamson's, for it does not call on cognitive limitations. See also Foss (1996c: 20) on this issue.

38 Bounded rationality must be understood as a limited resource, which is why individuals can economize on it. It is a somewhat awkward notion, for rationality is not usually considered as a resource, but as a feature of human beings (whether it is limited or not). "Confronted with the realities of bounded rationality, the costs of planning, adapting, and monitoring transactions need expressly to be considered," Williamson writes. "Which governance structures are more efficacious for which types of transactions? *Ceteris paribus*, modes that make large demands against cognitive competence are relatively disfavored" (Williamson 1985: 46).

39 Thomsen notes that researchers in the area of artificial intelligence disagree with Simon, they show that individuals are able to determine what is relevant in their environment (Thomsen 1992: 78–9).

40 Simon played an important role in the emergence of the theory of organization and in pointing out the deficiencies of the neoclassical approach. His contributions in this respect are very important. But he misled economists by putting the emphasis on the bounded rationality issue. "Framing the problem in this manner," writes Machovec, "misplaces the emphasis on the computational limits of man (and his machines) rather than on the open-ended ignorance of man, by which I mean that before one can profitably distill and correlate data, one must be in the right data base" (Machovec 1995: 172).

41 Williamson adopts the same perspective as Simon regarding the role of prices (see below). With respect to the use of rationality in Austrian economics (what Williamson calls "process" or "organic" rationality), Williamson writes: "Although transaction cost economizing is surely an important contributor to the viability of the institutions with which Austrian economics is concerned, and a joinder of the two approaches would be useful, the research agenda of organic rationality and transaction cost economics are currently rather different" (Williamson 1985: 47).

42 As Williamson puts it: "(1) [A]sset specificity refers to durable investments that are undertaken in support of particular transactions, the opportunity of which investments is much lower in best alternatives uses or by alternative users should the original transaction be prematurely terminated, and (2) the specific identity of the parties to a transaction plainly matters in these circumstances, which is to say that continuity of the relationship is valued, whence (3) contractual and organizational safeguards arise in support of transaction of this kind, which safeguards are unneeded (would be the source of avoidable costs) for transactions of the more familiar neoclassical (nonspecific) variety" (Williamson 1985: 55).

43 Williamson distinguishes four types of asset specificity (Williamson 1985: 95–6): site specificity (plants that are located next to each other); physical asset specificity (especially relevant to the internalization problem if assets are not mobile); human asset specificity (specificity that emerges in a learning-by-doing fashion); and dedicated assets (discrete investment made for a specific customer). It is interesting to notice that the concept of asset specificity was absent from Williamson's analysis in *Markets and Hierarchies*. In this early work, information impactedness and complexity are the key concepts (along with bounded rationality and opportunism) in the explanation of the emergence of organizations. "Information impactedness is a derivative condition that arises mainly because of uncertainty and opportunism, though bounded rationality is involved as well. It exists when true underlying circumstances relevant to the transaction, or related set of transactions, are known to one or more parties but cannot be costlessly discerned by or displayed for others" (Williamson 1975: 31). Williamson's rationale for the firm in *Markets and Hierarchies* has to do with moral hazard and adverse selection, and is, in that sense, closer to Knight's view than his 1985 explanation is. In 1975, listing the advantages of internal organization in relation to markets (Williamson 1975: 39), he does not give any importance to asset specificity, but puts forward the concepts of complexity, bounded rationality, opportunism, small-number situations and information impactedness. In the following decade, he replaced the first and the last notions by the well sorted out concept of asset specificity. To be sure, asset specificity is not entirely foreign to the notion of moral hazard, but the development of the former allowed Williamson to expose a much more coherent view of the fundamental transformation. Moreover, he did not drop the complexity issue completely (especially in his study of contracting), but he changed the emphasis. Williamson also abandoned, during the same period, the notion of "atmosphere" (Williamson 1975: 37–9) which appears to be less tractable (or even useless) in his later work.

44 Frequency and uncertainty are also important dimensions to take into account with respect to the existence of specialized governance structures. The issue of frequency has to do with the fact that specialized governance structures (specialized contracts, etc) are generally necessary to deal with non-standard transactions. In other words, when the parties know that the assets being transacted are specific, they try to set up a governance structure that might reduce the bargaining costs on each occasion when contract renewal takes place. However, a specialized structure comes at greater cost than general ones. Therefore, the greater the frequency of a transaction, the greater the benefits (i.e. economies on transaction costs) a specialized governance structure might bring about.

45 This point was suggested to me by Peter G. Klein in his comments on a previous version of this section (Sautet 1996).

46 It is important to mention that Williamson, in his 1985 book, does not make any reference to the rationale for the firm when prices do not qualify as a sufficient statistic.

47 An interesting part of Williamson's work, which makes us think that to a large extent his economics is open-ended, is the room that he makes for the existence of error. He mentions the existence of mistaken integration (Williamson 1985: 111, 119), but he does not give any explanation for it. What is certain is that he does not offer a Stiglerian analysis to explain errors and he seems to imply that in the world sheer error is possible.

48 We can find in *Markets and Hierarchies* one of the consequences of this mis-understanding of the information problem. Herein Williamson explains that he considers, for the sake of his analysis, that "in the beginning there were markets." From that assumption, he studies organizations from a market failure angle: "[A] presumption of market failure is war-ranted where it is observed that transactions are shifted out of a market into a firm" (Williamson 1975: 20). However, he explains that the assumption "in the beginning there was central planning" can also be made and in that case, the "analysis would appear instead to be preoccupied with internal organizational failures" (Williamson 1975: 21). Implicitly, Williamson considers that the study of market competition and central planning are symmetrical.

49 "Primary uncertainty is of a state-contingent kind, while secondary un-certainty arises 'from lack of communication, that is from one decision maker having no way to find out the concurrent decisions and plans made by others'" (Williamson 1985: 57).

50 This is also the view adopted by Hart, for instance, in his discussion of the feasibility of a complete contract, and who writes that "thinking, negotia-tion, and enforcement costs usually make such a contract prohibitively expensive. As a result, many of the terms of the relationship have to be negotiated by the parties as they go along" (Hart 1995 [1989]: 158).

51 Foss explains that in most modern organizational theory there are strong knowledge assumptions. "A more specific manifestation of strong knowl-edge assumptions," writes Foss, "is that while knowledge for organization purposes is assumed to be private, knowledge that relates to production is essentially assumed to be public" (Foss 1997a: 13).

52 As Foss puts it with respect to the absence of process analysis in the theory of the firm: "Although modern organizational economists are quite happy

to appeal to process adjustments (e.g. Williamson 1985) . . . the process itself is never really inquired into in detail" (Foss 1997a: 12).

53 The concept of transaction costs encompasses *"all* of the impediments to bargaining. Given this definition bargaining *necessarily* succeeds when transaction costs are zero" (Cooter and Ulen 1997: 81, emphasis in the original).

54 Some authors, like Demsetz, have realized that there is perhaps something wrong with the transaction costs analysis. However, it is not the concept of information costs that is problematic in Demsetz's criticism, but the misuse of the notion of transaction costs. "A more complete theory of the firm," writes Demsetz, "must give greater weight to information cost than is given either in Coase's theory or in theories based on shirking and opportunism" (Demsetz 1993 [1988]: 159). In fact he argues that transaction costs in themselves are not necessary to the explanation of firms: "Since firms may not be perfect substitutes in the production of goods and services, and since they generally will not be if information cost is positive, it might be in the interest of a firm to produce its own inputs even if transaction costs were zero and management costs were positive. The production cost of other firms might simply be so high as to make in-house production superior to relying on these other firms" (Demsetz 1993 [1988]: 164). As I argue below, there is no analysis in terms of the HKP in modern transaction costs economics, and the authors who venture themselves in criticizing the transaction costs framework stay in the equilibrium-always approach in which information costs play the dominant role.

55 In a recent working paper, Bryan Caplan (1999) tries to explain what, according to him, cannot be explained by the rational ignorance theory.

56 Alanson Minkler makes a similar point with respect to the discussion of "bounded rationality versus structural uncertainty." "If the world is characterized by bounded rationality in the Simon sense," writes Minkler, "then as information processing techniques advance incentive alignment problems will diminish. Relying on governance structures in this world to align incentives makes some sense. . . . If the world was instead characterized by structural uncertainty, then even if information processing costs fell to zero, incentive problems would still arise and ways to align incentives would still have to be found" (Minkler 1993: 581). Minkler neglects in his comments the notion of entrepreneurship.

57 Langlois and Robertson define dynamic transaction costs as the following: "[Dynamic transaction costs are] the costs of persuading, negotiating, and teaching outside suppliers. Another way to look at these transaction costs is as the costs of not having the capabilities you need when you need them" (Langlois and Robertson 1995: 35).

58 Langlois and Robertson (1995) argue that "the dominant transaction-cost theories of the boundaries of the firm are short-run theories that, unlike Marshallian price theory, have no long run correlative" (Langlois and Robertson 1995: 30). That is why the responses studied in the various modern transaction-cost models are outside of the passage of time, they are "static in an important sense. They take the circumstances of production as given and investigate comparatively the properties of market-contract arrangements, internal organization" (Langlois and Robertson

1995: 30). Langlois and Robertson provide a theory that connects the short and the long runs by introducing considerations on the capabilities theory of organizational learning. I try, in the following chapter, to provide a theory that will connect the emergence and the growth of the firm to the engine of change in the marketplace: the entrepreneur.

59 Lewin calls for the adoption of a more coherent approach. ("Occam's razor suggests the adoption of an alternative simpler system" Lewin (1998b: 16).)

60 Nelson and Winter understand the firm as a body of idiosyncratic and productive knowledge which is implemented in productive tasks through existing routines.

61 This view encompasses the notion of asset specificity, for it deals with all transactions that are to take place in a firm.

62 The notion of risk states that the universe is closed, i.e. the past contains all present and future states, but individuals are ignorant of the theories and facts that would permit them to make accurate predictions. The notion of uncertainty corresponds to the open-ended view of the world.

63 No profit can be made in a market without uncertainty. If all the risk could be appraised (no uncertainty) the "losses could be converted into fixed costs. Such special costs would . . . be costs merely, like any other necessary outlays, and would not give rise to profit, which is a difference between cost and selling price" (Knight 1965 [1921]: 199). Another way of stating this idea is to say that risk is a transformable form of uncertainty (into costs). Langlois and Cosgel give a new explanation of the dichotomy between risk and profit. According to them, one has to understand the role of "judgments" (as an exhaustive classification of states, or instances) in order to understand Knight's theory. Uncertainty is a "situation in which 'there is no valid basis of any kind for classifying instances'" (Langlois and Cosgel 1993: 459). In facing uncertainty, an agent first has to make a qualitative estimate (estimating the possible outcomes) and then, a subjective probabilistic estimate. These are two separate exercises of judgment. "When the categories of knowledge are unknown, they cannot form the basis of interpersonal agreement and market exchange [i.e. no subjective estimate of the probabilities is possible]" (Langlois and Cosgel 1993: 460). In such a situation, firms supersede markets.

64 One should note that it is not the same type of limitation as in Simon's work. In Simon, complexity is the major obstacle, in Knight, it is the emergence of genuine novelty.

65 As Kirzner also writes: "For much of its history the science of economics made important progress by abstracting from such apparently chaotic elements, and by therefore concentrating on only those features of the world that could fit into the model of a closed universe. Undoubtedly these contributions of economics were of enormous value and importance. Much that is central to the working of the market can indeed most easily be grasped by reference to the closed world model. But this approach to economic understanding has not been without costs. Principal among these costs has been the widespread tendency for economists to ignore and even to deny features of the world that do not fit into the closed world model. . . . If the phenomenon of advertising (and other similar phenomena intrinsic to the open-ended universe) are to be adequately

understood and evaluated, traditional economics must be regenerated,
enriched and deepened to encompass concepts of discovery, surprise, and
entrepreneurial competition" (Kirzner 1988: xxii). This is true of advertising and I contend that it is also true of the firm.

66 Foss (1994a) shows that Austrians cannot only complement contemporary
theories, but they can also develop a more genuine approach since they can
combine in their toolbox many different new and old tools: "(1) a distinction between planned and spontaneous orders; (2) the market process as a
process of entrepreneurial discovery; (3) property rights (incentives); (4)
specificity and complementarity of assets; (5) the subjectivity of costs . . . ;
(6) the private and tacit nature of knowledge . . . ; and (7) transaction and
information costs" (Foss 1994a: 55). But he does not really develop a
theory, he simply gives hints on how such a theory might be developed.

67 As Boudreaux and Holcombe explain, "the Coasian firm emerges only after
markets exist" (Boudreaux and Holcombe 1989: 147). In this view, firms
are not embedded in markets.

2 THE LACHMANNIAN PROBLEM, THE
PROMOTER AND THE EMERGENCE OF THE FIRM

1 Foss (1996b) also argues that the perfect competition framework has led to
an abandonment of a theory of production in the modern transaction-cost
approaches. As a result, the contractual view became "an analysis of which
incentives will bring the firm closest to its production frontier" (Foss
1996b: 17).

2 The papers of David O'Mahony (1979), Stavros Ioannides (1997), Nicolai
Foss (1997a) and Peter Lewin (1999) remain notable exceptions. The
literature on the issue is growing at a fast pace.

3 This view possibly finds its origin in Adam Smith, who did not sustain an
entrepreneurial approach to economic development and capital accumulation. As Machovec explains: "[i]n Smith, macroeconomic expansion and
the routine deepening of the division of labor were seen as spontaneous
generators of opportunities for technical change which self-interested
agents would exploit" (Machovec 1995: 110).

4 For an interesting account of the absence of entrepreneurship in the neoclassical theory of the firm, see Danny Le Roy (1997). Le Roy explains that
in neoclassical microeconomic theory the firm faces three optimization
problems: (a) choose the lowest cost factor mix to produce a given level
of output, (b) choose the output level to maximize profits, and (c)
choose the input factor mix consistent with maximized profits. It also
necessitates three notions (a) a production function, (b) constrained optimization as a characterization of rationality, and (c) perfect information
(or imperfect information with known distribution). If we consider the
entrepreneur as an innovator, as an arbitrageur or as a coordinator of
resources, explains Le Roy, "[a]ny attempt to include the perceptive entrepreneur will destroy the internal consistency of the neoclassical model" (Le
Roy 1997: 11). For the "interconnectedness and the consistency of the
model must be maintained if the theory is to function" (Le Roy 1997: 12).

5 As Casson puts it: "The entrepreneur believes that he is right, while everyone else is wrong. Thus the essence of entrepreneurship is being different –

being different because one has a different perception of the situation. It is this that makes the entrepreneur so important. Were he not present, things would have been very different" (Casson 1982: 14).

6 A famous attempt to introduce the entrepreneur in a general equilibrium framework is Schumpeter's book *The Theory of Economic Development* (Schumpeter 1961 [1934]). See *Breaking out of the Walrasian Box* by Rothbard (1987) for a critique of it.

7 A rare exception to the list above is Penrose (1995 [1959]: 31–3). She understands that economics must make a distinction between entrepreneurial and managerial activities if we are to have a theory of the firm. This issue is covered in Chapter 3 below.

8 Theodore Schultz (1975) tries to deal with the concept of entrepreneurship in a disequilibrium economy from a Chicagoan perspective. Even if he is right in noticing the necessity of entrepreneurial behavior in the received theory, his analysis of a disequilibrium framework remains within the walls of the Chicago approach. He sees the entrepreneur as a scarce resource: it is a human capital perspective. As he puts it: "Within such [equilibrating] models, the function of entrepreneurship would be much extended and the supply of entrepreneurial ability would be treated as a scarce resource" (Schultz 1975: 843). In his 1975 article, he was aware of Kirzner's approach, but he misunderstood it as the following passage shows: "Israel M. Kirzner presents a perceptive analysis of the state of economic theory with respect to the entrepreneur. He sees clearly the omission of the entrepreneur in received equilibrium theory, but he persists in holding fast to the zero profit concept in that theory and, as a consequence, fails to see the economic rewards accrue to those who bring about the equilibrating process" (Schultz 1975: 833).

9 There is a debate among Austrian economists on the notion of alertness and its use to explain the entrepreneurial function (see, for instance, Rothbard 1985). I do not think that the notion of alertness is incompatible with a Misesian understanding of entrepreneurship. On the contrary, the notion of alertness enriches the Misesian view by providing a greater semantic precision to the concept of entrepreneurship. It makes the Misesian analysis fully accountable for the emergence of novelty and treats entrepreneurship as a function rather than as an individual. In addition, even if some work remains to be done on the articulation of entrepreneurship and the institutional environment (to which the present work is a contribution), more recent work (for example Kirzner 1992a; Salgado 1999) has shown that the Kirznerian view of entrepreneurship is compatible with the existence of errors and losses in the marketplace.

10 As Pasteur said: "Dans le champs de l'expérimentation, le hasard ne favorise que les esprits préparés." (In the field of experimentation, chance only favors the prepared minds.) This amounts to saying that "people tend to perceive information which they are predisposed to recognize" (Shane 1999: 9).

11 This view does not rule out the possibility that some discoveries can be the result of sheer luck, and not of alertness to what is around the corner. Moreover, if it is true that only the prepared mind will tend to notice what has to be discovered, to prepare one's mind does not guarantee successful discovery.

12 The fact that a demand is waiting to be discovered does not mean that it is actual. Whether preferences can only be expressed in action (Rothbard 1993 [1962]) is not so much the problem here, what matters is that value scales (ordinal preferences) come into existence (even if they are not expressed in choice). In other words, they are discovered. This places limits on the use of utility functions in economics.

13 Many criticisms of this view have been made. One can see the purposeful activity of entrepreneurs in particular, and of individuals in general, as impossible to prove. Indeed, there is perhaps no proof of the existence of purposeful action and, as a result, the whole argument may rest on a leap of faith. The same can be said with respect to entrepreneurs' tendency to discover, i.e. their alertness. Moreover, one can reject the whole entrepreneurial approach and argue that non-optimizing behavior is (a) nonsense, and (b) useless to economics (Shmanske 1994).

14 The fact that the lure for profit brings about entrepreneurial behavior does not exclude other motives for discovery in the market system. However, the profit motive ensures that entrepreneurial behavior is socially beneficial. See Postrel (1998) for an exploration of the reasons for creativity and enterprising behavior.

15 Kirzner (1997a) explains why entrepreneurship is not equivalent to search behavior:

> An opportunity for profit cannot, by its nature, be the object of systematic search. Systematic search can be undertaken for a piece of missing information but only because the searcher is aware of what he does not know and is aware with greater or lesser certainty of the way to find out the missing information. . . . But it is in the nature of an overlooked profit opportunity that it has been utterly overlooked, i.e., that one is not aware at all that one has missed the grasping of any profit. . . . What distinguishes *discovery* (relevant to hitherto unknown profit opportunity) from *successful search* (relevant to the deliberate production of information which one knew had lacked) is that the former (unlike the latter) involves the *surprise* that accompanies the realization that one had overlooked something in fact readily available.
>
> Kirzner (1997a: 71–2)

16 "The discovery of a profit opportunity," writes Kirzner, "means the discovery of something obtainable for nothing at all. No investment at all is required; the free ten-dollar bill is discovered to be already within one's grasp" (Kirzner 1973: 48).

17 Kirzner expresses the same idea when he explains that the entrepreneurial function is speculative in essence.

> By itself, a decision simply to buy a group of resources, or their productive services, involves no essentially speculative element; neither does a decision to sell a finished product, once it has been produced. But the decision to buy a bundle of productive resources at one price in order to resell "them" (that is, the finished product for whose production these productive services suffice completely)

NOTES

later at a higher price, is essentially speculative. In a market there is
constant opportunity for this kind of decision to be made, and we
distinguish the "pure" function of making this kind of decision by
referring to it as the role of the entrepreneur.
Kirzner (1963: 17–18)

18 This based on Schumpeter's distinction between innovation and invention
(Schumpeter 1989a [1947]: 224).
19 Herein I distinguish two aspects of entrepreneurship that both stem
from the same understanding of the nature and role of the entrepreneur
as an arbitrageur. Entrepreneurship is crucially related to the HKP.
Certain authors have found two types of HKP: HKP 1 involving dispersed
knowledge, and HKP 2 involving novelty (Foss and Christensen 1996).
I believe, following Kirzner, that this distinction is superfluous. Kirzner's
notion of entrepreneurship (encompassing type I and type II) necessarily
involves a conception of knowledge that takes place in an open-ended
world (in which true novelty exists). Therefore, I sustain the view that
there is only one HKP, and it relates in my approach to two aspects of
entrepreneurship.
20 As Salgado puts it: "The misdirection of resources may have affected a
number of other genuine activities already under way whose profitability
depended on the availability of these resources" (Salgado 1999: 67). He
emphasizes here the effect of an original error on the allocation of other
resources in the marketplace.
21 As High puts it: "The same active mental processes which are taken to
adjust to change once it has occurred, will also originate change. Changes
in cost and revenue curves do not simply happen; they are the results of
purposeful attempts by consumers and producers to improve their situations. If we are not content to take the ends-means framework of agents
as given, then we should not be willing to take changes in tastes, technology, and resources as given" (High 1986: 115, emphasis removed).
22 In this respect, it might be interesting to consider the market system as an
orderly process of change. "As Austrians examine and debate these issues,"
write Boettke, Horwitz and Prychitko, "we should recall Hayek's neglected
The Sensory Order (1976 [1952]), and recognize that the mind is always in
the process of becoming. The way we understand our theory, the way we
put it to use, and the way we defend it changes as the nature of our knowledge and the problems we want answered change. Theoretical knowledge,
like the market process, is neither equilibrating nor disequilibrating, it is
rather an orderly process of change" (Boettke *et al.* 1994: 70).
23 It could be, for instance, indirect consequences of technological shocks
which, by decreasing certain transaction costs, make new activities
possible, which themselves create the need for firms.
24 Ioannides shows the same concern when he writes: "[T]he fact that the
market is perceived as fraught with error, ignorance and uncertainty –
i.e. the phenomena that give rise to entrepreneurial action – means that
the emergence of the firm through that action is entirely independent of
any consideration of transaction costs, since the latter assumes a given
ends-means framework within which the agent can calculate exactly the
relative costs of every available course of action" (Ioannides 1997: 11).

149

NOTES

25 On the one hand, I refer to the case of complete coordination when, in the economy, individuals' plans dovetail and all profit opportunities have been exhausted: there is no HKP (it is similar to the notion of final equilibrium). Kirzner defines a fully coordinated state of affairs as "one in which each decision made, within a demarcated set of decisions, each action taken by each individual in the demarcated set, correctly takes into account (a) the decisions and actions in fact being taken by everyone else in the set, and (b) the decisions and actions which the others might take were one's own actions to be different" (Kirzner 1997b: 6). On the other hand, I refer to the case of complete compatibility of plans when individuals' plans mesh, but profit opportunities are still waiting to be discovered: there is a HKP. In other words, disequilibrium can refer to two cases: (a) discoordination at the level of the underlying variables (profit opportunities are waiting to be discovered) but not at the level of current individuals' plans (plans mesh); and (b) discoordination at the level of underlying variables (profit opportunities are waiting to be discovered) *and* at the level of current individual plans (plans do not mesh).

26 As Lewin puts it: "Joint production would not be a problem were it not for the fact that production occurs over time" (Lewin 1997: 85).

27 One could also perhaps use the evenly rotating economy (ERE) (defined as a situation in which underlying and induced variables are constant and the time element is eliminated) as a foil to study the emergence of the firm. The problem with the ERE is that there is no entrepreneurial activity (Mises 1966: 702) and market prices coincide with the final prices (if it is conceivable). In such a context, it is impossible to show the link between the entrepreneurial function and the emergence of the firm.

28 Mises explains that the concept of the promoter "refers to a datum that is a general characteristic of human nature, that is present in all market transactions and marks them profoundly. This is the fact that various individuals do not react to a change in conditions with the same quickness and in the same way. . . . There are in the market pacemakers and others who only imitate the procedures of their more agile fellow citizens. The phenomenon of leadership is no less real on the market than in any other branch of human activity. The driving force of the market, the element tending toward unceasing innovation and improvement, is provided by the restlessness of the *promoter* and his eagerness to make profits as large as possible" (Mises 1966: 255, emphasis added).

29 "The entrepreneur hires the technicians, i.e. the people who have the ability and the skill to perform definite kinds and quantities of work. . . . The technician contributes his own toil and trouble, but it is the entrepreneur qua entrepreneur who directs his labor toward definite goals" (Mises 1966: 303).

30 As Kirzner explains: "the Austrian theory of entrepreneurial equilibration process relies . . . on some entrepreneurs being more alert than others (and it is the relative unalertness of the latter which is responsible for the errors which create the opportunities and the incentives for profit)" (Kirzner 1992a: 21).

31 The issue of who owns the capital in the firm is of little importance in this context, as this analysis focuses on entrepreneurship purely as a function. Therefore, the entrepreneur–promoter could be a capitalist – i.e. the owner

150

of some capital to be invested – or not, it does not change the analysis on
the function of the entrepreneur and the emergence of the firm. If the promoter is a capitalist, then he/she does not need to borrow capital from
someone else, he/she just borrows it from himself/herself. If the promoter
is not a capitalist, then he/she must borrow money from a capitalist, that is
to say, from someone who owns savings or who has access to funds. The
emergence of the firm can perfectly be understood without reference to
the problem of ownership of capital. All that is required is pure promoters
and pure capitalists. In the real world, all resource owners do exercise some
entrepreneurial alertness (and therefore earn entrepreneurial pure profits)
and all promoters do own, in general, some factor services of their own
(and therefore earn pure productivity returns). Our goal is to be as analytical as possible and to show that a theory of the emergence of the firm
does not require that promoters are capitalists; it just requires the isolation
of the entrepreneurial function. This issue is controversial among Austrian
economists, but if we understand, following Mises and Kirzner, the entrepreneurial function as pure arbitrage, then the entrepreneur is the one who
"pushes the button," that is to say, he/she is the one who realizes that
there is a price discrepancy in the price system and seizes the opportunity
and makes a profit (once all the costs have been taken into account). Finding funds can be part of his activity, even if it is true that capitalists are
often entrepreneurs as well. Edith Penrose makes the same point in *The
Theory of the Growth of the Firm* where she writes: "[M]any small firms
without adequate initial financial resources do succeed, do raise capital,
do grow into large firms," she explains. "And they do this, for the most
part, by virtue of a special entrepreneurial ability. There are many
examples testifying to the ingenuity of the superior businessman in
obtaining the funds he needs, and only if the requisite entrepreneurial
ability is lacking can one safely say that a firm cannot attract the required
capital" (Penrose 1995 [1959]: 37–8). See Kirzner (1992b) for a further
discussion.

32 This view can also be helpful to determine the limits of the firm. As
Richardson explains: "[T]he optimum size of the firm may be determined,
not so much by the scale economies associated with any particular operation, but by the number of operations which require planned coordination" (Richardson 1990 [1960]: 86). Penrose makes a similar
point: "It is the 'area of co-ordination' – the area of 'authoritative communication' – which must define the boundaries of the firm for our purposes,
and, consequently, it is a firm's ability to maintain sufficient administrative
co-ordination to satisfy the definition of an industrial firm which sets the
limit to its size as an industrial firm" (Penrose 1995 [1959]: 20).

33 This is why Mises explains that uncertainty of the future affects the
entrepreneur and not the employees: "In the changing economy changes
in the market structure may bring about differences between these two
magnitudes," writes Mises. "The ensuing profits and losses do not affect
the wage earner. Their incidence falls upon the employer alone. The
uncertainty of the future affects the employer alone" (Mises 1966: 625).
This concept of the firm is the "simple firm," i.e. a firm in which individuals do not participate in the discovery of new profit opportunities.

34 As Coase explains: "I have come to believe that the problems posed by
long-term contracts for commodities, to which I allude in 'The Nature
of the Firm,' do not in practice usually seem to result in vertical integration being the more efficient solution" (Coase 1993c [1988]: 68). Coase
gives an explanation of vertical integration in terms of costs assessment
which leaves aside the issue of opportunistic behavior: "What decides
whether vertical integration or a long-term contract represents the more
efficient solution depends on the absolute relation of the costs of these
alternative arrangements" (Coase 1993c: [1988] 70). Coase gives the
example of A. O. Smith, which has been an automobile frame manu-
facturer for decades, and which possesses highly specific assembly plants
where frames are built for many customers, among them General
Motors. This case makes him "skeptical about what general lesson could
be drawn from the Fisher Body case" (Coase 1993c [1988]: 71). Langlois
and Robertson make the same remark: "[T]he problem with the hold-up
view is that it is neither sufficient nor necessary as an explanation for integration. It is not sufficient because, in the absence of uncertainty and a
divergence of expectations about the future, long-term contracts, reputa-
tion effects, and other devices can remove the costs of arm's-length
arrangements. It is not necessary because, in the presence of uncertainty
and a divergence of expectations about the future, arm's-length arrangements can be costly even without highly specific assets" (Langlois and
Robertson 1995: 36).

35 This profit exploitation cannot be carried out through market contracts
for the reason that what is at stake is the overcoming of Knightian
uncertainty. I assume that prices may vary according to unpredictable
patterns, for entrepreneurs make prices change (assuming, there are no
information costs). Therefore, we cannot assume that the entrepreneur-
promoter could take an insurance against price variations of the inputs
needed, for instance.

36 On the issue of order and chaos, High explains that "[o]rder is a byproduct
of the competition for profit, which gives entrepreneurs an incentive to
discover and implement those divisions [of labor] that are productive on
net" (High 1986: 118). The lure for profit and a pure cost-benefit analysis
cannot adequately explain order in the marketplace because of reasons
explored above (type three error).

37 High explains that "[t]he development of market institutions is the result
of the operation of the market. The mere fact that money, monetary
calculation, business firms, and advertising emerge and persist in the
market belies the claim that the market is a strictly equilibrating process.
These institutions do not exist in general equilibrium. A theory that pos-
tulates a persistent movement toward general equilibrium is a theory that,
in an evolutionary sense, can only explain the disappearance of these institutions" (High 1986: 117, emphasis removed).

38 Vaughn also writes: "Capital [is] the outcome of conscious plans of entrepreneurs to construct equipment that would only yield a return in the
future. Hence the decision to invest in any particular kind of capital
equipment is a consequence of an entrepreneur's assessment of current economic conditions and his expectations about the future" (Vaughn 1994:
150–1).

39 Mises also makes this point but in different terms (Mises 1966: 392).

40 This idea is also emphasized in Rothbard: "Even the existence of one purely nonspecific factor is inconceivable if we properly consider 'suitability in production' in value terms rather than in technological terms" (Rothbard 1993 [1962]: 281).

41 As Lewin puts it: "Complementarity is a condition of plan equilibrium (stability), substitutability is a condition of plan disequilibrium (change)" (Lewin 1997: 72).

42 Penrose (1995 [1959]) also makes this point. As she puts it: "[I]f resources were completely non-specific, a firm could in principle produce anything." But this is not the case, for we observe that firms are relatively specialized. Penrose then adds that "[t]he selection of the relevant product-markets is necessarily determined by the 'inherited' resources of the firm" (Penrose 1995 [1959]: 82). It shows how an understanding of capital in terms of specific capital structure cannot be disentangled from a capabilities approach to the firm.

43 Substitution of factors is not the source of the firm, even if we assume that resilience (complementarity) and flexibility (substitution) are two aspects of the capital structure of the economy as a whole. On this issue, see Lewin and Phelan (1999: 28).

44 When substitution is possible among different capital goods, they can perform different functions, in other words, they have more than one specificity. Lachmann calls this property multiple specificity (see Lewin 1997: 72).

45 When some workers are hired on a daily basis by a manager to work in a factory, they are not specific to the exploitation. But the fact that some workers are not specific to a capital structure does not mean that the firm can exist without any specific assets. A firm, as a set of complementary inputs in time, must always involve the use of specific assets.

46 On the importance of causal-genetic explanations of systems, Maturana and Varela (1992) make the following remark: "The dynamics of any system can be explained by showing the relations between its parts and the regularities of their interactions so as to reveal its organization. For us to fully understand it, however, we need not only to see it as a unity operating in its internal dynamics, but also to see it in its circumstances, i.e., in the context to which its operation connects it. This understanding requires that we adopt a certain distance for observation, a perspective that in the case of historical systems implies a reference to their origin" (Maturana and Varela 1992: 58). Also see Cowan and Rizzo (1996) on causal-genetic explanations.

47 Of course uncertainty as the source of planned coordination is not a new theme in the literature. As I showed in the first chapter, Coase puts this argument forward when dealing with long-term contracts. David Teece (1976) also points out that uncertainty is a major source of vertical integration. As he puts it: "Difficulties arise only if program execution rests on contingencies that cannot be predicted perfectly in advance. In this case, coordinated activity is required to secure agreement about the estimates that will be used as a basis for action. Vertical integration facilitates such coordination," quoted in Langlois and Robertson (1995: 36). Loasby (1976; 1991) puts forward an explanation in terms of genuine

uncertainty, and, to a certain extent, so do Langlois and Robertson (1995). But most of this literature boils down to a theory of how does the firm "handle" parametric uncertainty. Knight saw the problem along the same lines, even if he was a special case (for he emphasized structural uncertainty and not entrepreneurship). As Knight put it: "When uncertainty and the task of deciding what to do and how to do it takes the ascendancy over that of execution, the internal organization of the productive group is no longer a matter of indifference or a mechanical detail. Centralization of this deciding and controlling function is imperative, a process of 'cephalization,' such as has taken place in the evolution of organic life, is inevitable, and for the same reasons as in the case of biological evolution" (Knight 1965 [1921]: 268).

3 CAPABILITIES, ENTREPRENEURSHIP, CENTRAL PLANNING AND THE GROWTH OF THE FIRM

1 "A commander in chief cannot take as an excuse for his mistakes in warfare an order given by his minister or his sovereign, when the person giving the order is absent from the field of operations and is imperfectly aware or wholly unaware of the latest state of affairs. It follows that any commander in chief who undertakes to carry out a plan which he considers defective is at fault; he must put forward his reasons, insist on the plan being changed, and finally tender his resignation rather than be the instrument of his army's downfall," quoted in Townsend (1970: 53).
2 Whether transaction costs are positive or not does not have any implications for the analysis in this chapter.
3 And, to a certain extent, Alfred Marshall and Harald B. Malmgren (1961).
4 Penrose wants to provide an answer to the following question: "[A]ssuming that some firms can grow, what principles will then govern their growth, and how fast and how long can they grow?" (Penrose 1995 [1959]: 7).
5 In other words: "There surely can be little doubt that the rate and direction of the growth of a firm depend on the extent to which it is *alert* to act upon opportunities for profitable investment. It follows that lack of enterprise in a firm will preclude or substantially retard its growth" (Penrose 1995 [1959]: 30, emphasis added).
6 She even refers to a new theoretical schema: "The economist's 'main conceptual schema' is designed for the theory of price determination and resource allocation, and it is unnecessary and inappropriate to try to reconcile this theory with 'organization theory'" (Penrose 1995 [1959]: 14).
7 She says, for instance, in very Smithian terms: "As a firm grows in size . . . it will reorganize its resources to take advantage of the more obvious opportunities for specialization" (Penrose 1995 [1959]: 72).
8 As she puts it: "Internal inducements to expansion arise largely from the existence of a pool of unused productive services, resources, and special knowledge, all of which will always be found within any firm" (Penrose 1995 [1959]: 66).
9 Alfred Chandler (1990a [1962]), even if he does not cite Penrose, uses exactly the same approach. A firm will have at some point in time some

NOTES

excess capacities that could become the source of further growth. The problem is (a) to realize the existence of these excess capacities; and (b) to find the best way to employ them. As he puts it: "The threat of excess capacity appears to have been a primary stimulus to initial combinations in most American industries" (Chandler 1990a [1962]: 29–30).

10 Although I used transaction cost economics in the asset-specificity approach as a foil to show the existence of a MTP, I could have done the same analysis with the measurement-cost view.

11 Foss, referring to the contractual approach, points this out:

> [the contractual] framework has led scholars within the theory of economic organization to:
> - largely neglect the role of tacit knowledge, implying that it becomes legitimate to assume that all knowledge for production purposes is shared among firms;
> - neglect the social aspect of much productive knowledge (with the same implication as above);
> - assume that production costs do not vary over firms for the same productive tasks – that is, what one firm can do, another firm can do equally efficient;
> - and, as a consequence of all this, not allow the boundaries issue to turn on differences in firms' endowments of productive knowledge, that is, their capabilities.
>
> (Foss 1996b: 17)

12 A similar point is made in Nelson and Winter (1982). See also Foss (1996c).

13 Prahalad and Hamel (1990: 82) define core competence as the "collective learning in the organization, especially how to coordinate diverse production skills and integrate multiple streams of technologies . . . Core competence is communication, involvement, and a deep commitment to working across organizational boundaries. It involves many levels of people and all functions. Core competence does not diminish with use. . . . [T]hey are enhanced as they are applied and shared."

14 We should not forget that these notions were set forth primarily by Hayek (1948) and Michael Polanyi (1962; 1967).

15 "With 'economies of diversity,' we associate the evolutionary argument that more variations increase the probability of finding an 'optimum' type of variation (at least within a given range), and the Schumpeterian argument that more diversity in terms of resources, competencies, technologies, etc increases the probability of making new combinations" (Foss and Christensen 1996: 20). These economies can be obtained by engaging in "asset creation" or "asset fission" (Foss and Christensen 1996: 21).

16 Even Williamson's efficiency hypothesis has evolved, he now includes competencies in his analysis. On this point see Foss (1996b: 13).

17 "Enterprise, or 'entrepreneurship' as it is sometimes called, is a slippery concept, not easy to work into formal economic analysis, because it is so closely associated with the temperament or personal qualities of individuals" (Penrose 1995 [1959]: 33).

18 Entrepreneurs possess entrepreneurial judgment that helps them to form an "image" of their environment (Penrose 1995 [1959]: 42). This understanding is obviously also influenced by Knight's notion of the entrepreneur.

19 She also treats uncertainty in terms of parametric uncertainty. There is no unknown ignorance in her system: the entrepreneur forms subjective probability estimates. See Penrose (1995 [1959]: 58–64).

20 The same is true for Cowen and Parker in their market-process approach to management. As they put it: "Entrepreneurs must seek out new markets, new products, and new understandings of the market environment. These entrepreneurial functions would be redundant if information were not costly to generate, process, interpret, and disseminate" (Cowen and Parker 1997: 55–6). See also (Cowen and Parker 1997: 43). Confusion can occur as their use of concepts like "discovery," "adaptation" or "entrepreneurial function" does not correspond to what is now generally accepted in Austrian economics.

21 According to Langlois and Robertson (1995), Morris Silver (1984: 17) is one of the exceptions. He gives a certain role to the entrepreneur with respect to innovation, but entrepreneurship is treated as a resource. Some authors in the capabilities approach assume the existence of an entrepreneur at some point in their theory, but it is only based on the fact that since "something" has to make the system work it might as well be the entrepreneur. As Lewin, for instance, puts it: "Organizational structure is here seen to be the result of entrepreneurial innovation" (Lewin 1998a: 27). But his claim is unsupported by the rest of his paper. "Entrepreneurial innovation" is mentioned to remind the reader that what makes the system change is the entrepreneur, but Lewin does not develop the idea further.

22 As the authors put it: "When the market cannot provide the right ancillary capabilities at the right time, vertical integration may result; and when the firm lacks the right ancillary capabilities at the right time, vertical specialization may occur" (Langlois and Robertson 1995: 35).

23 Foss and Christensen (1996: 19) make exactly the same point.

24 My contention remains valid, even if capabilities theories are supposed to account for phenomena that exist only in an equilibrium-always world.

25 On the subject of changes in the organization of production as a source of value, see Leijonhufvud (1986).

26 Andrew Carnegie, for instance, explains how, in his production of steel, he would have to rely on men who would have tacit knowledge: "The blast furnace manager of that day was usually a rude bully, generally a foreigner, who in addition to his other acquirements was able to knock down a man now and then as a lesson to the other unruly spirits under him. He was supposed to diagnose the condition of the furnace by instinct, to possess some almost supernatural power of divination, like his congener in the country districts who was reputed to be able to locate . . . water . . . by means of a hazel rod" (quoted in Hughes 1986 [1965]: 231).

27 It is worth noting that, herein, I do not formulate the knowledge problem that the firm encounters in the same fashion as Foss and Christensen (1996: 14). They see the whole knowledge issue in terms of HKP 1 and 2 and not in terms of the genuine ignorance of (a) profit opportunities in the marketplace and (b) the knowledge possessed by input-owners.

28 Williamson uses the term "accounting chicanery" (Williamson 1985: 140) to describe this phenomenon.
29 Another important development in the neoclassical approach to incentives is tournament theory, which emphasizes how agency costs may be reduced when employees compete for prizes.
30 Williamson explains that transfer prices cannot usually be replaced by market prices, for the reason that specific assets are usually involved (Williamson 1985: 139).
31 This is under the section: "Incentive compensation and profit sharing."
32 Kevin Murphy (1986) analyses the issue from an empirical point of view. He shows that there is, empirically, a positive relation between compensation and performance in managerial labor contracts. One can argue that this empirical approach does not measure more than the Robbinsian incentives which make managers work more (this is certainly true).
33 Leadership and rewards in kind could also be considered as entrepreneurial incentives if they fit in a general framework of rules within the organization, i.e. if they are not discretionary. Firms reward money-saving tips from workers, for instance, as the following excerpt from a Wall Street Journal article shows: "Cash awards for employee ideas grow in number and size of the top prizes. Commercial Inc. will start its Great Idea program July 5 to solicit money-saving tips from workers. In a trial, it got 3,000 suggestions. Top prizes are $10,000. General Motors recently doubled its top award to $20,000 and now includes some salaried employees. Also, first-line supervisors can win up to $1,000 for ideas. Previously, such workers didn't have incentives. . . . Eastman Kodak paid $3.6 million in awards last year, up 8.7% from 1982, and figures it saves $16 million from suggestions" (*Wall Street Journal*, 15 May 1984. Quoted in Williamson 1985: 143–4). Other examples of entrepreneurial incentives include Sam Walton, CEO of Wal-Mart, who created cash awards for employees who contributed to superior cost-saving service, and McDonald's under the guidance of Ray Kroc who set up an unusual franchising system (Cowen and Parker 1997: 63–4). It is sometimes difficult to say in which incentive category these kind of rewards fall into, but such borderline cases show that it is not easy to dismiss "high-powered incentives" in the firm.
34 Senior executives usually receive the following forms of income in a corporation: salaries, bonuses, stock options, (restricted) stock awards, phantom stock plans and stock appreciation rights (Milgrom and Roberts 1992: 425).
35 As the research coordinator of Standard Oil of Ohio puts it: "We employ many people who, if left to their own devices, might not be research-minded. In other words, we hire people to be curious as a group . . . We are undertaking to create research capability by the sheer pressure of money," in Daniel Hamburg (1963: 107), quoted in Williamson (1985: 141).
36 Cowen and Parker (1997: 65) make the distinction between collectively-based incentives and individually-based ones. The former are useful when enhanced cooperation is needed among various members of a specific group in the firm.

37 O'Driscoll and Rizzo define rule-following behavior as the following: "If, in situations of the general type X, a relatively specific action or a limited set of actions A is observed, then the agent's behavior can be characterized as 'rule-following.' The more general X is and the more specific A is (the more limited the set A), the more rule oriented is the behavior" (O'Driscoll and Rizzo 1986). As Kim (1998) explains, "O'Driscoll and Rizzo's definition of rule-following makes it clear that the concept of rule-following is not meant to contrast with random or purposeless action, but to contrast with the conventional economists' conception of human activity as case-by-case maximization" (quoted from Kim's dissertation draft, Chapter 5).

38 The notion of routines is certainly the best-known example of rules within the firm (Nelson and Winter 1982). The concept of rules can also be extended to include capabilities (Langlois 1995).

39 Hayek emphasized the coordinative properties of rules of conduct because they allow for adaptation to truly unexpected change. As Hayek puts it:

> It is not irrelevant to our chief purpose if in conclusion we consider briefly the role which abstract rules play in the coordination not only of the actions of many different persons but also in the mutual adjustment of the successive decisions of a single individual or organization. Here, too, it is not often possible to make detailed plans for actions in the more distant future (although what we should do now depends on what we shall want to do in the future), simply because we do not yet know the particular facts which we shall face. The method through which we nevertheless succeed in giving some coherence to our actions is that we adopt a framework of rules for guidance which makes the general pattern though not the detail of our life predictable.
> (Hayek 1964: 11; quoted in Kim 1998)

Following Kirzner and Langlois, I contend that abstract rules permit the adaptation to future circumstances in the sense that they may induce entrepreneurial activity.

40 Moreover, Hayek explains that: "The more complex the order aimed at, the greater will be that part of the separate actions which will have to be determined by circumstances not known to those who direct the whole, and the more dependent control will be on rules rather than on specific commands" (Hayek 1973: 50).

41 As Mises puts it: "The selective principle according to which the Catholic Church chooses its future chiefs is unswerving devotion to the creed and its dogmas. It does not look for innovators and reformers, for pioneers of new ideas radically opposed to the old ones. This is what the appointment of the future top executives by the old and well-tried present rulers can safeguard. No bureaucratic system can achieve anything else. But it is precisely this adamant conservatism that makes bureaucratic methods utterly inadequate for the conduct of social and economic affairs. Bureaucratization is necessarily rigid because it involves the observation of established rules and practices. But in social life rigidity amounts to petrification and death" (Mises 1983 [1944]: 103). This statement should not be understood as a denial of the need of hierarchy in firms. By stating the

limits of bureaucracy, Mises simply explains its *raison d'être*. He clearly shows, in another passage (Mises 1983 [1944]: 36), that organizations, if they are to be the source of novelty, cannot be like bureaucracies (this does not imply that organizations are of the same nature as markets).

42 Even if the constitutional approach is certainly closer to the transaction cost view than to the Hayekian analysis (Langlois 1995: 250).

43 See Langlois (1995) in which he explains that in the Hayekian analysis, firms and markets are both systems of rules of conduct.

44 Although, in the case where tips are expected, like in New York city for instance, they certainly only represent a return on investment (15% of the fare), and not a pure profit.

45 See Scott Shane (1999) for a development of the idea that prior knowledge plays an important role in entrepreneurial discoveries. As he puts it in a comment on a paper by Kirzner: "[P]eople do not discover opportunities through search, but through recognition of the value of new information which they happen to receive through other means. People tend to perceive information which they are predisposed to recognize because the prior information frames the new information . . . and creates the relevant cognitive schema for the processing of information. . . . Therefore, the opportunity discovery process is a recognition process that results from the intersection of some prior information (e.g. the existence of a problem), and the new information" (Shane 1999: 9, references removed).

46 Team entrepreneurship allows for the discovery of knowledge that no one (in the firm and in the team) possessed beforehand. In that sense, general rules are necessary to induce discoveries and commands are of a limited use, since discoveries cannot be planned. Team entrepreneurship means that individuals can make discoveries as members of a team that they could not have made otherwise. That is why they have never exploited their alertness themselves. For this alertness only comes about with teamwork.

47 As Foss puts it: "[C]apabilities are not bound to individual input-owners but are tied to the interaction of a number of input-owners and acquire some permanence over time" (Foss 1996b: 21). See also note 29 of Chapter 3.

48 See Nonaka and Takeuchi (1995) for a theory of organizational learning that stems, to a certain extent, from knowledge considerations that are familiar to Austrian economists. (Their approach is nevertheless entangled in a general "management approach," which generally lacks a comprehensive theory of information and individual action.)

49 On the subject of information and its treatment within the firm, also see Minkler (1993) and Cowen and Parker (1997), for instance.

50 Even if, like Penrose for instance, Ghoshal *et al.* see that entrepreneurship has certainly a fundamental role to play, the question is: which one? As they put it with respect to the megacorporation: "Local entrepreneurship in different business and markets requires a governance mechanism that stimulates discretionary behavior within the organization" (Ghoshal *et al.* 1995: 751).

51 See Berle and Means (1991 [1932]) for an early account of the problem.

52 See Williamson (1993 [1988]) for a discussion on the general office and internal capital markets.

53 This "permitted a single parent company to hold the majority of the stock of locally chartered subsidiaries and so provided an inexpensive and easy way for enterprises operating over a wide area to avoid these obstacles and still retain legal control over their geographically dispersed activities" (Chandler 1990a [1962]: 31).

54 With the notable exception of Ford before the Second World War. As Chandler puts it: "By concentrating on one model which came to be built largely in one plant, Henry Ford expanded enormously in size without creating many central office management problems" (Chandler 1990a [1962]: 301).

55 J. Kocka has argued that Siemens developed aspects of a multidivisional structure before the First World War, ahead of its more widely known adoption in the USA. See Schmitz (1993: 34) on that issue.

56 Simon was also certainly in agreement with Williamson and Chandler when Williamson's *The Economic Institutions of Capitalism* came out. Since then, the capabilities approach has perhaps changed the focus of the debate, but it is certainly the case that the core explanation of transaction cost economics is still held as the major explanation for the emergence of the M-form. See Langlois (1995), for instance.

57 As Williamson puts it: "Effective multidivisionalization . . . involves the general office in the following activities: (1) the identification of separable economic activities within the firm; (2) according quasi-autonomous standing (usually of a profit center nature) to each; (3) monitoring the efficiency performance of each division; (4) awarding incentives; (5) allocating cash flows to high-yield uses; and (6) performing strategic planning (diversification, acquisition, divestiture, and related activities) in other respects. The M-form structure is thus one that combines the divisionalization concept with an internal control and strategic decision-making capability" (Williamson 1985: 284).

58 Some Austrian economists have emphasized that Mises and Hayek had a different view of the central planning issue. Mises (and followers, like Rothbard) is supposed to have shown that the issue of central planning is a calculation problem (i.e. without ownership there are no prices of raw materials, and therefore, there is no rational planning possible because planners do not know the values of the various alternatives to society). Hayek is supposed to have emphasized a knowledge problem. Our view herein is to say that these two views are the two faces of the same coin: they are complementary. Indeed, even if one can understand the calculation issue without taking into account the radical ignorance problem, emphasized by Hayek, it is still the case that the calculation issue can be understood and subsumed under a more global knowledge problem. On this subject, see Boettke (1997d). See also Hayek (1948 [1935a]; 1948 [1935b]; 1948 [1940]), Kirzner (1992a), Lavoie (1985), Mises (1966), Salerno (1990) and Yeager (1994).

59 The calculation problem makes the issue even more difficult for the central planner.

60 Murray Rothbard (1993 [1962]: 547–8) makes the same point from a calculation perspective: "[W]e must conclude that complete vertical integration for a capital-good product can never be established on the free market (above the primitive level). For every capital good, there must

be a definite market in which firms buy and sell that good. It is obvious that this economic law sets a definite maximum to the relative size of any particular firm on the free market." See also Klein (1996) on that issue. Kirzner also explains that "[w]e may expect firms spontaneously to tend to expand to the point where additional advantages of 'central' planning are just offset by the incremental knowledge difficulties that stem from dispersed information" (Kirzner 1992a: 162). Strangely enough, this statement treats the problem of knowledge in marginalist terms.

61 In the words of Chandler: "If diversity rather than increased size of operations led to organizational inadequacies, then it becomes clearer why these four companies were among the earliest in the United States to consider structural reorganization. Du Pont was the first large chemical company to diversify its production on a major scale. General Motors was far and away the most diversified automobile company of its day. In the 1920s, Jersey's operations were geographically more widely scattered than those of any other American petroleum company. . . . Sears, although closely followed by Montgomery Ward, pioneered in combining over-the-counter sales with mail-order marketing on a national basis. These four companies were therefore among the earliest to face the complex management problems that came to confront so many large American firms in the post-World War II economic boom" (Chandler 1990a [1962]: 302).

62 See Minkler (1993) on the issue of firms and dispersed knowledge. Minkler seems to say that Austrian economists would have to recognize that organizations exist despite dispersed knowledge. I have argued otherwise in this chapter. He also argues that capabilities theories make use of structural uncertainty, but not of dispersed knowledge. I argue in this chapter that Austrian economics can certainly make use of capabilities theories and integrate them in a dispersed-knowledge framework.

63 As Langlois puts it: "Foresight is of limited usefulness, and it may be a positive detriment to the extent that it is based on a model formed from a set of past experiences that have become inappropriate. Thus firms exist not because they plan but because they planned" (Langlois 1995: 255).

64 As Townsend (1984) explains, managers can commit themselves to certain rules that are established on a permanent basis (a moral blinder) and which do not need to be restated each year.

65 I disagree with Cowen and Parker when they write: "There is no 'firm mode of organization' or 'firm mode of resource allocation' separate and distinct from the market mode" (Cowen and Parker 1997: 40–1). Planning is the distinguishing mark of the firm. It is not the same type of planning as in the case of a socialist economy though, for it requires external markets to function.

66 At Sears, the top manager, General Wood, was much more involved in structural issues, but he clearly benefited from the experience of du Pont and General Motors.

67 Chandler mentions the resistance to change and the fact that often young executives would be less reluctant to upset the old structural order. See Chandler (1990a [1962]: 314–23). It is interesting to realize that the issue of coordination is usually treated as a market issue (Langlois and Robertson 1995: 36–40), rather than an intra-firm problem (in relation

to the inner HKP). However, Foss (1997a) is an exception to the rule. There is no doubt that the coordination issue in the marketplace can be a source of the emergence of organization (that is the subject of my second chapter), but empirical evidence shows that structural issues can best be understood as the result of inner-coordination problem.

68 Chandler also mentions Pierre du Pont and Harry Haskell at du Pont; Frank Howard and Edgar Clark at Standard Oil NJ; and James Barker, Theodore Houser and Frazer at Sears.

69 Changing the structure made the strategy possible as "the new structure eased the problems of coordination and appraisal. Coordinating product flow and determining costs in relation to volume as well as adapting product design or make-up to changing demands were all left to the multifunction divisions, each operating in its own clearly defined market" (Chandler 1990a [1962]: 302).

70 Following Kirzner (1973: 68), I could say that the true entrepreneurial inkling belongs to the promoter who knew who to hire to make his company grow, but it is still the case that those who became aware were not the top executives.

71 As Reid puts it, regarding the evolution of the management at Harley-Davidson: "Most important, Harley has dropped the concept of white-collars thinking and blue-collars doing, a notion that has plagued American business practices but is anathema in Japan. The goal now is to have everybody thinking and doing. The color of their collars is irrelevant" (Reid 1990: 165; quoted in Minkler 1993: 573). Another example is Just-in-Time production in which workers accept the responsibility for making sure that the parts they receive and send contain no defects. See also Herb Kelleher's interview in the *Wall Street Journal* (Lancaster 1999) in which he explains that, as the CEO of Southwest Airlines, he has tried to "create a culture of caring for people [employees] in the totality of their lives." This explains the competitive advantage of Southwest Airlines.

72 It would be interesting to know what happened to the individuals who were at the origin of the structural changes at du Pont, General Motors, Jersey Standard and Sears. Chandler (1990a [1962]: 319) mentions that Pierre du Pont got hired by General Motors in the 1920s for his experience. Sloan and Brown became famous consultants and wrote a series of papers on the multidivisional firm. My guess is that most of the individuals who identified the structural problems in those four companies got promoted among the top executives of their companies.

73 As Cowen and Parker put it: "By using a set of (shadow) price signals to decision-makers located in profit or cost centers (for instance, departments and subsidiaries) of the firm, the firm can mimic the market mechanism" (Cowen and Parker 1997: 51). This analysis reminds us of Mises's analysis in the socialist-calculation debate. Mises (1966) is very clear on the fact that planners cannot mimic the market system. It seems that this criticism is also valid, to a certain extent, for the firm. Managers cannot mimic the market, because internal (transfer) prices only reflect costs and not real profit opportunities. There cannot be any profit discoveries made like in the marketplace, even if there can be entrepreneurial activity. Besides, as Cowen and Parker explain, internal prices are in practice "determined by negotiation across company divisions, or are simply imposed by managers"

(Cowen and Parker 1997: 52). This contention, if it depicts how managers can mimic market prices, falls under Mises's (and Williamson's) criticism. For a related development, see Kirzner (1997b) and Rizzo (1980a; 1980b).

74 This is part of a profound confusion in the market-process approach to management. Cowen and Parker attribute market-like properties to phenomena that, in fact, pertain to the realm of non-market entrepreneurship. As Kirzner (1979: 158–60) shows, it can be the case that Crusoe acts like an entrepreneur even if there is no market system on the island. By analogy, it means that innovations can take place within the firm (with respect to its structure) without inner markets (these innovations being ultimately driven by external ignorance).

75 Mises in his exposition of the roles of the entrepreneur and the manager explains that "if the manager is given a completely free hand, things are different. He speculates in risking other people's money. . . . It is precisely when he is rewarded by a share of the profits that he becomes foolhardy because he does not share in losses too" (Mises 1966: 306). This passage simply means that if one is to give to a manager a position in which he/she will be expected to act upon his/her own knowledge and seize profit opportunities, it must be done within the right "institutional framework," i.e. within a framework in which the manager is as responsible for his/her mistakes as an entrepreneur in the marketplace.

76 Sloan set up Inter-Divisional Committees at General Motors between 1922 and 1924 which would keep managers and staff specialists in contact with one another (Chandler 1990a [1962]: 307).

77 As Chandler puts it: "A steady flow of detailed reports on all aspects of a given division's financial performance and its share of the market provided both its manager and the general officers with a useful and continuing check on operating results and achievements. Comparisons were made with the results of similar units within the enterprise, such as the various automobile divisions of General Motors or the Territories at Sears, or with the past performance for similar seasons or with the divisional or general office estimates and forecasts for the same period" (Chandler 1990a [1962]: 311).

78 As Loasby puts it: "Different patterns of organization, we must never forget, may be expected to produce different patterns of knowledge. That is why these patterns, and their differences, are so important" (Loasby 1991: 55).

79 See Coase (1973) and Demsetz (1995) for further developments on accounting.

80 Koch Industries makes use of profit centers which have their own profit and loss statements. If they are run like a division of the company, which seems to be the case, it is fair to say that they foster entrepreneurial activity within the organization. See Cowen and Parker (1997: 47).

81 Rank Xerox, du Pont and General Electric, for instance, are experimenting with cluster-type structures. See Cowen and Parker (1997: 26).

82 Along the same lines, Koch Industries uses cross-functional teams and a form of matrix management. See Cowen and Parker (1997: 47).

83 In some firms, divisions do not have to buy from others within the group (Cowen and Parker 1997: 27), this certainly enhances entrepreneurial activity in the divisions, but it also encourages managers and staff to

do their best. It is therefore both a Robbinsian and an entrepreneurial incentive.

84 Some scholars, like P. Hayes, have argued that the German chemicals firm I. G. Farben, created in 1925, was already a vast decentralized organization with more than 50 semi-autonomous divisions, which operated under a "flexible system of widely dispersed authority," and in which "decisions were taken at the lowest level possible, and only the most precedential matters percolated upwards" (Quoted in Schmitz 1993: 34).

85 As Barnevik says, ABB is supposed to be "local and global, big and small, radically decentralized with central reporting and control" Ghoshal et al. (1995: 750).

86 As they put it: "The combination of such focus on employment relationship as the essence of a firm and on opportunism as the focal aspect of human nature has, then, naturally led to the view that control of opportunism is the central function of organizations, and hierarchy has emerged as the taken for granted – indeed, necessary – mechanism for the governance of firms" (Ghoshal et al. 1995: 754).

87 A future development of this work could explore the cases in which the inner HKP becomes an impediment to growth of the firm.

BIBLIOGRAPHY

Alchian, Armen A. (1984) "Specificity, Specialization, and Coalitions." *Journal of Economic Theory and Institutions*, 140: 34–49.

Alchian, Armen A. and Demsetz, Harold (1972) "Production, Information Costs, and Economic Organization." *The American Economic Review*, 62: 777–95.

Alchian, Armen A. and Woodward, Susan (1988) "The Firm is Dead; Long live the Firm." *Journal of Economic Literature*, 26: 65–79.

Arrow, Kenneth (1969) "The Organization of Economic Activity: Issues Pertinent to the Choice of Market Versus Non-market Allocation." In *Joint Economic Committee, the Analysis and Evolution of Public Expenditure: the PPB System*, vol 1, Washington DC: US Government Printing Office.

—— (1974) *The Limits of Organization*, New York: W. W. Norton.

—— (1994) "Methodological Individualism and Social Knowledge." *American Economic Review*, 84 (2): 1–9.

Barreto, Humberto (1989) *The Entrepreneur in Microeconomic Theory: Disappearance and Explanation*, London: Routledge.

Barzel, Yoram (1987a) "The Entrepreneur's Reward for Self-Policing." *Economic Inquiry*, 25: 103–16.

—— (1987b) "Knight's 'Moral Hazard' Theory of Organization." *Economic Inquiry*, 25: 117–20.

Baumol, William J. (1968) "Entrepreneurship in Economic Theory." *American Economic Review*, 58 (2): 64–71.

—— (1993) *Entrepreneurship, Management and the Structure of Payoffs*, Cambridge, MA: MIT Press.

Berle, Adolf A. and Means, Gardiner C. (1991) [1932] *The Modern Corporation and Private Property*, New Brunswick: Transaction Publishers.

Boettke, Peter J. (ed.) (1994) *The Elgar Companion to Austrian Economics*, Aldershot: Edward Elgar.

—— (1996) "Is the Transition to the Market Too Important to Be Left to the Market?" Unpublished working paper, Austrian Economics Colloquium, New York University.

165

—— (1997a) "Where Did Economics Go Wrong? A Hayekian Reading of Contemporary Economics." Unpublished working paper.

—— (1997b) "Where Did Economics Go Wrong? Modern Economics as a Flight From Reality." *Critical Review*, 11 (1): 11–64.

—— (1997c) "Coase, Communism and the 'Black Box' of Soviet-Type Economies." Unpublished working paper.

—— (1997d) "Economic Calculation: *The* Austrian Contribution to Political Economy." *Laissez-Faire: Revista de la Facultad de Ciencias Economicas Universidad Francisco Marroquin*, 7: 30–51.

Boettke, Peter J. and Prychitko, David L. (eds) (1994) *The Market Process: Essays in Contemporary Austrian Economics*, Aldershot: Edward Elgar.

Boettke, Peter J., Horwitz, Steven and Prychitko, David L. (1994) "Beyond Equilibrium Economics: Reflections on the Uniqueness of the Austrian Tradition." In Boettke, Peter J. and Prychitko, David L. (eds) *The Market Process: Essays in Contemporary Austrian Economics*, Aldershot: Edward Elgar, 62–79.

Boudreaux, Donald and Holcombe, Richard (1989) "The Coasian and Knightian Theories of the Firm." *Managerial and Decision Economics*, 10: 147–54.

Caplan, Bryan (1999) "Rational Ignorance vs. Rational Irrationality." Working Paper presented at the Austrian Economics Colloquium, New York University.

Casson, Mark (1982) *The Entrepreneur: An Economic Theory*, Oxford: Martin Robinson.

Chandler, Alfred (1977) *The Visible Hand*, Cambridge: The Belknap Press.

—— (1990a) [1962] *Strategy and Structure*, second edition, Cambridge, MA: MIT Press.

—— (1990b) *Scale and Scope*, Cambridge: The Belknap Press.

Cheung, Steven N. S. (1983) "The Contractual Nature of the Firm." *The Journal of Law and Economics*, 26: 1–22.

Coase, Ronald H. (1960) "The Problem of Social Cost." *The Journal of Law and Economics*, 3: 1–44.

—— (1964) "The Regulated Industries: Discussion." *American Economic Review*, 54 (3): 194–7.

—— (1972) "Industrial Organization: A Proposal For Research." In Fuchs, V. R. (ed.) *Policy Issues and Research Opportunities in Industrial Organization*, New York: National Bureau of Economic Research, 59–73.

—— (1973) "Business Organization and the Accountant." Reprinted in Buchanan, James M. and Thirlby, G. F. (eds) *L.S.E. Essays On Cost*, London: London School of Economics and Political Science, 95–132.

—— (1990) *The Firm, the Market and the Law*, Chicago: The University of Chicago Press.

—— (1992) "The Institutional Structure of Production." *The American Economic Review*, 82 (4): 713–19.

—— (1993a) [1937] "The Nature of the Firm." Reprinted in Williamson, Oliver E. and Winter, Sidney G. (eds) *The Nature of the Firm*, Oxford: Oxford University Press, 18–33.

—— (1993b) [1988] "The Nature of the Firm: Origin." In Williamson, Oliver E. and Winter, Sidney G. (eds) *The Nature of the Firm*, Oxford: Oxford University Press, 34–47.

—— (1993c) [1988] "The Nature of the Firm: Meaning." In Williamson, Oliver E. and Winter, Sidney G. (eds) *The Nature of the Firm*, Oxford: Oxford University Press, 48–60.

—— (1993d) [1988] "The Nature of the Firm: Influence." In Williamson, Oliver E. and Winter, Sidney G. (eds) *The Nature of the Firm*, Oxford: Oxford University Press, 61–74.

Conner, K. R. and Prahalad, C. K. (1996) "A Resource-Based Theory of the Firm: Knowledge vs. Opportunism." *Organization Science*, 7: 477–501.

Cooter, Robert and Ulen, Thomas (1997) *Law and Economics*, second edition, Reading, MA: Addison-Wesley.

Cowan, Robin and Rizzo, Mario J. (1996) "The Genetic-Causal Tradition and Modern Economic Theory." *Kyklos*, 49 (3): 273–317.

Cowen, Tyler and Parker, David (1997) *Markets In The Firm. A Market-Process Approach to Management*, London: The Institute of Economic Affairs.

Currie, Martin and Steedman, Ian (1990) *Wrestling With Time*, Ann Arbor: The University of Michigan Press.

Dahlman, Carl J. (1979) "The Problem of Externality." *The Journal of Law and Economics*, 22 (1): 141–62.

Deming, W. Edwards (1986) *Out of the Crisis*, Cambridge: Cambridge University Press.

Demsetz, Harold (1969) "Information and Efficiency: Another Viewpoint." *Journal of Law and Economics*, 12 (1): 1–22.

—— (1988) *Ownership, Control and the Firm*, vol. 1 of *The Organization of Economic Activity*, Oxford: Basil Blackwell.

—— (1993) [1988] "The Theory of the Firm Revisited." *Journal of Law, Economics and Organization*, 4: 141–62. Reprinted in Williamson, Oliver E. and Winter, Sidney G. (eds) *The Nature of the Firm*, Oxford: Oxford University Press, 159–78.

—— (1995) *The Economics of the Business Firm*, Cambridge: Cambridge University Press.

Downs, Anthony (1957) *An Economic Theory of Democracy*, New York: Harper.

Economist, The (1996) *The ABB of Management*, 6–12 January, p. 56.

Eggertsson, Thrainn (1990) *Economic Behavior and Institutions*, Cambridge: Cambridge University Press.

Ellig, Jerry (1993) "Internal Pricing for Corporate Services." *Working Papers in Market-Based Management*, Center for the Study of Market Processes, September.

Fama, Eugene F. (1980) "Agency Problems and the Theory of the Firm." *Journal of Political Economy*, 88: 288–307.

167

Fink, Richard and Cowen, Tyler (1985) "Is the Evenly Rotating Economy a Useful Construct?" *American Economic Review*, 75: 866–9.

Fisher, Franklin M. (1991) "Organizing Industrial Organization: Reflections on the Handbook of Industrial Organization." *Brookings Papers on Economic Activity: Microeconomics*, 201–25.

Foss, Nicolai J. (1993a) "More on Knight and the Theory of the Firm." *Managerial and Decision Economics*, 14: 269–76.

—— (1993b) "Theories of the Firm: Contractual and Competence Perspective." *Journal of Evolutionary Economics*, 3: 127–44.

—— (1994a) "The Theory of the Firm: the Austrians as Precursors and Critics of Contemporary Theory." *The Review of Austrian Economics*, 7 (1): 31–65.

—— (1994b) "The Two Coasian Traditions." *Review of Political Economy*, 6 (1): 37–61.

—— (1995) "On the Rationales of Corporate Headquarters." Working Paper. Institut For Erhvervs-Og Samfundsforskning, Handelshojskolen I Kobenhavn.

—— (1996a) "Harald B. Malmgren's Analysis of the Firm: Lessons for Modern Theorists?" *Review of Political Economy*, 8 (4): 349–66.

—— (1996b) "Capabilities and the Theory of the Firm." *Revue d'Economie Industrielle*, 77: 7–28.

—— (1996c) "Firms, Incomplete Contracts, and Organizational Learning." *Humane Systems Management*, 15 (1): 17–26.

—— (1997a) "Austrian Economics and the Theory of the Firm." Working Paper.

—— (1997b) "Evolutionary and Contractual Theories of the Firm: How Do They Relate?" *Rivista Internazionale di Scienze Sociali*, 29: 63–91.

—— (1997c) "On the Rationales of Corporate Headquarters." *Industrial and Corporate Change*, 6: 313–39.

—— (1997d) "Austrian Insights and the Theory of the Firm." In Boettke, Peter J. and Rizzo, Mario J. (eds) *Advances in Austrian Economics*, 4: 175–98.

Foss, Nicolai J. and Christensen, Jens F. (1996) "A Process Approach to Corporate Coherence." DRUID Working Paper No. 96–7.

Friedman, Milton (1953) *Essays in Positive Economics*, Chicago: The University of Chicago Press.

Ghoshal, Sumantra, Moran, Peter and Almeida-Costa, Luis (1995) "The Essence of the Megacorporation: Shared Context, not Structural Hierarchy." *Journal of Institutional and Theoretical Economics*, 151 (4): 748–59.

Grant, R. M. (1996) "Towards a Knowledge-Based Theory of the Firm." *Strategic Management Journal*, 17: 109–22.

Grossman, Sanford J. and Hart, Oliver D. (1986) "The Costs and Benefits of Ownership: A Theory of Vertical and Lateral Integration." *Journal of Political Economy*, 94: 691–719.

Hamburg, Daniel (1963) "Invention in the Industrial Laboratory." *Journal of Political Economy*, 71: 95–116.

BIBLIOGRAPHY

Harper, David (1996) *Entrepreneurship and the Market Process*, London: Routledge.

Hart, Oliver D. (1993) [1988] "Incomplete Contracts and the Theory of the Firm." In Williamson, Oliver E. and Winter, Sidney G. (eds) *The Nature of the Firm*, Oxford: Oxford University Press, 138–58.

—— (1995) [1989] "An Economist's Perspective on the Theory of the Firm." *Columbia Law Review*, 89 (7): 1757–74. Reprinted in Williamson, Oliver E. (ed.) *Organization Theory*, expanded edition, Oxford: Oxford University Press, 154–71.

Hayek, Friedrich A. (1948) [1935a] "Socialist Calculation I: The Nature and History of the Problem." Reprinted in *Individualism and Economic Order*, Chicago: The University of Chicago Press, 119–47.

—— (1948) [1935b] "Socialist Calculation II: The State of the Debate." Reprinted in *Individualism and Economic Order*, Chicago: The University of Chicago Press, 148–80.

—— (1948) [1937] "Economics and Knowledge." Reprinted in *Individualism and Economic Order*, Chicago: The University of Chicago Press, 33–56.

—— (1948) [1940] "Socialist Calculation III: The Competitive Solution." Reprinted in *Individualism and Economic Order*, Chicago: The University of Chicago Press, 181–208.

—— (1948) [1945] "The Use of Knowledge in Society." Reprinted in *Individualism and Economic Order*, Chicago: The University of Chicago Press, 77–91.

—— (1964) "Kinds of Order in Society." *New Industrialist Review*, 3 (2): 3–12.

—— (1973) *Law, Legislation and Liberty*, Volume I, Chicago: The University of Chicago Press.

—— (1976) *Law, Legislation and Liberty*, Volume II, Chicago: The University of Chicago Press.

—— (1976) [1952] *The Sensory Order*, Chicago: University of Chicago Press.

—— (1977) [1958] "The Creative Powers of a Free Civilisation." In *Essays on Individuality*, Indianapolis: Liberty Press, 259–89.

—— (1978) "Competition as a Discovery Procedure." In *New Studies in Philosophy, Politics, Economics and the History of Ideas*, London: Routledge, 179–90.

High, Jack (1986) "Equilibration and Disequilibration in the Market Process." In Kirzner, Israel (ed.) *Subjectivism, Intelligibility and Economic Understanding*, New York: New York University Press, 111–21.

Hodgson, Geoffrey M. (1989) "Institutional Economic Theory: the Old Versus the New." *Review of Political Economy*, 1 (3): 249–69.

Holmström, Bengt R. and Tirole, Jean (1989) "The Theory of the Firm." In Schmalensee, Richard and Willig, Robert D. (eds) *Handbook of Industrial Organization*, vol I, Amsterdam: North-Holland, 61–133.

Hughes, Jonathan R. (1986) [1965] *The Vital Few: The Entrepreneur and American Economic Progress*, expanded edition, Oxford: Oxford University Press.

Ioannides, Stavros (1997) "Towards An Austrian Perspective on the Firm." Working paper presented at the EAEPE conference, Athens, Panteion University.
—— (1999) "Towards an Austrian Perspective on the Firm." *Review of Austrian Economics*, 11 (1–2): 77–98.
Jensen, Michael C. and Meckeling, William H. (1976) "Theory of the Firm: Managerial Behavior, Agency Costs and Ownership Structure." *Journal of Financial Economics*, 3: 305–60.
Kaldor, Nicholas (1934a) "The Equilibrium of the Firm." *Economic Journal*, 44: 70–91.
—— (1934b) "A Classifatory Note on the Determinateness of Equilibrium." *Review of Economic Studies*, 2: 122–36.
Kay, Neil M. (1984) *The Emergent Firm: Knowledge, Ignorance and Surprise in Economic Organization*, New York: Saint Martins Press.
Kim, Yisok (1998) *The Obviation of Coordination Problem by Way of Decoupling*, doctoral dissertation, New York University.
Kirzner, Israel M. (1963) *Market Theory and the Price System*, Princeton, NJ: D. Van Nostrand Company, Inc.
—— (1973) *Competition and Entrepreneurship*, Chicago: University of Chicago Press.
—— (1979) *Perception, Opportunity, and Profit: Studies in the Theory of Entrepreneurship*, Chicago: University of Chicago Press.
—— (1985a) *Discovery and the Capitalist Process*, Chicago: University of Chicago Press.
—— (1985b) "Review of the Economics of Time and Ignorance." *Market Process*, 3 (2). Reprinted in Boettke, Peter J. and Prychitko, David L. (eds) *The Market Process: Essays in Contemporary Austrian Economics*. Aldershot: Edward Elgar, 38–44.
—— (1988) *Foreword: Advertising in an Open-Ended Universe*. In Ekelund, Robert B. Jr. and Saurman, David S. *Advertising and the Market Process*, San Francisco: Pacific Research Institute for Public Policy, xv–xxii.
—— (1989) *Discovery, Capitalism, and Distributive Justice*, Oxford: Basil Blackwell.
—— (1992a) *The Meaning of Market Process*, London: Routledge.
—— (1992b) *Commentary: Entrepreneurship, Uncertainty and Austrian Economics*. In Caldwell, Bruce J. and Boehm, Stephan (eds) *Austrian Economics: Tensions and New Directions*, Boston: Kluwer Academic Publishers, 85–102.
—— (1994) "A Tale of Two Worlds: Comments on Shmanske." *Advances In Austrian Economics*, 1: 223–6.
—— (1997a) "Entrepreneurial Discovery and the Competitive Market Process: An Austrian Approach." *Journal of Economic Literature*, 35: 60–85.
—— (1997b) "Coordination as a Criterion for Economic 'Goodness'." Unpublished working paper presented at the Austrian Economics Seminar at New York University.

—— (1997c) *How Markets Work: Disequilibrium, Entrepreneurship and Discovery*, London: IEA Hobart Paper, No. 133.

Klein, Benjamin, Crawford, R. G. and Alchian, Armen (1978) "Vertical Integration, Appropriable Rents and the Competitive Contracting Process." *Journal of Law and Economics*, 21: 297–326.

Klein, Peter G. (1996) "Economic Calculation and the Limits of Organization." *The Review of Austrian Economics*, 9 (2): 3–28.

Knight, Frank (1965) [1921] *Risk, Uncertainty and Profit*, New York: Augustus Kelley.

Koppl, Roger (1994) "Ideal Type Methodology in Economics." In Boettke, Peter J. (ed.) *The Elgar Companion to Austrian Economics*, Aldershot: Edward Elgar, 72–6.

Lachmann, Ludwig M. (1976) "From Mises to Shackle: An Essay on Austrian Economics and the Kaleidic Society." *Journal of Economic Literature*, 14 (1): 54–62.

—— (1977a) [1959] "Professor Shackle on the Economic Significance of Time." Reprinted in Grinder, Walter (ed.) *Capital, Expectations, and the Market Process*, Kansas City: Sheed Andrews and McMeel, 81–93.

—— (1977b) [1947] "Complementarity and Substitution in the Theory of Capital." Reprinted in Grinder, Walter (ed.) *Capital, Expectations, and the Market Process*, Kansas City: Sheed Andrews and McMeel, 197–213.

—— (1977c) [1969] "Methodological Individualism and the Market Economy." Reprinted in Grinder, Walter (ed.) *Capital, Expectations, and the Market Process*, Kansas City: Sheed Andrews and McMeel, 149–65.

—— (1978) *Capital and Its Structure*, Kansas City: Sheed Andrews and McMeel.

Lancaster, Hal (1999) "Kelleher's Main Strategy: Treat All Employees Well." *Wall Street Journal*, 31 August.

Lang, Nancy (1990) "Desert Bloom." *Beverage World*, 109: 26–8.

Lange, Oskar (1938) "On the Economic Theory of Socialism." In Lippincott, Benjamin E. (ed.) *On The Economic Theory of Socialism*, Minneapolis: The University of Minnesota Press, 55–143.

Langlois, Richard N. (1986) "Rationality, Institutions and Explanation." In Langlois, Richard N. (ed.) *Economics as a Process*, Cambridge: Cambridge University Press, 225–55.

—— (1989) "What Was Wrong With the Old Institutional Economics (And What Is Still Wrong With the New)?" *Review of Political Economy*, 1 (3): 270–98.

—— (1992) "Orders and Organizations: Toward an Austrian Theory of Social Institutions." In Caldwell, Bruce J. and Boehm, Stephan *Austrian Economics: Tensions and New Directions*, Boston: Kluwer Academic Publishers, 165–83.

—— (1994) "Risk and Uncertainty." In Boettke, Peter J. (ed.) *The Elgar Companion to Austrian Economics*, Aldershot: Edward Elgar, 118–22.

—— (1995) "Do Firms Plan?" *Constitutional Political Economy*, 6 (3): 247–61.

Langlois, Richard N. and Cosgel, Metin M. (1993) "Frank Knight on Risk, Uncertainty, and the Firm: A New Interpretation." *Economic Inquiry*, 31 (3): 456–65.

Langlois, Richard N. and Robertson, Paul. L. (1995) *Firms, Markets and Economic Change*, Routledge: London.

Lavoie, Donald C. (1985) *Rivalry and Central Planning: The Socialist Calculation Debate Reconsidered*, Cambridge: Cambridge University Press.

Le Roy, Danny (1997) "Is There a Need For Entrepreneurship? An Assessment of the Role of the Entrepreneur Within the Neoclassical Theory of the Firm." Unpublished working paper presented at the Southern Economic Association Meetings in Atlanta.

Leijonhufvud, Axel (1986) *Capitalism and the Factory System*. In Langlois, Richard N. (ed.) *Economics As a Process*, Cambridge: Cambridge University Press, 203–23.

Lewin, Peter (1997) "Capital in Disequilibrium: Investigating the Dynamics of the Market Economy." Preliminary draft.

—— (1998a) "Capital Structures and Organizational Structure: An Austrian Market-Process Theory of the Firm." Unpublished working paper presented at the Austrian Economics Colloquium, New York University.

—— (1998b) *An Austrian Theory of the Firm*, unpublished working paper.

—— (1999) *Capital in Disequilibrium*, London: Routledge.

Lewin, Peter and Phelan, Steven (1999) "Rent and Resources: A Market Process Perspective." Working paper presented at the Austrian Economics Colloquium, New York University.

Libeskind, J. P. (1996) "Knowledge, Strategy and the Theory of the Firm." *Strategic Management Journal*, 17: 93–107.

Loasby, Brian J. (1976) *Choice, Complexity and Ignorance*, Cambridge: Cambridge University Press.

—— (1982) "The Entrepreneur in Economic Theory." *Scottish Journal of Political Economy*, 29 (3): 235–45.

—— (1991) *Equilibrium and Evolution: An Exploration of Connecting Principles in Economics*, Manchester: Manchester University Press.

Lucas, Robert E. (1981) *Studies in the Business Cycle Theory*, Cambridge: MIT Press.

Machlup, Fritz (1967) "Theories of the Firm: Marginalist, Behavioral, Managerial." *American Economic Review*, 57: 1–33.

Machovec, Frank M. (1995) *Perfect Competition and the Transformation of Economics*, London: Routledge.

Malmgren, Harald B. (1961) "Information, Expectations and the Theory of the Firm." *Quarterly Journal of Economics*, 75: 399–421.

Manne, Henri G. (1966) *Insider Trading and the Stock Market*, New York: The Free Press.

March, James G. and Simon, Herbert A. (1958) *Organizations*, New York: John Wiley.

172

Marengo, Luigi (1992) "Structure, Competence and Learning in an Evolutionary Model of the Firm." In *Papers on Economics and Evolution*, edited by the European Study Group for Evolutionary Economics, Freiburg.

Mathews, Don (1998) "Management vs. the Market: An Exaggerated Distinction." *The Quaterly Journal of Austrian Economics*, 1 (3): 41–6.

Maturana, Humberto R. and Varela, Francisco J. (1992) *The Tree of Knowledge*, revised edition, Boston and London: Shambhala.

McNulty, Paul J. (1984) "On the Nature and Theory of Economic Organization: The Role of the Firm Reconsidered." *History of Political Economy*, 16: 233–53.

Menger, Carl (1985) *Investigations into the Method of Social Sciences, With Special Reference to Economics*, New York: New York University Press.

Milgrom, Paul and Roberts, John (1992) *Economics, Organization and Management*, New York: Prentice Hall, International edition.

Minkler, Alanson P. (1993) "The Problem with Dispersed Knowledge: Firms in Theory and Practice." *Kyklos*, 46 (4): 569–87.

Mises, Ludwig von (1966) *Human Action: A Treatise on Economics*, third revised edition, Chicago: Henry Regnery.

—— (1980) [1951] *Profit and Loss*. In Mises, Ludwig von *Planning for Freedom*, Spring Mills: Libertarian Press.

—— (1983) [1944] *Bureaucracy*, Cedar Falls: Center for Futures Education.

Murphy, Kevin J. (1986) "Incentives, Learning, and Compensation: a Theoretical and Empirical Investigation of Managerial Labor Contracts." *Rand Journal of Economics*, 17 (1): 59–76.

Nelson, Richard and Winter, Sidney G. (1982) *An Evolutionary Theory of Economic Change*, Cambridge, MA: Belknap Press.

Nonaka, Ikujiro and Takeuchi, Hirota (1995) *The Knowledge Creating Company*, Oxford: Basil Blackwell.

O'Driscoll, Gerald P. Jr. and Rizzo, Mario J. (1986) "Subjectivism, Uncertainty and Rules." In Kirzner, Israel (ed.) *Subjectivism, Intelligibility and Economic Understanding*, New York: New York University Press.

—— (1996) [1985] *The Economics of Time and Ignorance*, second edition, New York and Oxford: Basil Blackwell.

O'Mahony, David (1979) *The Firm: An Austrian Approach*, unpublished lecture, delivered at Rutgers, Newark, NJ.

Penrose, Edith (1995 [1959]) *The Theory of the Growth of the Firm*, third edition, Oxford: Oxford University Press.

Polanyi, Michael (1962) *Personal Knowledge: Towards a Post-Critical Philosophy*, New York: Harper Torchbooks.

—— (1967) *The Tacit Dimension*, Garden City, NY: Doubleday Anchor.

Popper, Karl (1982) *The Open Universe: An Argument for Indeterminism*, Totowa, NJ: Rowman and Littlefield.

Postrel, Virginia (1998) *The Future and Its Enemies: the Growing Conflict Over Creativity, Enterprise, and Progress*, New York: Free Press.

Prahalad, C. K. and Hamel, Gary (1990) "The Core Competence of the Corporation." *Harvard Business Review*, 66: 79–91.

Reder, Melvin W. (1982) "Chicago Economics: Permanence and Change." *Journal of Economic Literature*, 20: 1–38.

Reid, Peter (1990) *Well Made in America*, New York: McGraw-Hill.

Richardson, George B. (1972) "The Organization of Industry." *The Economic Journal*, 82, 883–96. Reprinted in Richardson, George B. (1990) *Information and Investment*, second edition, Oxford: Oxford University Press, 224–42.

—— (1990) [1960] *Information and Investment*, second edition, Oxford: Oxford University Press.

Rizzo, Mario (ed.) (1979) *Time, Uncertainty, and Disequilibrium*, Lexington: Lexington Books.

—— (1980a) "Law Amid Flux: the Economics of Negligence and Strict Liability in Tort." *The Journal of Legal Studies*, 9: 291–318.

—— (1980b) "The Mirage of Efficiency." *Hofstra Law Review*, 8 (3): 641–58.

—— (1996a) "Real Time and Relative Indeterminacy in Economic Theory." Paper presented at the Austrian Economics Seminar at New York University.

—— (1996b) "Introduction: Time and Ignorance After Ten Years." In O'Driscoll, Gerald P. Jr. and Rizzo, Mario J. (1996) [1985] *The Economics of Time and Ignorance*, second edition, New York and Oxford: Basil Blackwell.

Robbins, Lionel (1932) *An Essay on the Nature and Significance of Economic Science*, London: Macmillan.

Rothbard, Murray N. (1979) "Comment: The Myth of Efficiency." In Rizzo, Mario (ed.) *Time, Uncertainty, and Disequilibrium*, Lexington: Lexington Books, 90–5.

—— (1985) "Professor Kirzner on Entrepreneurship." *Journal of Libertarian Studies*, 7 (2): 281–6.

—— (1987) "Breaking Out of the Walrasian Box: Schumpeter and Hansen." *Review of Austrian Economics*, 1: 97–108.

—— (1993) [1962] *Man, Economy and State*, third edition, Auburn, AL: Ludwig von Mises Institute.

Rumelt, Richard (1984) "Towards a Strategic Theory of the Firm." In Lamb, Richard B. (ed.) *Competitive Strategic Management*, Englewood Cliffs, NJ: Richard D. Irwin.

—— (1987) "Theory, Strategy and Entrepreneurship." In Teece, David J. (ed.) *The Competitive Challenge: Strategies for Industrial Innovation and Renewal*, Cambridge, MA: Ballinger.

Salerno, Joseph (1990) "Ludwig von Mises as Social Rationalist." *The Review of Austrian Economics*, 4: 26–54.

Salgado, Gilberto G. (1994) "Profit, Losses and the Coordination of Economic Activities." Unpublished working paper presented at the Austrian Economics Seminar at New York University.

—— (1999) "The Economics of Entrepreneurial Error." Ph.D. dissertation, New York University.

Sautet, Frédéric E. (1996) "From the Ashes of the Present Theory of the Firm: An Austrian Approach." Unpublished working paper presented at the Southern Economic Association Meetings in Washington DC (November).

—— (1997a) "Towards an Entrepreneurial Theory of the Firm." Unpublished working paper presented at the Austrian Economics Seminar at New York University.

—— (1997b) "The Hayekian Knowledge Problem and the Emergence of the Firm: The Simple Firm as a Locus of Exploitation of a Profit Opportunity." Unpublished working paper presented at the Southern Economic Association Meetings in Atlanta (November).

—— (1998) "The Hayekian Knowledge Problem and the Growth of the Firm." Unpublished working paper presented at the Austrian Economics Seminar at New York University.

Sautet, Frédéric E. and Foss, Nicolai J. (1999) "The Organization of Large, Complex Firms: An Austrian View." Unpublished working paper presented at the Austrian Economics Seminar at New York University and at Peter Boettke's Seminar George Mason University.

Schmitz, Christopher J. (1993) *The Growth of Big Business in the United States and Europe, 1850–1939*, Cambridge: Cambridge University Press.

Schultz, Theodore W. (1975) "The Value of the Ability to Deal with Disequilibria." *The Journal of Economic Literature*, 13 (3): 827–46.

Schumpeter, Joseph A. (1961) [1934] *The Theory of Economic Development: An Inquiry Into Profits, Capital, Credit, Interest, and the Business Cycle*, New York: New York University Press.

—— (1989a) [1947] "The Creative Response in Economic History." Reprinted in Clemence, Richard V. (ed.) *Essays on Entrepreneurs, Innovations, Business Cycles and the Evolution of Capitalism*, New Brunswick, USA: Transaction Publishers, 221–31.

—— (1989b) [1948] "Science and Ideology." Reprinted in Clemence, Richard V. (ed.) *Essays on Entrepreneurs, Innovations, Business Cycles and the Evolution of Capitalism*, New Brunswick, USA: Transaction Publishers, 272–86.

Shane, Scott (1999) "Prior Knowledge and the Discovery of Entrepreneurial Opportunities." Unpublished working paper. Forthcoming in *Organizational Science*.

Shmanske, Stephen (1994) "On the Relevance of Policy to Kirznerian Entrepreneurship." *Advances In Austrian Economics*, 1: 199–222.

Silver, Morris (1984) *Enterprise and the Scope of the Firm*, London: Martin Robertson.

Simon, Herbert A. (1957) *Models of Man: Social and Rational*, New York: Wiley.

—— (1972) "Theories of Bounded Rationality." In McGuire, C. B. and Radner, Roy (eds) *Decision and Organization*, New York: American Elsevier, 161–76.

Stigler, Georger J. (1957) "Perfect Competition, Historically Contemplated." *Journal of Political Economy*, 65 (1): 1–17.

Stiglitz, Joseph E. (1994) *Whither Socialism?*, Cambridge, MA: MIT Press.

Teece, David J. (1976) *Vertical Integration and Vertical Divestiture in the U.S. Oil Industry: Analysis and Policy Implications*, Standford: Standford University Institute for Energy Studies.

Teece, David J., Rumelt, Richard P., Dosi, Giovanni and Winter, Sidney (1994) "Understanding Corporate Coherence: Theory and Evidence." *Journal of Economic Behavior and Organization*, 23: 1–30.

Thirlby, G. F. (1973) [1946] "The Ruler." Reprinted in Buchanan, James M. and Thirlby, G. F. (eds) *L.S.E. Essays On Cost*, London: London School of Economics and Political Science, 165–98.

Thomsen, Esteban F. (1992) *Prices and Knowledge*, London: Routledge.

Townsend, Robert (1970) *Up the Organization*, New York: Alfred A. Knopf.

—— (1984) *Further Up the Organization*, New York: Alfred A. Knopf.

Vanberg, Viktor (1992) "Organizations As Constitutional Systems." *Constitutional Political Economy*, 3 (2): 223–53.

Vaughn, Karen I. (1994) *Austrian Economics in America: the Migration of a Tradition*, Cambridge: Cambridge University Press.

White, Lawrence (1992) "Afterword: Appraising Austrian Economics: Contentions and Misdirections." In Caldwell, Bruce J. and Boehm, Stephan (eds) *Austrian Economics: Tensions and New Directions*, Boston and Dordrecht: Kluwer, 257–68.

Williams, Philip L. (1978) *The Emergence of the Theory of the Firm from Adam Smith to Alfred Marshall*, New York: St Martin's Press.

Williamson, Oliver E. (1975) *Markets and Hierarchies*, New York: Free Press.

—— (1985) *The Economic Institutions of Capitalism*, New York: Free Press.

—— (1988) "Economics and Sociology of Organization: Promoting a Dialogue." In Farkas, George and England, Paula (eds) *Industries, Firms and Jobs*, New York: Plenum, 159–85.

—— (1989) "Transaction Cost Economics." In Schmalensee, Richard and Willig, Robert D. (eds) *Handbook of Industrial Organization*, vol I, Amsterdam: North-Holland, 136–82.

—— (1993) [1988] "The logic of economic organization." *Journal of Law, Economics and Organizations*. Reprinted in Williamson, Oliver E. and Winter, Sidney G. (eds) *The Nature of the Firm*, Oxford: Oxford University Press, 90–116.

Winter, Sidney (1993) [1988] "On Coase, Competence and the Corporation." Reprinted in Williamson, Oliver E. and Winter, Sidney G. (eds) *The Nature of the Firm*, Oxford: Oxford University Press, 179–95.

Witt, Ulrich (1995) "Do Entrepreneurs Need Firms? A Contribution to a Missing Chapter in Austrian Economics." Unpublished working paper presented at the Austrian Economics Seminar at New York University.

Womack, James, Jones, Daniel and Roos, David (1990) *The Machine that Changed the World*, New York: Macmillan.

Yeager, Leland E. (1994) "Mises and Hayek on Calculation and Knowledge." *The Review of Austrian Economics*, 7 (2): 93–109.

INDEX

Dahlman, Carl 43
Deming, Edwards 124
Demsetz, Harold 2, 44, 53, 58, 70,
   90–1, 97, 100
departmental structure 110–11
discovery 15, 46, 49, 54, 62, 70, 80,
   86, 95, 118, 120–1; and Coase
   18; of dispersed knowledge 13,
   59–60; and the emergence of the
   firm 72, 75–77; and error 64–5;
   in the firm 122–7; and incentives
   in the organization 100–7; and
   Williamson 31, 40–1; see also
   entrepreneur and entrepreneurship
disequilibrating tendencies 68
disequilibrium 15–16, 49–50, 52,
   54, 68, 71, 73, 81, 87, 96, 115,
   133–4; analysis 12–13; in Coase
   25; and entrepreneurship 59, 61;
   and error 64; in Williamson
   40–2
Downs, Anthony 44
Du Pont 111, 122–3, 125

economic problem 6, 8, 10, 13, 15,
   28, 37, 40, 42, 53, 59–60, 68,
   80, 84, 89, 104
economies: of scope 92; of diversity
   92
Eggertsson, Thrainn 43
emergence: of the firm 71–7
entrepreneur: entrepreneur-manager
   58; entrepreneur-promoter 74,
   82, 99–100, 116; in Langlois 118;
   as a manager in Coase 24; in
   Penrose 93; as the prime mover
   57–9; and resource owner 73;
   role in the process view 15; in
   Williamson 41–2; see also
   discovery
entrepreneurship: in the firm 106–7,
   122–6; and the M-form 115; in
   teams 107; type I and type II 63;
   see also discovery
equilibrative tendencies 63–4
equilibrium: argumentum a contrario
   8, 13; description of reality 8;
   general 7–9, 12–13; indictment 9;
   instrumental approach 8; as a
   method of contrast in Coase 20

equilibrium concept: Coase's use of
   20–1; in Williamson 32–33, used
   as a foil in Williamson 35–6, used
   as a description of the world in
   Williamson 36
error: entrepreneurial 64–6; first type
   64–5, second type 65, third type
   66; over-optimism 65;
   over-pessimism 64
exploitability thesis 75–7

Fetter, Frank 48–9
Fink, Richard 7
firm: Coase's definition of 58;
   complex 87, 99; discovery
   mechanisms within it 122–6;
   distinctive nature of 81–2;
   entrepreneurial 86; four rationales
   for the existence of 5–6; as an
   institution and an institutional
   structure 78, 120; as a locus of
   exploitation and of discovery 86;
   as a nesting of entrepreneurs
   105–6; as a non-price planned
   coordination 76; as a problem
   solving structure 91;as a pulling
   together of entrepreneurial
   alertness 76; resource-based
   theories of 47–50, 77, 87; as a
   specific capital structure 79–81
Fisher, Franklin 16
flattening: of organizational
   structures 123
flexibility 22; flexibility effect 91
Ford 117
Foss, Nicolai 18–19, 22, 29, 32,
   40, 56–7, 80, 90–2, 95, 97,
   126
Friedman, Milton 8

General Motors 122–3
Ghoshal, Sumantra 108, 130
Grant, R. 90
Grossman, Sanford 9
growth: of the firm 98, 107,
   111–13

Hamel, Gary 90
Harley Davidson 124
Harper, David 86, 91

INDEX

Hayek, Friedrich 4, 14, 36–7, 56,
  68, 79, 82, 98–9, 104, 106, 116,
  122, 125
Hayekian Knowledge Problem
  13–14; double 98–100, 116–18
Hewlett-Packard 121
High, Jack 67
Hodgson, Geoffrey 30; see also
  rationality (bounded)
Holcombe, Richard 18, 24, 50, 54,
  59
Hughes, Jonathan 1
hunch: entrepreneurial 60; see also
  Schumpeter, Joseph

ignorance 94; concept of 44–5;
  known 70; sheer 71
incentives: entrepreneurial 101–5;
  high-powered 101, low-powered
  101; and the M-form 120;
  Robinsian 100–1
incomplete contracts 90–1, 109
information 12, 59, 63, 69–71, 78,
  89–91, 105–6; in Coase 21–3; and
  cost–benefit analysis 15; in
  Grossman and Stiglitz 9; and the
  HKP 13–4; and the M-form
  116–18, 122, 126–7; and
  transaction cost 43–6; in
  Williamson 27, 31, 36–8, 40;
  see also knowledge
innovation: and entrepreneurship 63;
  and firms 86, 93; and the M-form
  113, 118, 122
institution, see firm
institutional stability 78
intrapreneur, see corporate
Ioannides, Stavros 56

Jersey Standard 122–3

Kaldor, Nicholas 68
kaleidic world 67–8, 75
Kay, Neil 15
Kirzner, Israel 12, 14, 37, 46, 50–1,
  57, 59–2, 64, 68–9, 73, 93, 96,
  100–1, 104–5, 109, 116, 120; on
  advertising 52–3; and the
  allocative paradigm 53; on
  ignorance 45

Klein, Benjamin 74
Klein, Peter 27
Knight, Frank 11–12, 19, 24; and
  the theory of the firm 50–2, 55;
  see also risk and uncertainty
knowledge 11, 44–5, 89–92; tacit
  and social 90–1; and Asea Brown
  Boveri 129–31; and capabilities
  94–5; and discovery in the firm
  122–6; and entrepreneurship 15;
  and entrepreneurial incentives
  104–5; and HKP 13–14, 59–69,
  71–7, 98–100; in Knight 50; and
  the M-form 108–10, 116–18;
  M-form and the creation of 127;
  substitution effect 91; in
  Williamson 36–8, 40;
Koopmans, Tjalling 38

labor: non-specific 74; specific 75
Lachman, Ludwig 67–8, 72, 75,
  77–81, 82
Lachmannian problem 63–9,
  78–81
Langlois, Richard 12, 46, 51, 53,
  86, 90, 92–3, 95, 104, 106, 118,
  125
learning 105, 109, 126, 129; by
  discovering 94, 107;
  organizational 90–2
Lewin, Peter 47–9, 62, 77, 79
Libeskind, J. 90
Loasby, Brian 11, 59, 78, 90

M-form 108–31, 109, 112, 120,
  122, 125; and dissemination of
  new knowledge 127; and the
  double Hayekian knowledge
  problem 116–8
Machlup, Fritz 55
Machovec, Frank 7, 9, 12
McNulty, Paul 55
management: enterprising 87–9,
  93–4; market-based 124
Manne, Henri 109
Marengo, Luigi 92, 95
market: failures 53; in the firm 125;
  as a rivalrous process among
  entrepreneurs 72–3; theory
  problem 7–16

179

F. Thomsu. Press Knowledge
(1992)

O'Driscoll & Rizzo (1996)
Economics of Time & Ignorance

Lightning Source UK Ltd.
Milton Keynes UK
UKOW051307120112

185250UK00001B/57/A